Scottish Men of Letters
and the New Public Sphere,
1802–1834

The Bucknell Studies in Eighteenth-Century Literature and Culture

The Bucknell Studies in Eighteenth-Century Literature and Culture aims to publish challenging, new eighteenth-century scholarship. Of particular interest is critical, historical, and interdisciplinary work that is interestingly and intelligently theorized, and that broadens and refines the conception of the field. At the same time, the series remains open to all theoretical perspectives and different kinds of scholarship. While the focus of the series is the literature, history, arts, and culture (including art, architecture, music, travel, and history of science, medicine, and law) of the long eighteenth century in Britain and Europe, the series is also interested in scholarship that establishes relationships with other geographies, literature, and cultures for the period 1660–1830.

Recent Titles in This Series

http://www.bucknell.edu/universitypress/

Scottish Men of Letters and the New Public Sphere, 1802–1834

Barton Swaim

Lewisburg
Bucknell University Press

Associated University Presses
2010 Eastpark Boulevard
Cranbury, NJ 08512

The paper used in this publication meets the requirements of the American National Standard for permanence of paper for Printed Library Materials Z39.48-1984.

Library of Congress Cataloging-in-Publication Data

Swaim, Barton, 1972–
    Scottish men of letters and the new public sphere, 1802–1834 / Barton Swaim.
    p. cm.
Includes bibliographical references and index.
ISBN 978-0-8387-5716-1 (alk. paper)
    1. Scottish literature — 19th century — History and criticism.   2. Periodicals — Publishing — Scotland — History — 19th century.   3. Scotland — Intellectual life — 19th century.   4. Literature publishing — Scotland — History — 19th century. 5. Politics and literature — Scotland — History — 19th century.   6. Authors and publishers — Scotland — History — 19th century.   7. Scottish periodicals — History — 19th century.   I. Title.
PR8550.S93   2009
820.9'9411 — dc22   2008026503

PRINTED IN THE UNITED STATES OF AMERICA

Contents

Abbreviations

BEM	*Blackwood's Edinburgh Magazine*
CER	Francis Jeffrey. *Contributions to the Edinburgh Review*, 4 vols. London: Longman, Brown, Green, and Longmans, 1844.
CL	Thomas and Jane Welsh Carlyle. *The Collected Letters of Thomas Carlyle and Jane Welsh Carlyle*. Edited by Charles Richard Sanders, Clyde de L. Ryals, and others, 32 vols. Durham, North Carolina: Duke University Press, 1970- .
ER	*Edinburgh Review*
FR	*Foreign Review*
LLJ	Henry Cockburn. *Life of Lord Jeffrey*, 2 vols. Edinburgh: Adam and Charles Black, 1852.
NLS	*National Library of Scotland*
QR	*Quarterly Review*
WPW	John Wilson. *The Works of Professor Wilson*. Edited by James Ferrier, 12 vols. Edinburgh: Blackwood and Sons, 1865
WTC	Thomas Carlyle. *The Works of Thomas Carlyle*. Edited by H. D. Traill. Centenary Edition, 30 vols. London: Chapman and Hall, 1896–99.

Scottish Men of Letters
and the New Public Sphere,
1802–1834

Introduction: Nine Tenths of the Public Sphere: Scottish Men of Letters, 1802–1834

PERIODICAL CULTURE

IN THE FIRST ISSUE OF THE *LONDON MAGAZINE,* IN 1820, THE EDITOR explained the decision to revive a defunct periodical of the same name. "We have been induced to revive the Title of a once well-known but discontinued Magazine, and to appropriate it to our new undertaking, in consequence of its occurring to us as singular, that, while secondary towns of the Kingdom give name and distinctions to popular journals, the METROPOLIS should remain *unrepresented* in the now strenuous competition of Periodical Literature."[1] By "secondary towns of the Kingdom" the editor meant Edinburgh. In 1820 the *Edinburgh Review* had been the most respectable periodical work in Britain for nearly a generation, despite having provoked the creation of a Tory rival in 1809 in the form of the London-based *Quarterly Review;* and only three years before, in 1817, another Scottish periodical, *Blackwood's Edinburgh Magazine,* had appeared to much fanfare as a brash and irreverent counterpart to the *Quarterly.* Scotland, it seemed to the *London'*s editor, dominated "Periodical Literature" to an astonishing degree — a perception made all the more real by the fact that he himself was a Scot: John Scott, from Aberdeenshire. It is, of course, well known that Scots were vastly overrepresented in periodical publication throughout the nineteenth century. John Gross, in his classic study of nineteenth- and twentieth-century "men of letters," observes correctly that

> it would be hard to exaggerate the part played by Scotsmen in the development of the English periodical press. They helped to create not only the great quarterlies and monthlies, as is well known, but the weeklies as well: the first editors of the *Spectator,* the *Economist* and the *Saturday Review,* for example, were all Scotsmen. And right through the nineteenth century critics and essayists made their way south across the border. Lockhart, Masson, Andrew Lang, William Archer are a few random instances. The list could be easily expanded — and it would become positively daunting if one were

11

allowed to include the second generation of the diaspora: men like Ruskin, who still spoke with traces of a Scots accent, or Macaulay, whose features in repose struck Carlyle as those of "an honest, good sort of fellow, made out of oatmeal."[2]

Confining such a list to the first thirty years of the nineteenth century, it would include, preeminently, Francis Jeffrey, Henry Brougham, and Francis Horner, who with the English cleric Sydney Smith founded the *Edinburgh Review;* Sir Walter Scott, an early contributor to the *Edinburgh* whose anger at what he considered its Jacobinical tendencies inspired him to help found the *Quarterly Review;* R. P. Gillies, the Edinburgh advocate and German literature scholar who founded the *Foreign Quarterly Review* in 1827; William Tait, the Edinburgh publisher and founder of the *Tait's Edinburgh Magazine,* which for some years competed with the radical London periodicals; William Fraser, the publisher from Inverness who founded *Fraser's Magazine;* and Thomas Campbell, the first editor of the *New Monthly Magazine* in 1824. Nineteenth-century Scottish periodicals also provided an outlet for women writers who, owing at least in part to social disapproval of literary women and the easily-maintained anonymity offered by periodicals, contributed a great deal to the Edinburgh periodical press's success: among them Constance Gordon-Cumming, Charlotte Dempster, Margaret Oliphant, and Christian Isobel Johnstone.[3]

The Scots' famous facility in periodical-writing had its origins in the latter half of the eighteenth century, when Scottish publishing firms experienced unprecedented vibrancy, thus emboldening them to experiment with periodical publication. In the period from 1774 to 1815 Edinburgh publishers grew faster than their London counterparts. Scottish publishers made available an average of 193 titles per year in the 1770s; by 1815 the number had increased to 565. In the same period, London publishers went from 372 in 1772 to 580 in 1815.[4] The first reason for this vibrancy was the fact that several Scottish booksellers, principally Andrew Millar, William Strahan, and the quasi-Scot Thomas Cadell, had established highly successful firms in London and had used their Scottish connections to become the primary publishers of the Scottish Enlightenment—which in turn allowed the Edinburgh firms with which they were connected to ally themselves with the much stronger London market.[5] The boom in Scottish publishing during this period was also the result of *Donaldson* v. *Becket,* 1774, the outcome of a lengthy legal battle between Scottish booksellers and London booksellers in which the House of Lords at last determined the former's right to reprint titles whose copyright had expired. The profits Scottish firms made on inexpensively produced "classics" allowed them to experiment with periodicals, and by the end of the century Edinburgh's publishers were putting out all manner of journals and magazines; in 1802, for example, when Archibald Constable began publishing the *Edinburgh*, he was already publishing the *Farmer's Magazine*, the *Scots Magazine*, and the *Edinburgh Medical and Surgical Journal*.[6] Obviously London was the greater hub of periodical activity, but residents of Edinburgh were, *per capita*, better represented by literary periodicals than Londoners were. In the year 1800 there were seven literary periodicals of substantial circulation published in London, whereas in Edinburgh there were two.[7] Yet London, with a population of 960,000 in that year, was at least fourteen times larger than Edinburgh, with only 66,000.[8] At the turn of the eighteenth and nineteenth centuries, the idea of contributing poems, squibs, letters, or essays would have been normal to the average educated person living in Edinburgh in a way that wasn't quite the case among Londoners.

Equally important, however, is the degree to which London's periodical reviews and magazines were written and run by Scots. In 1756 Tobias Smollett founded the ministerialist *Critical Review*, which competed impressively with the venerable *Monthly Review*. Of the *Critical's* five or six chief contributors, three were Scots: Archibald Hamilton, John Armstrong, and Patrick Murdoch. Hume also contributed. Founded by John Murray in 1783, the *English Review* was, as Derek Roper has noted, "owned, edited, and in great part written by Scots" such as the notoriously alcoholic slasher Gilbert Stuart, its first editor.[9] The first editor of the radical *Analytical Review* was Thomas Christie, native of Montrose; among its most frequent contributors were James Currie (biographer of Burns) and Alexander Geddes. The Scot William Rose, co-founder with Ralph Griffiths of the *Monthly Review*, was that periodical's most frequent contributor; and John Ferrar, poet, literary critic, and medical doctor from Jedburgh, wrote voluminously for the *Monthly* as well. Between 1802, when James Mill moved to London, aged twenty-nine, and 1811, when his history of India was published, he contributed a huge number of articles to the *Anti-Jacobin Review*, the *Monthly*, and the *Edinburgh* to support his family. A number of Scots began as *Monthly* reviewers and became *Edinburgh* reviewers once the latter was begun: James Mackintosh was among the *Monthly's* chief reviewers in the 1790s, and among the *Edinburgh's* in the 1810s; Lockhart Muirhead, principal librarian at Glasgow University from 1795 to 1827, wrote often for both periodicals, as did Joseph Lowe, from Brechin.[10]

Henry Cockburn, among many others, would later complain that Scottish authors left for London in the 1820s; but although there is some truth in the claim, London—and especially Grub Street—had teemed with Scots throughout the latter part of the eighteenth century. Many of these Scots, determined to make a go at a literary career in the capital, were obliged to write for periodicals just to make ends meet.[11]

The affinity for periodicals of all kinds in eighteenth-century Scotland was no doubt largely a consequence of the desire felt by many Scots after 1707 to know what was happening in Britain's capital. In 1831 Carlyle professed shock at hearing of a "Review of Reviews" ("all Literature has become one boundless self-devouring Review," he wrote in "Characteristics"), but by that time periodicals about periodicals had been published in Edinburgh for at least a century. *The Gleaner,* a typical transmitter of periodical information begun and ended in 1795, contained "Original Essays in prose and verse, with Extracts from various publications, particularly Reviews, and other periodical works."[12] The *Scots Magazine* itself contained extracts from the London periodical press, and many Scottish publishers "not infrequently recommended their periodicals to the public on the ground that in them could be found the best of all that was published in the London and other contemporary serials."[13]

The sheer number of periodical publications sprouting up in the 1780s and '90s, within and outwith Edinburgh, is remarkable. In the space of just five years, between 1786 and 1791, no less than five periodicals were started in Aberdeen: *The Caledonian Magazine* (two runs); *The Aberdeen Magazine; The Northern Gazette, Literary Chronicle and Review;* and *The Aberdeen Magazine, Literary Chronicle and Magazine.*[14]

In the early-nineteenth century, by contrast, the Scots' dominance in periodical-writing was greater though less quantifiable. What occurred from 1802, with the founding of the *Edinburgh,* until roughly halfway through the 1830s, when most of the notable Scottish periodical-writers had emigrated to London—Carlyle left for good in 1834—was much more than a matter of large numbers of Scottish people involving themselves in periodicals, however essential that predilection was. Marilyn Butler's assertion is no exaggeration: "The most essential fact about 'English' criticism of the period"—and that includes much more than literary criticism—"is . . . that it is predominantly Scottish."[15] So it was thought by many at the time, anyhow. Examining the comments of observers of the cultural and political scenes around 1815 or so, one discerns a sense of alarm, even exasperation, that Scots were wielding so much influence over public debate through periodicals. Thus one correspondent writes: "A man who has been observant of the change which has taken place in the tone and character of public opinion within these last twenty years cannot but perceive how infinite a portion of this change is *demonstrably* chargeable upon the influence of *two* publications only, the Edinburgh Review and the Morning Chronicle."[16]

Both periodicals were, or at least were understandably seen to be, Scottish. The *Morning Chronicle* had been founded by a group of Scots and, at the time of this correspondent's complaint, was edited by the Aberdonian James Perry. Another remark, this one by a tireless Scoto-phobe called Samuel Taylor Coleridge, indicates something of the nature of what was happening. In *The Courier* in 1811, he responded to an observation made in the *Morning Chronicle* that England could learn from Scotland. "We are likewise gratified with another discovery, that England has yet much to learn from Scotland, which is rather extraordinary, as half the ushers in the countless English boarding-schools have been Scotchmen for near a century past, a full half of the newspaper writers, and two thirds of the reviewers. Now Newspapers and Reviews, joined to the small incipient quantity brought away from school, form nine tenths of the erudition of nine tenths of the readers throughout England."[17] Now, the complaint that Scots were coming south in fearful numbers, taking jobs rightfully belonging to Englishmen and generally making nuisances of themselves, was an old one, its high point having been reached in the 1760s with John Wilkes's satirical periodical, the *North Briton.* For Coleridge, though, the intellectual (as opposed to social or political) aspect of this onslaught is most pronounced. Scots in his view had acquired disproportionate influence over the intellectual development, over the fundamental outlooks, of the literate classes in England. This he could not abide, not only because he was personally averse to Scots, though he certainly was that, but also because his intellectual clericalism revolted against the belief that knowledge of all kinds ought to be given the widest possible circulation, a belief both advocated and exemplified by the periodical-writing Scots among Coleridge's contemporaries. Children were instructed by Scots in school. Adults imbibed the views of Scots through newspapers and periodical reviews. Scots were now responsible for "nine tenths of the erudition"—of the knowledge, the informed opinions—"of nine tenths of the readers throughout England." It is almost as if, according to Coleridge's obviously hyperbolic outburst, Scots had come somehow to occupy what Jürgen Habermas called the "public sphere"—which is to say, that realm in which issues of social or cultural importance were discussed among informed people who were heeded and judged according to the reasonableness and cogency of their views rather than according to their power or status.

Indeed Habermas's analysis of eighteenth- and nineteenth-century European cultural history is, I believe, the most useful conceptual framework in which to understand the development decried by Coleridge, at least as it pertained to periodicals. The overriding purpose of the following chapters is to examine the means by which Scottish "men of letters" or, as we would now say, intellectuals, dominated the public sphere through periodical-writing during the first three decades of the nineteenth century.[18] And although, as the above-quoted complaints make clear, newspapers played a vital role in this development, I shall deal exclusively with periodical reviews and literary magazines, for it was mainly through these latter media, in which the combination of intellectual substance and popular accessibility proved most successful, that Scots achieved what could be called without exaggeration a dominant position in the public sphere. The most efficient way in which to address this subject, I find, is to examine in detail four of the most prominent Scottish periodical-writers of the period, namely Francis Jeffrey, founder and editor for twenty-seven years of the *Edinburgh Review*; John Wilson, *Blackwood's Magazine*'s most frequent and famous contributor and intermittently its editor; John Gibson Lockhart, originally with *Blackwood's* and later editor of the *Quarterly Review*; and Thomas Carlyle, whose fame began with essays published in the *Edinburgh*, *Fraser's*, and the *Foreign Quarterly*. By examining each of these writers with a view to elucidating the manner in which certain cultural conventions and institutions of Scotland influenced their writing, and indeed even impelled them to write in the periodical medium in the first place, I have tried to present a broader view of a period when Scottish periodicals, and Scottish periodical-writers generally, influenced the cultural disposition of British society as never before. I have not attempted to explain the precise manner in which these writers used their influence, only how their influential positions came about to begin with — how, in other words, the rise to prominence of Scottish periodicals and periodical-writers during this period was more than a merely interesting coincidence.

A brief description of Habermas's famous work, together with several relevant qualifications to his argument, will be necessary to convey the ways in which Scots came to dominate a sphere supposedly resistant to domination by individual participants. Habermas argues that in early modern Europe "private" realms began to separate. During the Middle Ages power had been exercised by what he calls "representative public-ness," or more commonly representational culture, in which outward displays of power—royal insignia, commissioned art, palatial architecture—signified sole authority.[19] With the rise of finance and trade capitalism, and the increasingly widespread exchange of information and commodities, a private realm developed in which a financially independent middle class began to recognize the authority of the state instead of the crown, a development exemplified by the separation of the state coffers from the royal purse, and by that of the bureaucracies from the court.[20] The emergence of this private realm tended, over the course of the eighteenth century, to "objectify" a public sphere in which those private individuals participated in discussions of public issues through rational argument, thus undermining the tenets on which the nobility and divine-right monarchy had based their authority to rule.[21] This public sphere of rational argument manifested itself in many forms, initially in private correspondence and official news reports, then in salons, coffeehouses, public houses, public concerts, literary societies, Freemason societies, and periodicals.[22] With the proliferation of such media, British statesmen became more and more aware that in some cases and in some ways they would have to appeal for their authority to "the public"; hence the term "public opinion" began to circulate around the middle of the century, and in 1792 Fox used the phrase in the House of Commons itself.[23]

Habermas intended to explain the origins of (as many on the continental Left in the 1960s saw it) the political lassitude and cultural superficiality of contemporary Western society by charting a transition "from cultural discourse (*Räsonnement*) to consumption."[24] Accordingly, in Habermas's avowedly Marxist reading, the bourgeois public sphere proved to have been false in its promise of all-inclusiveness: from the mid-nineteenth century civil society began to develop into a sphere of mere competing interests, an arena made to order by and for the bourgeoisie. But although there is manifestly a great deal of truth in Habermas's portrayal of eighteenth-century European historical development, I take exception to his Marxist interpretation, and wish therefore to register three relevant qualifications to his brilliant work. First, Habermas's characterization of the public sphere as fundamentally in opposition to existing political authority, arising as it does from his historically over-determined analysis, is mistaken.[25] Those existing authorities, especially the nobility, participated in and facilitated the development of the public sphere: they were, after all, the most educated people in society, and many of them understood that the expansion of power through print and other media was inevitable. To focus on the subversive dimensions of the public sphere, as James Van Horn Melton has written, "overlooks the resilience and adaptability of the Old Regime society and institutions, which were quite capable of recognizing the communicative potential of the public sphere." On the contrary, "one could just as easily see the social intermingling of noble and bourgeois as having contributed to a process of social integration, fusing the propertied classes of society into a new elite by creating new criteria for social distinction and exclusion based on education and taste."[26] Or, as T. C. W. Blanning has put much the same point, "Just as the public sphere was socially heterogeneous, so was it politically multi-directional. It was not an agenda but a space in which all kinds of opinions could be expressed, *including those which were supportive of the status quo.*"[27] Indeed, Blanning's study demolishes the notion of the public sphere as necessarily adversarial by delineating the many ways in which European power-holders, from monarchs down, skilfully manipulated the institutions and media of the allegedly bourgeois public sphere. But to the point. The logical corollary to this new understanding of the public sphere is essential to any interpretation of nineteenth-century periodical-writing, especially Scottish periodical-writing: that reviewers and magazine-writers were just as often motivated by the desire, not to destroy or undermine, but to transform the dominant understanding of cultural and political authority in such a way as to make room for themselves. Following this reasoning, Mark Parker has recently and persuasively interpreted British magazine-writing of the 1820s (the *London, Blackwood's,* the *New Monthly, Fraser's*) as in many ways an "aspiration to gentility": "Other aristocratic signs and protocols, such as political privilege, feudal sports, travel, or classical education, could not be so easily obtained, but the gentility provided by 'Literature' was within reach."[28] Just such an "aspiration to gentility" may be applied with equal, perhaps even greater, applicability to Scottish periodical-writers as a whole from the late-eighteenth century forward; the Scots, after all, had the additional burden of having come from a part of the country thought by many to be a cultural non-entity.

Second, Habermas's scheme mistakenly posits what he calls a "literary precursor" to the public sphere, or a "public sphere in the world of letters."[29] What began as a forum for the discussion of literary and artistic matters at the beginning of the eighteenth century, the obvious example in Britain being the *Spectator* and other such polite periodicals, gave way by the last third of the century to more directly political debates. But this order could just as feasibly be reversed.[30] This will surprise neither historians of the English civil war nor scholars of

Romantic literature: open and hard-hitting political arguments raged throughout the 1640s and '50s, while the discussion of literary subjects became more prevalent and more politically charged after 1789. This is a significant point because, as is well known, discussions of politics and discussions of literature are increasingly difficult to distinguish from each other in nineteenth-century periodical criticism. In Jeffrey's reviews of Wordsworth, to take an example relevant to this study, some knowledge of the reviewer's political stance, or rather stances, is vital to any assessment of that notorious conflict (although, as I shall argue, the commonly accepted depiction of Jeffrey's politics is quite mistaken).

Finally, while the language of equality was undeniably bound up with the nascent public sphere throughout the eighteenth century, Habermas, again owing to the Marxist premises of his analysis, overplays the degree to which its champions represented themselves as unselfinterested co-equals. Thus he speaks of the representation "of the selfish *bourgeois* in the guise of the unselfish *homme*," as though anyone had claimed that under the new dispensation people would shed their selfishness; elsewhere he speaks of the "allegedly universal interest of property-owning private people."[31] In such a Marxist interpretation any bourgeois or "capitalist" institution—private property, the judicial system, parliament, private firms, the family—may be said to have falsely claimed to represent universal interests; but in truth every person and institution in every society in any era may be designated likewise. The effect in Habermas's reading is to heighten the sense of disillusion in the book's latter chapters, but such interpretations do not (in my view) help one to distinguish historical eras, or illuminate the progression from one to another. Nor is this particular reading consistent with the available evidence. Certainly in post-revolutionary France, where the egalitarian project was at its most open, many forms of exclusion were unashamedly maintained, as a number of studies showed in the 1980s.[32] And in Britain before the French Revolution, as Jon Klancher has contended, many prominent writers projected an image of the public sphere more accurately thought of as concentric circles that "describe both the 'unbounded equality' of exchange within each circle and the distinctions between circles—the way all ranks are intricately connected, yet also distinct."[33] Hence even the rhetoric of those who promoted the public sphere in the eighteenth century, quite apart from their practice, never approached the egalitarianism portrayed by Habermas. The Scottish writers discussed in the following chapters adopted just such a contradictory disposition in their writing.

Owing to their undeniable (if slowly diminishing) status as outsiders in Great Britain, as also to their sense of having come from a country in which all people could (so they chose to believe) acquire education and therefore status, these Scots applied latitudinarian language liberally, yet their own rhetorical and critical demeanor was emphatically, flagrantly *not* latitudinarian. In the following analysis, then, these Scots' departures from the ideals of the public sphere will not be presented as having been motivated or necessitated by the development of capitalism; instead their aims and practices will be linked to the particular ways in which Scottish culture had transformed in the century after the Union. And for the same reasons, Habermas's critique will not be explicitly relied upon as an interpretive tool, but rather as a general and mostly tacit framing device.

I intend to stress both the continuity and the discontinuity of these writers' discursive practices with respect to public-sphere liberalism in its eighteenth-century form—"public-sphere liberalism" meaning, roughly, the ideal of equality between participants in discussion and the elevation of reasonableness over appeals to authority in debate.[34] Jeffrey, Wilson, Lockhart, and Carlyle drew heavily on the language and ideals of public-sphere liberalism, while also relying on rhetorical habits that contradicted those same ideals—which rhetorical habits, furthermore, enabled these Scots to negotiate the public sphere in such a way as effectively to grant privilege to their own writing. The public sphere, to repeat, was never, even at its high noon in the late eighteenth century, wholly or even largely defined by strict egalitarianism or, in other words, by the notion that all participants must be granted the same consideration given to all others merely by virtue of their desire or ability to participate in good faith. The public sphere had always been, as Geoff Eley has observed, "an arena of contested meanings, in which different and opposing publics maneuvered for space," and "this element of contest was not just a matter of coexistence, in which such alternative publics participated in a tolerant pluralism . . . questions of domination and subordination—power, in the economic, social, cultural, and political dimensions—were also involved."[35] The Scottish men of letters of the early nineteenth century both understood these dynamics and helped to create them.

It may seem dubious to designate Scots as a definable group, one of many "publics" jockeying for some corporate privileged status in the public sphere. But although writers such as Jeffrey and Lockhart were not attempting in any direct way to further the interests of Scotland or the Scottish people, they did bring to their writing many shared assumptions, assumptions that shaped their writing and, in turn, shaped British culture generally. As Alexander Broadie has remarked with regard to the Scottish Enlightenment, "Scots who think about politics, economics, social structures, education, law or religion are bound to have in mind the politics, economics, society, education, law or religious life of Scotland, and these national considerations are bound to influence what they write."[36] By treating Scottish periodical-writers as in some measure products of Scottish education and culture, it is possible, I believe, not only to understand why their writing took the form it did, but also cautiously to draw some conclusions about why British culture took the shape *it* did in the nineteenth century. Certain attitudes and preoccupations prompted these writers to address their readers in a way that, at the time, rivetted many and offended many more, and these attitudes and preoccupations in turn affected the nature of the public sphere as it evolved throughout the nineteenth century. Leith Davis has discussed the ways in which Scottish writers of the eighteenth and early-nineteenth centuries participated with English writers in a "literary dialogue over the nature of Britain," a dialogue in which "Scottish and English writers"—the former, especially, wishing to stake their claims in an increasingly dominant British culture—". . . attempted to articulate an identity by sometimes denying but more often acknowledging the contradictions within that identity."[37] In the following chapters I wish to present a similar kind of "dialogue" (though from an exclusively Scottish point of view). Scottish periodical-writers discovered several means by which to respond to the London-centered culture around them on terms set by that culture, while at the same time transforming those terms in such a way that advantage effectively accrued—at least temporarily—to themselves.

EXCHANGE AND DOMINATION

What generated the phenomenon of Scottish preeminence in early-nineteenth-century periodical-writing is hardly a new question. Several observers have attributed it to the nature of Scottish university education. Oxford and Cambridge tended to stress classics and mathematics, whereas Scottish universities stressed philosophy, logic, and classical rhetoric, and were far less specialized in their approach. Scottish universities, as Joan Milne and Willie Smith have argued, "aimed to produce a mind that was intellectually flexible, articulate and wide ranging."[38] Walter Bagehot must have been the first to point this out:

"the teaching of Scotland," he wrote in his 1855 essay "The First Edin-burgh Reviewers," "seems to have been designed to teach men to write essays and articles. . . . The particular, compact, exclusive learning of England is inferior in this respect to the general, diversified, omnipres-ent information of the north."[39] Bagehot's point seems plausible in light of the fact that the generalist or "philosophical" approach in Scottish university education was most pronounced during the late-eighteenth and early-nineteenth centuries.[40] Moreover, many of the most promi-nent figures in Scottish periodical-writing had been motivated by a more mundane concern: they were lawyers who for a variety of reasons had too few clients to live comfortably. The lawyers Jeffrey, Brougham, and Horner were all, at least partly owing to their known Whig politics, without much work in early 1802.[41] Lockhart and Wilson were both fledgling advocates when they took up magazine-writing.[42] Lockhart complained (in the voice of Peter Morris) that younger lawyers in the Scottish courts could hardly find enough work to live on.[43] In 1825, just before leaving for London to take his post as editor of the *Quarterly Re-view*, Lockhart, asked to make a toast at a farewell dinner given by friends from the Edinburgh bar, began by quipping, "You know very well that I am no speaker; for, if I had been, there would have been no occasion for this parting."[44]

To this must be added the fact that England in general and London in particular had never had a cohesive and easily distinguishable group of men of letters, whereas Scotland had. The question of why British society never produced its own version of France's radicalized homme de lettre is an old and complex one, bound up as it is with the "Whig" conception of British political history, but it is safe to say that no radical or even reformist "intelligentsia," to use an anachronistic term, ever arose in eighteenth-century London (and certainly not in eighteenth-century Oxford and Cambridge). Yet something of precisely that de-scription formed the engine of the Scottish Enlightenment.[45] One of the distinguishing characteristics of eighteenth-century British intellectual history was that its intellectual enclaves were dispersed over the whole country, and were not, as in France, concentrated in the capital city.[46] The point here is that London, an exponentially bigger and wealthier city than Edinburgh, but not a place notoriously rife with well-known writers, was therefore not a place to which Scottish writers felt they had to emigrate in order to make names for themselves by their writings.

But these considerations, while certainly relevant, reveal little about what made the Scots' writings themselves uniquely persuasive in the arena of literary and cultural criticism at the beginning of the century.

Any account of this must, of course, begin with the success of the *Edinburgh Review* in the 1800s. Circulation numbers can conceal as much as they reveal, but the journal's dramatic numerical rise was truly remarkable: by 1807 it had surpassed all the major London reviews by selling seven thousand copies, while the venerable and still influential *Monthly Review* sold only five thousand. In 1814 the *Edinburgh* sold thirteen thousand copies; in 1818, twelve thousand—more than any other periodical (of which numbers are extant, anyhow) save William Cobbett's *Political Register* after 1816 when it was published in a twopenny edition.[47] But the more important if less quantifiable part of the story has to do with the enormous influence it acquired almost instantaneously. Within a matter of five or six years the *Edinburgh* achieved a level of prestige and cultural authority totally foreign to any of the older reviews and magazines. The reasons for this shocking success have been discussed many times for the past two centuries, often unhelpfully. For years scholars concerned with the subject, unwisely relying on the testimonies of the early *Edinburgh* reviewers themselves, assumed that the eighteenth century's reviewers had been mere hacks serving the interests of their bookseller-employers, and that the *Edinburgh*'s supposedly apparent "independence" made it attractive to readers of reviews. But, as Derek Roper has definitively argued, the pre-1802 reviewers could not possibly have got away with puffing books published by the publishers of the same periodicals in the way often described.[48] What made the *Edinburgh* different was, rather, its selectivity. The earlier periodicals had aspired towards encyclopedic knowledge; they were intended to be bound, stored, and shelved precisely as encyclopedias were.[49] The *Edinburgh* reviewers, by contrast, announced at the head of the first issue that their journal would be distinguished "rather for the selection, than for the number of its articles." "The final number of the *Analytical* had reviewed sixty-five works; in October 1802 the *Monthly* reviewed forty-four, the *Critical* sixty, and the *British Critic* seventy-seven. The *Edinburgh*, which as a quarterly might have been expected to deal with three times as many works as these monthly journals, reviewed twenty-nine."[50] The *Edinburgh*, then, achieved authority because it presented itself authoritatively: other journals reviewed everything, it seemed to say, whereas we will tell you what is important.

The subject of authority touches upon the crucial characteristic of Scottish periodical-writing at this period. For authority in its discursive manifestation, at least as I am using the word—the power to command deference to opinions and positions mainly by virtue of the fact that those opinions and positions appear under the name of a certain writer or in the pages of a certain periodical publication—goes against the grain of public-sphere liberalism. Not that the notion of discursive authority was new in 1802. Even in that seemingly most egalitarian realm of "periodical literature," authority in this sense had existed. In the 1790s, for example, many reviewers, evidently troubled by the huge quantity of printed material in circulation, began claiming their right through criticism to disallow kitsch from finding any significant readership: "by brandishing what the *Gentleman's* called 'the correcting lash of criticism,' reviewers would be able to offer an informal type of censorship based on their power to persuade."[51] "Based on their power to persuade," yes, but based also on the fact that their reviews appeared in respected and venerable journals: such is the nature of periodical criticism of any kind, in any era.

This, however, was a different order of authority from what appeared in the *Edinburgh* and later in *Blackwood's*. The Scots, I shall argue in chapter 1, understood the nature of the public sphere almost by instinct. A great majority of educated Scots right through the first quarter of the nineteenth century accepted without qualm the belief that Scottish education was, and had long been, widely available on the basis of ability rather than wealth or rank. Yet these same writers were just as quick to depart from the ideals of discursive equality and reciprocity, and this for a variety of reasons. The first and most obvious reason has to do with the reality, stubbornly persistent throughout the eighteenth century and into the nineteenth, that Scots remained "North Britons" and that Scotland remained what Cockburn called, with pride, "a remote part of the kingdom."[52] The Scottish landed elite, merchant and professional classes, and intelligentsia all wanted to participate in British cultural and political life; indeed the chief reason why Scots became so prevalent among the British Empire's administrators, to take only the most striking instance of the Scots' southern-directed ambition, is precisely this desire to make Great Britain into more of an equal partnership.[53] For the periodical-writer, invoking the values of equality as opposed to privilege and unfounded authority might come naturally, and might even provide a means by which to lay claim to some personal respectability or literary legitimacy. But the ambition to achieve "respectability" and "legitimacy" also lends itself easily to the ambition to achieve ascendancy, and within the first six years of the *Edinburgh's* publication Jeffrey secured something like critical omnipotence for the journal—what in theory no participant in any liberal public sphere can possess—by asserting the virtues and inevitability of the "diffusion of knowledge"; i.e. the first prerequisite in any notion of a public sphere.

It is probably true that the *Edinburgh* reviewers' realization that the public sphere could be both promoted and dominated had as much to do with their Whig outlook as their Scottishness. Scott understood this when he remarked in 1822 that the "new Whigs" of the *Edinburgh Review* have "a great belief in the influence of fine writing and think that a nation can be governed by pamphlets and reviews."[54] Of course by this date Scott had himself been fully engaged in trying to govern the country through journalistic commentary. The "philosophic Whigs" may have been the first to grasp the governable nature of the nascent public sphere, but Scots of other political outlooks caught on almost immediately; they sensed a disjunction between the ideal of the public sphere and the way it was practiced. "Only in this ideal discursive sphere is exchange without domination possible," Terry Eagleton has written, "for to persuade is not to dominate, and to carry one's opinion is more an act of collaboration than of competition."[55] Perhaps, but it is also true that the public sphere had never been "ideal" (a point with which Eagleton would agree, if not to the extent I would claim).

The public sphere had never been ideal, moreover, for the principal reason that it had involved real people and had existed in the real world in which everyone was (is) primarily interested in themselves: it could be used for any number of purposes by those who understood its institutions. The first and most basic form of reasonable interchange to take place within most of those institutions—coffeehouses and the like—was the conversation itself, that is, the spoken conversation. The strictures of politeness, as will be discussed in chapter 2, decreed the manner in which people were expected to take part in these conversations, and those strictures were also applied to the institutions whose medium was not oral but written, especially the periodical. The affinities between engaging in polite conversation and writing in periodicals are readily apparent quite apart from eighteenth-century notions of politeness. The critic Clive James has recently summed up his own job this way: "The role of the freelance man of letters . . . is to accept—and to act on the acceptance—that he is engaged in a perpetual discussion, an interminable exchange of views in which he cannot, and should not, prevail."[56] The very fact that the periodical is an ongoing affair, seemingly perpetual, implies the contingent nature of the views expressed in it. But James's statement is normative ("cannot, and should not"); other men of letters may not feel obliged to forego the attempt to prevail, and in fact Scottish men of letters of the early-nineteenth century—beginning their writing careers at the end of a long period during which the rules of politeness had been rigidly adhered to by middle-class Scots—did not feel so obliged. Accordingly many of them, though still fixated on conversational ability, became more interested in the individual's ability to "shine" than with reciprocity or strict politeness, and this new style of conversation appeared strikingly in the reviews and essays they wrote. Their bearing as critics became, in time, more like that of the twentieth-century American literary critic Edmund Wilson. "The implied position of the people who know about literature," Wilson believed, ". . . is simply that they know what they know, and that they are determined to impose their opinions by main force of eloquence or assertion on the people who do not know."[57] The new and more individualistic attitude to conversation was promoted most vigorously by John Wilson in *Blackwood's*, where conversational fluency becomes a particularly Scottish (as opposed to English or faux-English) talent, but a similar brand of Scottish cultural promotion is evident in the very style of the *Edinburgh Review*. In fact, a large part of what made that journal so original, and thus successful and influential, was precisely this underlying "national vanity," to use Jeffrey's phrase for it, in which Scottish intellectuals wished to portray themselves as adept communicators.

On Wilson I have taken a very different approach from that taken by Andrew Noble in an essay for the recent *History of Scottish Literature* series. Noble's forthrightly Marxian (if not Marxist) interpretation treats Wilson's role in what the author describes as "Tory Hegemony," the rise of a sentimentalized political conservatism that purportedly dominated Scottish culture during the nineteenth century.[58] My own analysis of Wilson's writing is not necessarily incompatible with Noble's, whose invectives tend in any case to resist falsifiability in the way such interpretations do. Still, it should be pointed out that Wilson's public persona was far from comprehensively admired by the representatives of conservatism Noble disparages. One Evangelical minister, John Dunlop, a leader in the temperance movement, scrawled out a gleeful poem upon Wilson's death in 1854. Part of it runs: "While 'Toryism' rears its front / And 'Moderatism' thrives upon't / While Scottish Drink absorbs the praise / So long men Wilson's glory raise."[59] As poetry it could hardly be worse, but it illustrates the point that no writer whose celebrity relied so entirely on the image of alcoholic hilarity and wild heuristic criticism can fairly be described primarily as a force for stale conservatism or traditional morality. (It may help to recall, too, that a young critic called R. L. Stevenson once penned a rapturously favorable review of an 1876 edition of Wilson's "Noctes Ambrosianæ.") Wilson did promote a kind of cultural hegemony, and his importance in Victorian Scotland is a subject worth pursuing (though it shall not be pursued here). But this "hegemony" was part of a much wider propensity among literary Scots throughout the first decades of the century to claim fluency and eloquence, and by extension intelligence and genius and wit, as Scottish property.

In the two subsequent chapters, 3 and 4, the public sphere as an analytic tool is less in evidence, but the subjects dealt with there do have relevance to the nineteenth-century public sphere. Chapter 3 deals specifically with John Gibson Lockhart, whose decades-long concern with the question of what the status of imaginative literature ought to be reveals much about the notorious conflict between English bards and Scotch reviewers, which is to say between the poets of Romanticism and Scottish literary critics. When dealing with these poets the Scottish periodical-writers tended to promote a conception of the public sphere that seemed to contrast with their own practice. In response to claims by the most prominent Romantic poets to possess some special knowledge and therefore (at least by implication) a more elevated status in society, their Scottish antagonists contended that imaginative writers, even when their works warrant praise, do not possess higher knowledge and thus deserve no special recognition. Here the effects of anonymity are especially evident, for these writers were for the most part free of the necessity of making their essays and reviews cohere; each piece had to be taken on its own. Not only that, but anonymity allowed the Scottish men of letters to be "literary" without advertizing that potentially embarrassing epithet. Their rejection of the Romantic poets' elevation of imaginative writing, as it turns out, had much to do with their own belief, an inheritance from late-eighteenth Scottish culture, that writing imaginative works—not necessarily reading poetry or fiction, but actually writing in those forms—was an intrinsically unsound enterprise. It is generally known that many Scottish people in the eighteenth century, especially (but not only) the more conservative Presbyterians, remained suspicious of poetry and fiction long after most people in polite society not only approved of them but enthused over them. Scottish literature itself reflects this antagonism.[60] It has rarely been acknowledged, however, that suspicion of imaginative writing, or at least suspicion of the activity of writing works of the imaginative order, was more than the preoccupation of religious extremists. In truth, writing poems and fiction was frowned upon by socially eminent people from business and professional fields as well as from Evangelicals in the Kirk, and these apprehensions, rather than being pervasively rejected or ignored, tended to push young men (and some women, for overlapping though distinct reasons) into the anonymous world of periodical-writing. Thus the ambiguous position occupied by imaginative literature in Scotland at the turn of the eighteenth and nineteenth centuries helped to produce a generation of periodical-writers who, in resisting the claims of Romanticism, in effect promoted the idea that imaginative literature ought to have something to say to everyone—an updated form of equality-centered public-sphere liberalism. In this respect, I believe, the Scottish men of letters exposed a contradiction between the poetics and the politics of the Romantic movement in Britain. Yet they themselves were caught in a contradiction. These Scottish critics, while averse to the claims consciously made by poets of this period, tacitly accepted the truth of those claims: accepted, that is, Romantic conceptions of the importance and sway of imaginative literature. They believed poets to be—or that poets could be, and certainly that poets had been—unacknowledged legislators. As for Lockhart, he solved the problem by invoking the old idea of the amateur, the genteel writer who writes principally to amuse himself because, crucially, he does not take himself seriously as a writer. The flagrant anachronism of that ideal, the fact that Lockhart himself was in some respects still a Calvinist, and the fact that his pretensions to good breeding were not quite credible, induced him to modify his conception of amateurism into something more realistic, and that something was not given substantial definition until his 1837–38 biography of Walter Scott.

In this chapter on Lockhart, and especially in chapter 4 on Carlyle, I have tried to take seriously one aspect of Scottish culture during this era, an aspect too often ignored or clumsily handled in recent scholarship, namely that Kirk ministers exercized a great deal of influence over the outlooks, dispositions, self-understandings, and aspirations of a great number of Scottish people. This fact is corroborated by many sources. Here are three:

> In England I maintain that (except amongst Ladies in the middle class of life) there is no religion at all. The Clergy of England have no more influence over the people at large than the Cheesemongers of England have. In Scotland the Clergy are extremely active in the discharge of their functions, and are from the hold they have on the minds of the people a very important body of men. The common people are extremely conversant with the Scriptures, and really not so much pupils, as formidable critics to their preachers; many of them are well read in controversial divinity. They are perhaps in some points of view the most remarkable nation in the world, and no country can afford an example of so much order, morality, oeconomy, and knowledge amongst the lower classes of Society.[61]

Among the people of Scotland, conversation turns much more frequently, and much more fervently, on the character and attainments of the individual clergyman, than is at all usual with us in England.

   . . . The slavish wonderment with which they [the Methodists] are gazed upon by the goggling eyes of their mechanical followers, is a very different sort of thing from the filial respect with which the Moncrieffs, Inglises, and Chalmerses of Scotland, are regarded by the devout descendants of the old establishers of Presbytery.[62]

Very venerable are those old Seceder Clergy to me, now when I look back on them. [*Crossed out:* More Christian-looking speakers of the word I never saw. Learned people, many of them, too; continually studious about what belonged to their business, in the theory or in the practice. Well-mannered, peaceably dignified people, poor but true and wise; of a pious rustic simplicity, or steadfast courtesy, silently resting on nature and the intrinsic fact against all comers.] Most of the figures among them, in Irving's time and mine, were hoary old men. Men so like what one might call antique "Evangelists in Modern Vestiture, and Poor Scholars and Gentlemen of Christ," I have nowhere met with in Monasteries or Churches, among Protestant or Papal Clergy, in any country in the world.[63]

Now although there may be more to these passages than what appears on the surface ("Peter Morris" is not always Lockhart, for one thing), taken together they give a fair idea of the ministerial class's highly influential status in Scotland, a status not confined to rural parishes or rigidly orthodox circles. Chapter 4 is an attempt to determine how this reality might have contributed to the Scottish dominance in periodical literature. The principal form in which the Scottish minister distinguished himself and communicated with his congregation, the sermon, is after all totally antithetical to the ideals of equality and reciprocity. And the sermon, omnipresent in Scotland, was in effect a form of essay—not, however, a polite essay in the eighteenth-century tradition, but an essay characterized by direct claims to authority. The discursive demeanor that animated the Presbyterian sermon also animated the essays of Scottish periodical-writers from Jeffrey forward. In the case of Carlyle this was literally so: essay-writing was for him another means of projecting the power of the pulpit. But, I will argue, other Scottish writers were similarly influenced by this form, and although in cases other than Carlyle's this is not always entirely provable, it does meet the demands of common sense. Nearly all the Scottish periodical-writers of this period heard sermons with hebdomadal regularity from childhood—thus for instance the essayist and German scholar R. P. Gillies began his writing career at age fourteen by writing sermons, and John Wilson, who as a child was educated in a manse, once preached to his family using a chair as a pulpit.[64]

Interpreting periodical-writing presents a unique dilemma between treating the discourse of individual authors, on the one hand, and that of individual periodicals or groups of periodicals, on the other. The first of these is entirely legitimate and often unavoidable, and it underpins one of the truly great reference works of nineteenth-century historical and literary scholarship, the *Wellesley Index to Victorian Periodicals*. It is still true, as *Wellesley*'s editor Walter Houghton wrote in 1974, that "an anonymous paper attacking the Thirty-nine Articles . . . would mean one thing if it were written by T. H. Huxley and something quite different if the author was the Bishop of London."[65] Houghton's approach is limited, however, by the facts that the writing in question was sometimes composed in collaboration, that anonymity and pseudonymity often allowed authors to write what they didn't believe or knew to be untrue or half-true, and that authors took for granted their readers' familiarity with a host of contemporary and often ephemeral realities. Klancher has addressed this problem by treating the individual journal as a source of what at one point he calls "a powerful transauthorial discourse" that echoes through the periodical's "protean collocation of styles, topics, and voices."[66] Such an approach has many advantages, not least that it sheds light on the specific ways in which periodical journals affected the development of Britain's social and political cultures. And yet, as I will note on two occasions in the following pages, it is difficult not to suspect that this approach lends itself easily to misinterpretations of individual pieces because they seem to fit into some analytic paradigm or preconception. This may be because the writer's other works are given insufficient attention, thus luring the interpreter into attributing an intention in glaring contrast to the writer's, or because the essay or review under consideration seems noteworthy from a twenty-first-century viewpoint but was atypical of, or even totally anomalous in, the journal in which it appeared.

Although I can hardly claim to have solved this dilemma, I have tried to keep in mind the difficulties inherent in both approaches. The fact that I view Scottish periodical-writers as a generally circumscribable group rather than specific periodicals and their pools of contributors has made it necessary, on the one hand, to concentrate on specific authors. Jeffrey, Wilson, Lockhart, and Carlyle each brought his own viewpoint and ambition to his journalism; those viewpoints and ambitions were closely linked to their own experiences, and those experiences were bound up with a specific national culture. There is no contradiction, it seems to me, between recognition of this and the indisputable fact that these writers were also media through which competing and even mutually exclusive forms of discourse expressed themselves. I would even suggest that these two factors appear almost comfortably together in the work of individual periodical-writers who wrote under the cloak of anonymity: they were permitted both to say what they liked (within perimeters set by editors and publishers) and to contradict what they had written on previous occasions. By examining many of an individual periodical-writer's works published over a long period, it is entirely possible, I believe, to configure a general outlook or, more specifically, a persisting project or aim. I have tried to draw out those outlooks and aims that bear some appreciable relationship to late-eighteenth-century Scottish culture, and in that way to frame the Scots' dominance of nineteenth-century periodical literature as a natural consequence of interaction among a specific set of social and political realities.

On the other hand, there is always an element of what Parker has called "irreducible rhetoricity" in any periodical publication: "A writer's intentions are only part of the meaning of the work in a periodical: a work in such a setting enters a variety of relations with other articles and ongoing institutional concerns that give subtle inflection to its meaning," including "appeals to what often goes without saying in a particular magazine or review, innuendo familiar to its circle of readers, exaggeration discernible only by reference to the standard line of the periodical."[67] Recognition of this point is especially important in examining Jeffrey's writing, not only because he entertained certain assumptions about his readers and wrote accordingly, but also because he was editor of the journal for which he wrote. Ever fretful about the success of the journal, he had a greater interest in and control over the way readers perceived it. Carlyle, by contrast, cared little about the success of the journals in which his writing appeared, and was much more concerned about combatting societal trends that he felt he alone had detected. Yet both Jeffrey's and Carlyle's rhetorical styles are—so I shall try to demonstrate—products of a national culture. And so, to sum up, each of the writers dealt with in this study were influenced by, and in turn capitalized on, certain aspects of late-eighteenth- and early-nineteenth-century Scottish culture, and those cultural influences, discernible to one degree or another in the work of each, combined to forge a rhetorical approach that practically guaranteed the Scottish men of letters a dominant place in the public sphere.

1

"A mere intellectual bazaar": The *Edinburgh Review* in (and as) the Public Sphere, 1802–1808

Scottish Writers and the Educated Populace

Little has yet been written on the ways in which Scottish writers of the late-eighteenth and early-nineteenth centuries helped to formulate the concept of the "public sphere"—which is to say, Scottish writers *as* Scottish writers, not simply the odd Scottish writer (Hume, say) among British writers generally. This paucity in recent scholarship is strange since, as anyone who has dealt with Scottish writing of this era will know, there are few convictions more commonly expressed by them than their belief in the existence of a literate and basically educated population in Scotland. Writers and intellectuals presupposing such a belief, however justified or mistaken they may have been in matters of historical fact, would have been well-prepared to take part in discussions of the idea of a public sphere; or so it would seem. Put otherwise, those who promoted the notion of a Scottish "democratic intellect," however mythical that notion was, would have been instinctively comfortable with the notion of an arena in which discussions of public moment were carried on between reasonable people by means of rational argument, without regard (or with less regard than in earlier periods) to wealth and rank. Whether the available evidence supports the period's presuppositions about Scottish education has been closely scrutinized in recent years, but the fact that Scottish people up to and including the early-nineteenth century adopted those presuppositions, even incorporating them into their sense of Scottish identity, is beyond dispute.[1] Indeed, as T. C. Smout has observed with regard to the first quarter of the nineteenth century, "It is hard to think of any subject on which Scots were so united as this determination to praise and to attribute wonders to the national tradition of education."[2]

In the latter eighteenth and early-nineteenth centuries the belief took, roughly speaking, two forms: a sentimentalized form in which the Scottish population at large, and especially the lower class, appeared as literate and intellectually well-equipped; and a more specific and politically oriented form in which the putative fact of an educated general population was assumed, understood to be a result of specific historical circumstances, and (on subjects of governmental policy) presented as the basis for some governmental initiative or broad political approach. These two views could be described as, respectively, the Scottish Tory view and the Scottish Whig view, though the distinction should not be pushed too far.

First, the Scottish Tory view. It appears in Smollett's fiction, where for example Matthew Bramble notes that the Scottish peasantry "are content, and wonderfully sagacious—All of them read the Bible, and are even qualified to dispute upon the articles of their faith"; and Roderick Random, when asked how he knows Latin, Greek, philosophy, and mathematics, replies that "it was not to be wondered at if I had a tolerable education, because learning was so cheap in my country, that every peasant was a scholar."[3] During the alarmism of the 1790s, of course, few on either side of the political spectrum would have dared to romanticize the lower classes with too much gusto, but at the beginning of the nineteenth century, many conservative writers felt free at least to romanticize the poor. A remark by Mary Brunton in her journal upon returning to rural Scotland from London in 1815 is typical: "Our cottages range in vile rows, flanked with pig-styes, and fronted with dunghills; but our cottagers have Bibles, and can read them."[4] In his novel *Reginald Dalton,* Lockhart created a Scottish coach driver, whose speech is pronouncedly lower-class, but whose knowledge of Ovid is somehow comprehensive.[5] Again, Lockhart mused in 1821 that the two most educated classes in Scotland were the shepherds of the Borders and the weavers of Glasgow: "They have both of them their libraries supported by voluntary subscriptions—& rich to an extent of which no Englishman could form any idea—these people read & think—they all consider reading as the natural occupation of their leisure hours. . . . They lie all day long on the hills wrapt in their plaids reading—what do you think—why the latest Quarterly Review or Ivanhoe or the Doge of Venice—whatever was a month or two before read by the first men in London.[6]

Another Tory and Blackwoodian, Wilson pushed this romanticized version of the well-read Scottish peasant as far as he could; his once-popular collection of stories *Lights and Shadows of Scottish Life* (1822) brims with such characters. There, as well as in his *Blackwood's* contributions, Wilson often used the sentimentalized Scottish peasant-scholar to advance his own version of Scottish cultural nationalism; Burns and the Ettrick Shepherd provided easy subjects.[7] Scott himself claimed to consider the common people of Scotland the best-educated in the world, and to Samuel Johnson's famous remark that in Scotland "learning is like bread in a besieged town: every man gets a little, but no man gets a full meal," Scott replied that "it was better education should be divided in mouthfuls, than served up at the banquet of some favoured individuals, while the great mass were left to starve."[8]

The second, more Whiggish and utilitarian view has a more substantive intellectual foundation, and accordingly was used for more directly political aims. Its expression often translated into political and institutional reform, as though the fact (as it was believed to be) of a basically educated populace in Scotland might help to relieve apprehensions about making that populace yet more educated. By the first years of the nineteenth century Scotland had become a locus of progressive thought and philanthropy on universal literacy and education. Scottish Evangelicals urged mass literacy, primarily for the purpose of Bible-reading, as one of the chief means by which social problems could be redressed; and utilitarians such as Robert Owen advocated universal education as the chief instrument of social progress. Gaelic school societies were started to improve education in the Highlands, and were eventually, in view of immigration from rural to metropolitan areas, propagated in the cities as well. At the same time, "sessional schools" were started by the Church of Scotland as a parish-based solution to political disaffection by equipping the poor with literacy and other skills.[9] Rev. Henry Duncan of Ruthwell, George Miller, and Thomas Dick were all zealous promoters of adult education, which would, as the first *Scottish Cheap Repository* put it in 1807, "[excite] a taste for reading and diffusing useful instruction among the vulgar"; and although they were hardly egalitarians, the record of their activities does indicate a widespread excitement among the Scottish middle and (to some extent) upper classes about the potential societal advantages of "diffusing" knowledge among the country's poor.[10] The first "working-class libraries" in Britain, after all, were begun in Scotland during the 1780s and '90s.[11] The Mechanics' Institute, the forerunner of which had been Anderson's College in Glasgow, begun in 1796, and later the Society for the Diffusion of Useful Knowledge, co-founded by Henry Brougham in 1827, were both originally Scottish ideas—part of the "March of Intellect," or what the earlier Cobbett called "Scotch feelosophy" and what English critics such as Coleridge and Lord Eldon thought inimical to societal order.[12] True, some adult-educationists in England, especially Hannah More, shared these Scots' belief in society's duty to educate the "vulgar," but "the standard bearers in Scotland exhibited a more whole-hearted faith in the effectiveness of education than did Mrs. More."[13] At the very least, the Scots were less divided on the issue than were the English elite.

An excellent instance of what I am calling the Scottish Whig view appears in Robert Henry's *History of Great Britain.* Henry accounts for the putative learning of the common people of Scotland by a set of political circumstances initiated by the Scottish Parliament: "By an act of parliament . . . every freeholder of substance was obliged to keep his eldest son at some grammar school till he had acquired a perfect knowledge of the Latin language, and then to put him three years to some university to study philosophy and the laws." Thus, Henry concludes, "a competency at least of learning became gradually more general among the gentlemen, and even among the common people of Scotland, than in any other country of Europe."[14] Henry's ostensibly historical treatment holds political implications not very difficult to discern. John Millar's treatment of the same subject—that is, how education became so pervasive among the Scottish people—is yet more politically suggestive. A Whig professor at Glasgow University famous (and notorious) for his liberal political views, Millar argues in his history of the English constitution that the parish school system was not the source of "intelligence, sagacity, and disposition to learning, in the common people of Scotland," but that the parish school system was itself the result of a complex set of economic and political circumstances.

> The peculiar spirit with which the Scots had overturned the Roman Catholic superstition, gave a peculiar modification to their intellectual pursuits. The great ferment excited over the whole nation, the rooted antipathy to the former ecclesiastical doctrines, produced a disposition to inquire, and to embrace no tenets without examination. . . . Even the common mass of the people took an interest in the various points of theological controversy; became conversant in many abstract disquisitions connected with them; and were led to acquire a sort of literary curiosity.
>
> The activity and vigour of mind which had thus been excited, produced a general attention to the propagation of knowledge by a liberal education.[15]

Millar's discussion exhibits a characteristically Whig viewpoint in its underlying conviction that intellectual progress or "improvement" had come about, and by implication could come about again, through the interaction of specific cultural and political forces. What is important in the present context is that Millar simply assumes that "the common people of Scotland" had in fact exhibited "intelligence, sagacity, and disposition to learning"; indeed the force of his argument depends entirely on that assumption.

And that is what characterized much of Scottish cultural criticism from this period. An unquestioning belief in the existence of an educated and intellectually-equipped Scottish populace, encompassing even "the common people," provided support for some other contention about how the world works or should work. James Mill relied on the assumption to put forward his controversial views on education, arguing in the *Edinburgh Review*, for instance, that the "intellectual and moral values" of the English populace were inferior to those of the Scottish; England had outstripped Scotland in every respect, he thought, but not in educating its masses. "We desire our opponents [those who wished to revamp the Scottish education system] to tell us, in what respect the circumstances of the English population have not been more favourable than those of the Scottish, except in the article of schooling alone?"[16] Mill would soon use the Scottish model as evidence for his views on democratizing all of Britain's educational system.[17] As did other Scots. In an 1802 pamphlet entitled *The General Diffusion of Knowledge One Great Cause of the Prosperity of North Britain*, Alexander Christison contended that Scotland's economic success and political stability were fruits of the country's policy of educating all of its subjects, even its poorest.[18] Again, in 1818, speaking for a bill before a Commons committee on education, Henry Brougham made deft use of the stereotype of common Scottish people as well-educated: "Go where you will in the world, the name of a Scotchman is still found — combined . . . , perhaps, *with some qualities which sincere regard for that good people restrains me from mentioning,* but certainly with the reputation of a well-educated man!"[19] Like Mill, Brougham seems willing to concede the truth of any unfavorable estimation of the Scottish people apart from the suggestion that education is not common among them.

In light of these considerations it is not surprising to detect a difference between the way Scottish writers treated public-sphere concepts and the way English writers treated them. This issue deserves analysis. The word "diffusion," as applied to "knowledge" and "learning," had emerged in British writing of the 1780s and '90s as a kind of cultural keyword. For "diffusion," defined as "spreading abroad, dissemination (of abstract things, as knowledge)," the *OED* lists the first instance as having appeared in Hume's 1741 *Essays:* "universal diffusion of learning among the people." Such phrases as "dissemination of knowledge" and "diffusion of knowledge" were intimately bound up with the notion of a public sphere, evoking as they did the image of education being dispersed in ever-expanding concentric circles. Jon Klancher has explained how pre-1789 British periodicals generated the idea of a public sphere largely by fostering an intimacy between writers and readers and by addressing their audiences in terms of familiarity and parity; and while the periodicals' language was often modified according to the particular audience they wished to reach (merchants, clergy, landed gentry), the hope was to broaden their influence by consolidating successive readerships.[20] The French Revolution, however, obliterated that hope by fragmenting British society into disparate and mutually suspicious social and political groupings, and in doing so made it necessary for periodical-writers to discover their audience's "reading habit," or cultural and ideological disposition, and work to consolidate it.[21]

One important distinction not sufficiently recognized in Klancher's book, however, is that between Scottish and English writers in the 1800s and early 1810s. Owing largely to their assumptions about widespread education among the Scottish population, Scottish writers of this period tended to persist in the use of universalist language, though at least in part for reasons suggesting self-concern rather than universalist altruism. Even Tory and otherwise traditionalist Scots failed to respond to the radical and reformist discourse of this decade in the robust manner of, say, High Church Anglicans: the ever-expanding "diffusion of knowledge" implicit in their own understanding of Scottish society, coupled with their need to employ the discourse of "diffusion" as a means of establishing their place in the British republic of letters, softened and blunted the counterarguments they might otherwise have used. As for reform-minded writers from Scotland such as Millar and Brougham and Mill, their handling of public-sphere discourse was proficient and profuse for the same reasons. It is true that the ideas of the "diffusion" were central to reform movements in England during the 1790s: radical figures such as Thomas Paine, Mary Wollstonecraft, and the young Wordsworth all espoused versions of a public sphere that would function through the constantly widening dissemination of knowledge.[22] But in England the idea of a liberal public sphere of print was very far from universally espoused—it was generally associated with Dissenters such as Joseph Priestley and radicals such as William Godwin, even if conservative periodicals invoked conceptually related ideas from time to time; and in any case there were many critics of public-sphere ideologies (Burke chief among them) whose arguments were both uncompromising and much read.[23] Public-sphere theorists in England, though differing in approach, formed a distinct group with particular aims, all converging on the issue of electoral reform.

The case was different with the great majority of this era's Scottish writers. For not only were they accustomed to equate the idea of diffusing knowledge with the actual historical development of their own country, but they also had a vested interest, as Scots, in promulgating that same idea. By celebrating the emergence of an open arena in which rational argument counted for more than rank or wealth—or, indeed, country of origin or associated accent—Scots were by implication laying claim to a place at the center of Britain's cultural life. That is why Scottish reformists and radicals of the 1780s and '90s, those most energetic in the cause of expanded knowledge and rights, promoted an emphatically British rather than Scottish political identity.[24]

Postulating a liberal public sphere helped to earn Scottish people (to change the metaphor) a place at the table. And no one did this with more subtlety and sophistication than Francis Jeffrey of the *Edinburgh Review*. What he did in the process was, in effect, to buy the table and place his contributors around it.

THE *EDINBURGH REVIEW* AS PUBLIC SPHERE

From its first number in October 1802, to October 1809 when it provoked the creation of the *Quarterly*, the *Edinburgh Review* dominated the public sphere of print culture in Britain.[25] There was, quite simply, no serious rival to the *Edinburgh*. The absence of alternative printed viewpoints is strikingly clear in the famous episode in which Lord Buchan, in a highly eccentric ceremony, kicked the offending issue of the *Edinburgh Review* out of his house into the street, "to be trodden under foot by man and beast."[26] The article Buchan found unsettling, "Don Pedro Cevallos on the French Usurpation of Spain," will be discussed in due course; here it is sufficient to note that he felt compelled physically to attack the journal itself. Buchan was an unusual man, but that kind of behavior seems inexplicable apart from the fact that the *Edinburgh*'s words were taken by a great many people to be peremptory, inerrant.

The journal's founders were surprised by its instantaneous popularity, as all their correspondence at the time makes clear. Yet the journal's success cannot have taken them completely by surprise. Anyone who starts a political or literary periodical does so in the belief that it has a good chance of success because the views he means to promulgate are largely or totally absent from the domain of print culture. That was the case with the first *Edinburgh* reviewers, but their venture, rather than simply promoting a new viewpoint or set of opinions, had the effect — for a time — of actually replacing the domain of cultural criticism as it existed in Britain. The language of public-sphere interchange, and the concomitant notions of "diffusion" and "dissemination" of knowledge and learning, were deployed to brilliant effect — primarily by Jeffrey, whose articles tended to take pride of place in each number either by appearing first or by treating the most contentious and prominent subjects in contemporary discussion, but also by Brougham and Francis Horner. The concept of diffusing knowledge, despite its suggestions of decentralization and dispersal of authority, provided the *Edinburgh Review* with a powerful tool for the imposition and exercise of its own authority — a dynamic that could not have taken place (so this chapter is meant to show) apart from the Scottish provenance of the journal's founders, and especially its editor.

The first *Edinburgh* reviewers, as has often (and correctly) been said of them, were the purest products of the Scottish Enlightenment. The ideas of diffusion were a central component of their education. Dugald Stewart, who taught Brougham and Horner at Edinburgh University, and whose lectures Jeffrey attended subsequent to his time as a student, routinely made the highest claims for the power of diffusion, referring for instance to "the present age, when the press has to so wonderful a degree emancipated human reason from the tyranny of ancient prejudices, and has roused a spirit of free discussion, unexampled in the history of former times."[27] Stewart believed that the diffusion of knowledge would counter the ill effects of the division of manual labor by creating a division of intellectual labor: "Different individuals are led, partly by original temperament, partly by early education, to betake themselves to different studies . . . and when the productions to which they give birth are, by means of the press, contributed to a common stock all the varieties of intellect, natural and acquired, among men are combined together into one vast engine, operating with a force daily accumulating, on the moral and political destiny of mankind."[28]

Horner, in an essay read to the Speculative Society in 1797 — its title, "On the Political Effects of the General Diffusion of Knowledge" — expresses Stewart's conception of societal progress in terms of the individual:

> Were an individual . . . to acquire science without this communication with
> society, his knowledge, however extensive and however accurate, would not

be accompanied with that beneficial influence over his mind, which philosophy is found to operate over national character. It would not beget liberality
of sentiment, for no opinion had ever been proposed to him different from
his own; it would not beget *independence* of sentiment, for he had never experienced what it is to unshackle the understanding . . . ; and with all his store
of knowledge, he could not ever possess the facility of distinguishing, among
contradictory opinions, the true from the false, because, from the manner in
which that knowledge had been impressed upon his mind, he had not
learned how to elicit truth from the heterogeneous systems and conflicting
prejudices of the world.[29]

To put it otherwise, one learns through disagreement and debate, and
salutary societal progress is effected through the same process writ
large. Liberality and *"independence* of sentiment" are attained by encoun-
tering opinions "different from [one's] own": thus does "philosophy,"
by training people to distinguish "the true from the false," improve "national character." The *Edinburgh Review,* especially in its first decade, affected to be the forum (note the definite article) in which that process
took place.

The *Edinburgh's* authority has usually been attributed, first, to its independence from the dictates of booksellers and, second, to its authoritative or "magisterial" tone. The first of these, as noted previously, is
a myth, perpetuated by the reviewers themselves. The second is true,
although the reviewers' posture of infallibility has as much to do with a
shift in the way Scotland's polite classes thought about conversation
(the topic of the next chapter) as with the arrogance of the *Edinburgh*
reviewers themselves. But the other source of that authority lay in the
periodical's strategy throughout its first years of presenting itself *as*
British culture — as the public sphere made palpable; as both the generator of disseminating knowledge and the landscape on which that dissemination took place. Ina Ferris is right, therefore, to say that the
Edinburgh Review "sought to forge a unity that would replace the disinte-
grated public sphere" after the French Revolution, but it is not quite
the case that Jeffrey and his contributors achieved that unity by "attempting to shape and control the reading practices so as to counter the
disseminative force of the entry of new groups of readers."[30] It was not
"new groups of readers" the *Edinburgh* reviewers wanted to counter; on
the contrary, they wanted to create new groups of readers, and in any
case fully expected such groups to emerge with or without their help.
Rather they wished to keep new periodicals out of bounds, which was
different.

Here it is best to speak of Jeffrey instead of the *Edinburgh* reviewers as a group, for it was he, primarily, who effected this policy. As the journal's major contributor, as intrusive collaborator on articles not his own, and as editor and arranger of the reviews in each number, Jeffrey may fairly be considered responsible for the general tone and overarching structure of individual numbers of the journal.[31] In that capacity he managed to convey to his journal's readers the impression that the grand and inevitable process of the dissemination of knowledge was taking place in the pages before them—in the *Edinburgh Review* itself. Jeffrey's writing combined with his editorial practices amount to a stylistic gambit in which he fostered in his readers' minds an impression of the *Edinburgh* as a broad forum for the expression of different viewpoints, which viewpoints would, when allowed to conflict and merge with each other, synthesize into truly wise counsel to modern Britons.

The first place to look when assessing the nature of this authority is not in the *Edinburgh* reviews themselves, but in the published writings of readers who, offended by the journal's increasingly obvious political commitments, attempted to describe the nature and origin of the authority they resented. The very fact that one commentator could write that the *Edinburgh* "glories in abusing the privilege which public admiration . . . has conferred upon it" suggests that he entertained a view of the periodical as a kind of public trust or chartered institution on the order of the BBC.[32] Especially insightful in this regard are a few of Walter Scott's observations. Until 1809 a contributor himself, albeit an increasingly uncomfortable one, Scott felt he could no longer maintain relations with a publication that impugned the motives of the British government with respect to its Spanish policy and averred the justice of revolution in Spain and, by implication, Britain. "No genteel family *can* pretend to be without it," he admitted to John Murray in November of that year, but was delighted nonetheless that after "Cevallos" "subscribers are falling off like withered leaves. . . . there never was such an opening for a new Review."[33] Writing to William Gifford in October of the same year, anticipating their forthcoming periodical, Scott discusses what in his view had made the *Edinburgh* so successful. "In Edinburgh or I may say in Scotland there is not one out of twenty who reads the work that agrees in political opinion with the Editor, but it is ably conducted & how long the generality of readers will continue to dislike the strain of politics so artfully mingled with topics of information & amusement is worthy of deep consideration. But I am convinced it is not too late to stand in the breach."[34] Scott supposes that Jeffrey has thus far managed to prevent rival journals from appearing by blending political discussion into apolitical articles of "information & amusement." His language—he speaks of an "opening" and of "stand[ing] in the breach"—suggests that Scott had till now thought of the *Edinburgh* as something like an occupying force under which no dissent was practically possible.

A year or two before, a Tory reader had complained in a pamphlet of the reviewers' inconsistency on political matters. In it he vows to lay those opinions before the world, "that the world may judge, whether they, who are so ready to find out inconsistencies in others, are themselves consistent and steady in their opinions."[35] As he does so, however, it becomes clear that what actually perturbs him is not the *Edinburgh*'s inconsistency but its consistently Whig alignment in political discussion. But even on that point he is denied the satisfaction of making his allegation sting by the fact that the reviewers had not always taken the Whig side: he complains that "its authors have uniformly taken the side adopted by one party," yet finds it necessary to qualify the claim with a bothersome footnote: "In justice to the author, the article on the proposed reform of the Court of Session in Scotland . . . must be excepted from this remark."[36] Thus did Jeffrey—the author so awkwardly excepted from the writer's complaint—neutralize the force of accusations that the *Edinburgh* had somehow abrogated its responsibilities as a public forum. Another pamphleteer, an outraged Tory responding to the "Cevallos" article, offered his own uncharitable theory on how the reviewers had attained their power, namely by speaking forcefully and peremptorily on "literary" matters, then, having trained readers unquestioningly to accept their assertions, deftly assuming the same authority on political matters.[37]

To be fair, these exasperated Tories had been accustomed to dealing with the respectable but thoroughly predictable and Court-oriented Whiggism of the *Monthly Review*. At the time of the *Edinburgh*'s first issue, the *Monthly*, founded in 1749 by Ralph Griffiths, had for some years been unofficially conducted by Griffiths's son, George Edward Griffiths; and the latter had imposed strict uniformity on his reviews—not only uniformity of style, purging all individual stylistic traits, but consistency of political opinion as well, even to the point of altering new contributions to match opinions published formerly.[38] This was true, to varying degrees, with the other Reviews as well.[39] Simply put, nothing matched the ostentatious heterogeneity of the *Edinburgh Review*—"The multiplicity of our essence, and our hypostatic disunion," wrote Horner, "have been quite understood from the very first."[40] The *Edinburgh* cultivated a belief among its readers that diverse viewpoints were always given fair consideration in its pages, and that any one opinion found there, however disagreeable in itself, had at least been arrived at fairly and reasonably. Hazlitt's portrayal of the journal's "studied impartiality," written much later in *Spirit of the Age* (1825), attests to the durability of this popular conception of the *Edinburgh Review:* "It takes up a question, and argues it *pro* and *con* with great knowledge and boldness and skill; it points out an absurdity, and runs it down, fairly, and according to the evidence adduced."[41] Here was a public sphere for a world that had recently become too fractured to maintain a public sphere. Indeed, in the decade from the beginning of the revolutionary wars to 1802, the British public, Parliament, and government had become embroiled in a war of ideas, as E. V. Macleod has called it, comparable in its ferocity and sheer ideological heterogeneity (though not in its readiness to settle disputes by force) to the Civil War more than a century before.[42] The sense of fragmentation and disunity consequently felt by much of the reading public lent itself to the belief that what was needed was some form of corporate intellectual enterprise in which disparate opinions could meet under the rules of reasonable debate.

To create a journal of this kind would have been a delicate task for anybody; it was especially so for a resolutely Whig editor working with a circle of Whig contributors in a decidedly Tory town. It is therefore not surprising to find Jeffrey, after having failed to maintain this parallel arena by allowing the journal to bear too hard in a Whig-radical direction, nonetheless depicting that failure as though the *Edinburgh* had been too much of an arena, not too little of one. Writing to Horner in 1815, he conceded that he may have given his contributors too much "latitude" on political subjects. "Perhaps," he says, "it would have been better to have kept more to general views," in other words to have confined political discussions to abstract principles and refrained from taking sides by name with people within the Whig party.

> But in such times as we have lived in, it was impossible not to mix them, as in fact they mix themselves, with questions which might be considered as of a narrower and more factious description. In substance it appeared to me that my only absolute duty as to political discussion, was, to forward the great ends of liberty, and to exclude nothing but what had a tendency to promote servile, sordid, and corrupt principles. As to the *means* of attaining these ends, I thought that considerable latitude should be indulged, and that unless the excesses were very great and revolting, every man of talent should be allowed to take his own way of recommending them. In this way it always appeared to me that a considerable diversity was quite compatible with all the consistency that should be required in a work of this description,

and that doctrines might very well be maintained in the same number which were quite irreconcilable with each other, except in their common tendency to repress servility, and diffuse a general spirit of independence in the body of the people.[43]

It is significant that Jeffrey does not say—what was in fact true, as Horner knew—that Brougham had been allowed too much freedom in the expression of his democratic views, and had created demand for a Tory rival. Instead Jeffrey frames the matter in terms of "latitude," as if his contributors had strayed, not in one particular direction, but in too many different directions. "[E]very man of talent," he says, had been "allowed to take his own way," and so it was inevitable that different positions were taken "in the same number which were quite irreconcilable with each other." The result was that these writings, taken together, tended "to repress servility, and diffuse a general spirit of independence in the body of the people": thus the process by which the public sphere leads to greater equity and justice is attributed to the periodical itself. Or, as Jeffrey put it in retrospect, the *Edinburgh* had "proportionally enlarged the capacity, and improved the relish of the growing multitudes to whom . . . [its reviews] were addressed, for 'the stronger meats' which were then first provided for their digestion."[44]

But although Jeffrey avoids admitting that the *Edinburgh*'s intermittent flirtations with radicalism had alienated a large and influential segment of its readership, it is not true, as Tory readers seem to have thought, that the periodical offered diversity only on questions of "information & amusement" but democratic Whiggism on questions of politics and public policy. Scott and the disgruntled pamphleteers believed they understood what they considered the *Edinburgh*'s artifice, and in a limited way they did—only they failed to see that they themselves were being quietly pacified for the *Edinburgh* Whigs' political ends. In any case it took them six years to realize that if they wanted their views circulated at all they would have to start their own quarterly.

Two of Jeffrey's reviews, both from 1807, illustrate the rhetorical sophistication with which he managed to disarm Tory antipathy and thus preserve his and his journal's authority. The first instance, a review of an anti-French tract by James Stephen entitled *The Dangers of the Country*, appeared in that year's first number. For the first ten pages of this long review, Jeffrey quotes with apparently unqualified approval from Stephen's diatribe—about the bellicose intentions of France, the wickedness of its Revolutionary regime, the lack of integrity among its present political elite—so much so that it is difficult to remember that one is reading a Whig periodical. Only after ten pages of approving Stephen's diatribes does Jeffrey come to his own observations, which concern the overhaul of Britain's patronage system—a major plank in the Whig reform platform.[45] While ostensibly Jeffrey has used Stephen to illustrate the ways in which Britain can "avoid the fate" of France, Stephen's tract has nothing to do with domestic issues in Britain: Jeffrey has countenanced its almost totally unrestrained invective against revolutionary France in order to raise the issue of reform without inviting a credible accusation of radicalism.

The second instance appears in Jeffrey's review of a reprint of William Cobbett's periodical, the *Political Register*. This review-essay played an important role in distancing the younger segment of the Whig establishment from Cobbett's brand of Parliamentary reform.[46] Jeffrey, suddenly sounding like Burke, contends that Cobbett's proposals for reform would unbalance the constitution; he even argues that sinecures, which he had castigated in the previous number's review of Stephen's *Dangers of the Country*, do not represent the threat to constitutional democracy claimed by Cobbett.[47] The contradiction is spectacular, especially in light of such remarks as that in a letter to Horner, written at about the same time, in which Jeffrey conjectures that the "actual government of the country is carried on by something less, I take it, than 200 individuals, who are rather inclined to believe that they may do anything they please, so long as the more stirring part of the community can be seduced by patronage."[48] John Clive argues that Jeffrey's conservative reasoning on this point was owing to comments in the *Political Register* slighting the personal character of Dugald Stewart, for whom Jeffrey had the highest respect, and who used the same argument in lectures Jeffrey is known to have attended.[49] However that may be, Philip Flynn is certainly correct when he observes that Jeffrey wanted to prevent Cobbett, with his histrionic tirades and political unreliability, from discrediting the reform movement, and so "in order to combat Cobbett's influence . . . Jeffrey drew a picture of British representative government in which . . . he himself did not wholeheartedly believe."[50] Still, there is more to Jeffrey's *volte face* than this. The article on Cobbett was written, in its own words, "for the purpose of reducing his [Cobbett's] *authority* to its just standard," and that italicized "*authority*" reveals what was actually at stake.[51] In 1807, Cobbett's advocacy of reform, apart from its rhetorical overkill, corresponded in almost every respect to what was then appearing with regularity in the *Edinburgh Review*. The *Political Register*, though intentionally appealing to the working classes, appealed also to middle-class intellectuals; its author enjoyed

"more influence . . . than all the other journalists put together," complains Jeffrey. To prevent Cobbett from gaining any further influence,
then, Jeffrey could not simply out-Cobbett Cobbett; it would not be
sufficient, that is, to demonstrate how the *Edinburgh* could endorse democratic measures and inveigh against corruption just like the *Register*
did, for that would put the two periodicals on the same plane, whereas
Jeffrey wanted his periodical to *be* the plane. He chose instead to remind the *Edinburgh*'s readers that Cobbett was merely an individual, the
Political Register little more than his personal newsletter. By holding up
Cobbett's one-man periodical to a broadly conservative argument in the
generally pro-reform and occasionally quasi-radical *Edinburgh Review*,
and then questioning Cobbett's right to speak with "*authority*," Jeffrey
reminds his readers that the *Edinburgh Review* is a diverse institution, a
broad arena in which rational argumentation is conducted fairly and by
many intelligent people—not a mere series of tracts written by one
gifted but volatile person. Or, to put it in more practical terms: prop-
ping up the notion of constitutional equipoise in the face of Cobbett's
rhetorically excessive writings on constitutional reform provided Jeffrey with a cost-free way in which the *Edinburgh* could mollify its increasingly disaffected Tory and aristocratic readership without
simultaneously alienating readers otherwise sympathetic to Cobbett's
arguments.

"Cevallos," however, went too far in the opposite direction, and so
gave Conservatives the evidence they needed to denounce the *Edinburgh*
as having lent itself to insurrectionism. The question of that article's authorship is a complicated one. Jeffrey claimed to some that he had written most of it, and to others, such as Horner and Scott, that Brougham
(who later included it in his collected contributions) had written it.[52] It
seems doubtful, in any case, that Jeffrey could have written any of the
truly provocative passages, not only because he was ordinarily so conscientious concerning the journal's political stances, but also because
those passages are written in a bitterly polemical style not his.[53] The
more conciliatory and inclusive rhetoric that appears at the end of these
passages, however, suggests itself as an attempt on Jeffrey's part to en-
sure that the *Edinburgh* did not permit any of its constituencies to break
away. "Now, who are the persons thus committed to these most whole-
some and truly English principles of government? Are they a few speculative men—a few seditious writers or demagogues—or a popular
meeting here and there—or are they even a political party in the state?
No such thing. Men of all descriptions—of all ranks in society—of
every party—have joined, almost unanimously, in the same generous

and patriotic sentiments, and have expressed them loudly and man-fully."[54]

That attempt failed, of course, and in less than a year the *Edinburgh Review* was one of two. In December 1808 Jeffrey wrote nervously to Horner that he had heard how angry some had been about the article; but what troubled him most, it seems, was not that he had lost a few important subscribers but that those "persons of consideration" were preparing rival journals:

> The Tories having got a handle are running us down with all their might . . . Walter Scott and William Erskine, and about twenty-five persons of consideration, have forbidden the Review to enter their doors. The Earl of Buchan, I am informed, opened his street door, and actually *kicked* it out! Then, Cumberland is going to start an anonymous rival; and, what is worse, I have reason to believe that Scott, Ellis, Frere, Southey, and some others are plotting another. You must see, therefore, that it is really necessary for us now to put on a manful countenance, and to call even the *emeriti* to our assistance. I entreat you to do an article for me during the holidays. . . . You shall have your choice, of course, of a subject . . . only no party politics, and nothing but exemplary moderation and impartiality on all politics. I have allowed too much mischief to be done from my mere indifference and love of sport; but it would be inexcusable to spoil the powerful instrument we have got hold of, for the sake of teasing and playing tricks.[55]

With Jeffrey as its editor and major contributor the *Edinburgh* had indeed become a "powerful instrument." It had managed for several years to preserve the popular idea that it, and it alone, was capable of determining the confines of respectable debate, a feat accomplished by the editor's policy of allowing the journal to imitate the dynamics of free and open public debate. Drawing its legitimacy from the concept of decentralized and expanding knowledge, the *Edinburgh* ironically acquired the authority of a chartered institution. Its supporters continued to promote this account of the *Edinburgh* long after the *Quarterly Review* emerged as a counterbalance in 1809. Hence Thomas Love Peacock's satirical portrait of Mr. Mac Quedy, the typical Scottish philosophical Whig and *Edinburgh* reviewer. When one character mentions to him "a set of gentlemen in your city," Mac Quedy interrupts him—"Not in our city, exactly; neither are they a set. There is an editor, who forages for articles in all quarters, from John O'Groat's house to the Land's End. It is not a board, or a society: it is a mere intellectual bazaar, where A., B., and C. bring their wares to the market."[56]

What Peacock recognized was the *Edinburgh* reviewers' success in presenting their periodical as something other than an organ for the propagation of a particular outlook: they denied that they were a "set," or that they represented the political approach or interests of Scotland or Edinburgh; it was rather a marketplace of ideas. By the time of *Crotchet Castle* (1831) Peacock was disparaging the *Edinburgh* as the principal manifestation of the March of Mind he despised. As a young satirist in the 1810s, however, he had read the *Edinburgh* avidly and used it as a source for ideas. "Peacock grew up on the *Edinburgh Review*," observes Marilyn Butler, "but treated it as an anthology of contemporary opinions rather than as a model to follow."[57] But although Peacock may never have deferred to the *Edinburgh*'s judgments in the enthusiastic way many others did, his conception of the journal as "an anthology of contemporary opinions" was precisely the one Jeffrey would have wanted him to have — and probably accounted for whatever esteem Peacock did have for the *Edinburgh*.

This conception of the review as independent, uncommitted, objective — in short, olympian — became the standard to which later reviews aspired. The *Fortnightly Review*, for example, founded in 1865 as an ideologically neutral publication in which contributors would appear under their real names, announced that its "object . . . is to become an organ for the unbiassed expression of many and various minds on topics of general interest in Politics, Literature, Philosophy, Science, and Art . . . . Each contributor . . . is allowed the privilege of perfect freedom of opinion, unbiassed by the opinions of the Editor or of fellow-contributors." "We propose," ran another of its ads, "to remove all those restrictions of party and of editorial 'consistency' which in other journals hamper the full and free expression of opinion." The *Fortnightly* nonetheless began as, and remained, a liberal, at times radical periodical; conservatism was all but excluded.[58] Similarly olympian in intention was the Metaphysical Society and its periodical outgrowth *The Nineteenth Century*. Sir James Knowles had begun the Society in 1869 in order to provide a "forum" — his word — in which the country's best minds could engage in informed discussion (members included Tennyson, Ruskin, FitzJames Stephen, Leslie Stephen, Gladstone, and Lord Arthur Russell), and the *The Nineteenth Century*, at its height one of the late Victorian era's two or three most venerated and authoritative journals, was begun in 1877. The idea that a periodical's perceived openness was essential to the cultivation of its own authority had been seized upon before: Swift, to take the best example I am aware of, had tried to present his arguments in the Tory-funded *Examiner* as measured and fair by inserting "letters" from ostensibly Whig readers — "letters" which, however, were by comparison petty and ill-reasoned.[59] But Swift's tactic was clumsy and obvious, and was in any event the product of his naïve and rather self-serving belief that narrow "factional" interests were invariably represented by those of the partisan alliance opposite from his own.

Not until the Victorian era did intellectual periodicals begin deliberately to derive influence from the impression they conveyed of being open institutions in which, through serious and unfettered engagement, disinterested insight might be found.[60] They owed more to Jeffrey than, to judge from most Victorian references to him, their editors and proponents were prepared to admit.

DIFFUSION AND AUTHORITY

The irony implicit in Jeffrey's use of public-sphere concepts and arguments extends beyond his well-planned unpredictability in political discussion. The appeal of diffusion as an ideal, after all, lay in the notion that an increasing number of people, through formal education and the widening availability of printed material, were capable of influencing public decision-making. But despite its seeming altruism there was always a potent element of self-interest below the surface: *Knowledge and learning have come our way, now give us power.* Taking that view, however, made it practically difficult to avoid also advocating that those presently benefiting from literacy and education should likewise be granted a measure of influence, most obviously the franchise: *They have knowledge and learning, now give them power.* To take this latter step depended on who "they" were and what "they" wished to do with their power; and a number of nineteenth-century intellectuals, though sympathetic to the ideal of the liberal public sphere, were not prepared to sanction its growth in practice. Habermas discusses those liberal writers whose outlook demanded that they assent to the idea of a public sphere, but who "were forced almost to deny the principle of the public sphere of civil society even as they celebrated it." Inasmuch as, by the middle of the nineteenth century, the public sphere had not fulfilled the hopes of liberals who had foreseen an all-inclusive realm of rational argument, some began to abandon the idea of an historical progression towards a political public sphere "in favour of a common sense meliorism," a compromise position of one form or another.[61] Habermas discusses John Stuart Mill and Alexis de Tocqueville in this regard, both of whom lamented that the public sphere had become little more than an arena of competing interests, and advocated straightforwardly elitist systems that would use public opinion only to the extent that it was informed.[62]

But while Mill's and Tocqueville's qualifications may have been unique in their fullness and coherence, they were not totally original in applying hierarchical and supposedly illiberal strictures in their formulations of liberalism. Jeffrey's reviews, which began appearing before either of these were born, sought to deal with the problems of liberalism while maintaining the ideals of open interchange among equals. There is an important difference between him and intellectuals such as Mill and Tocqueville, however: Jeffrey was not a political philosopher, or a philosopher of any kind for that matter, and he made no attempt to unify his productions or limit the contradictions between them; indeed to a certain extent (as shown already) he cultivated contradictions, which in any case he had little incentive to avoid since his writings always appeared anonymously. Jeffrey enjoyed the freedom of preserving the ambivalence with which he regarded the benefits of diffusion. But the particular contradictions he maintained in his reviews, appearing as they did in successive issues of a periodical, had the added effect of maintaining that periodical's ability to issue credible decrees in a rapidly diversifying print culture, and in that way was an essential part of the political maneuvering discussed earlier. Thus on some occasions Jeffrey optimistically, even triumphantly, claims that greater numbers of people presently experience the benefits of education and learning, and that political governance and cultural life have as a result improved on all fronts. The implication is plain. If those improvements have been brought about by the diffusion of understanding on matters of public concern, then the *Edinburgh Review*, as generator of that very, must also be credited in large measure with having made those societal improvements possible. Taken another way, however, that reasoning leads in the opposite direction. The *Edinburgh Review* becomes merely one receptacle of dissemination among many others, the *Gentlemen's Magazine*, say, or Cobbett's *Political Register*. Thus on other occasions, and it would seem for that reason, Jeffrey reverses himself completely: the liberal public sphere is being taken advantage of by shams, print media have become so widely available that any charlatan can circulate his opinions, however conspicuously fatuous, and consequently no one really knows what to believe. This latter argument echoed the anxieties of many eighteenth-century conservative reviewers.[63] But it was also an integral part of the typically more progressive *Edinburgh*'s critical discourse. When the founders announced in the first number that their periodical would be distinguished "rather for the selection, than for the number of its articles," they were distinguishing their project from that of the more encyclopedic reviews of previous decades, but they were also reserving the right to review what they considered worthless books whose existence revealed the extent of corruption infiltrating the public sphere. The *Edinburgh* reviewers were hardly unique in this; many writers at the end of the eighteenth century "could no longer ignore the fact that a broader, more inchoate public now threatened to dwarf the literary public they had once championed," and so took to denouncing it.[64] In Jeffrey's writing, this line of attack served to re-gather whatever authority he may have yielded by proclaiming the virtues of diffusion.

Jeffrey's ability to tergiversate in so flagrant a manner was in an important sense an outworking of his Whig disposition. As a Whig, he was well prepared to use the supposed virtues of shifting and conflicting viewpoints for the benefit of his enterprise.[65] Utility and adaptability were the great principles of the so-called Scientific Whigs in Scotland (Lord Kames, Adam Smith, John Millar, Adam Ferguson, et al.), and in that sense, at least, Jeffrey was merely allowing his own political disposition to unfurl in the periodical he edited.[66] Most eighteenth-century Whigs tended to hold well-defined ideologies of any kind in suspicion; one thinks of Burke's insistence in the *Reflections* that "circumstance" rather than the "abstractions" of philosophers should govern decision-making at any given time.

Even so, Jeffrey's Whig orientation can easily be overstated. He had a prickly relationship with the Whig party, hardly noticing (according to Cockburn anyhow) such seemingly momentous occurrences as its accession to power in 1806.[67] Nor was the *Edinburgh* under his editorship, either before or after 1808, a "Whig organ" as is sometimes stated.[68] In fact, while Jeffrey's political beliefs, variously expressed depending on the issue at hand, lay most often within mainstream Whiggism, in his reviews and letters he took occasional excursions into the ideological territory of the "Mountain" Whigs and even into radicalism — provoking Sydney Smith on one occasion to taunt Jeffrey for indulging in "that pernicious cant that all men are equal": "I believe you take your notions of the state of opinion in Britain, from the state of opinion among the commercial and manufacturing population of your own country."[69] In a speech in 1823 Jeffrey claimed that the "Peterloo" massacre four years before had forced him to alter his views on suffrage: "For the peace of the country, it is indispensable that public opinion should have a direct and powerful influence; if not, the state of things which exists will be productive only of discord and disorder, and will

lead ultimately to violence."[70] But it is clear from evidence within and
without his published works that he had espoused robustly democratic
views since the early days of the *Edinburgh Review* and before. In his
commonplace book, kept from 1796 to 1800, he summarizes some of
what he had read on the conflicts in America between Federalists and
Anti-federalists, and declares his sympathy for the latter, the "true re-
publicans" as he calls them, who were opposed to the new constitution
as "too Aristocratical"; the Anti-federalists are misnamed, since "their
object is only to make the govt more democratical."[71] Analogous sentiment appears in a letter of 1795: "I have set to a new history of the
American war, and read Mrs. Woolstoncroft's [*sic*] French Revolution
and other democratical books with great zeal and satisfaction."[72] Again,
he wrote to Horner in 1806 that "The antiquity of our government, to
which we are indebted for so many advantages, brings this great com-
pensating evil along with it; there is an oligarchy of great families—
borough-mongers and intriguing adventurers—that monopolises all
public activity, and excludes the mass of ordinary men nearly as much
as the formal institutions of other countries."[73] Accordingly, the majority of Jeffrey's political reviews during the *Edinburgh*'s first decade contended, with varying degrees of directness and intensity, for the justice
of substantially expanded political power: "If the people have risen into
greater consequence," he wrote in 1811 on the lessons of the French
Revolution, "let them have greater power."[74] In this light Clive's conclusion that Jeffrey was a mainstream Whig who championed electoral
reform because it was the only way to avoid civil unrest, though true as
far as it goes, seems less than adequate.[75] The inconsistent expressions
of democratic and almost radical ideas may be more fruitfully understood, rather, as intellectual consequences of Jeffrey's use—also inconsistent—of the rhetoric of public-sphere liberalism. Having asserted his
journal's authority by making the case that disseminated knowledge
had led to greater political equity and sounder public policies, he was
forced from time to time to invest those abstract arguments with contemporary political meaning.[76] And in reversing himself by decrying the
liberal public sphere as a formerly successful enterprise gone awry, or
even as a false hope, Jeffrey was able both to enhance the political com-
prehensiveness of his journal and precipitate anxiety among his readers
to the effect that nowadays it was unsafe to trust the opinions of just
any periodical—better to stick with the *Edinburgh Review*.

It is difficult to know whether and to what degree Jeffrey intended
his tergiversations to have such an effect—especially during the time
leading up to the journal's initial publication, when its astounding suc-

cess was unforseen, and when Jeffrey himself claimed to be pessimistic about its prospects on at least three occasions.[77] According to Brougham he predicted that the second *Edinburgh Review* would prove short-lived as the first.[78] But despite his pessimism (or possibly because of it—he had nothing to lose), Jeffrey began the first issue by arguing, with boldness approaching bravado, that the "writings" of intellectuals do, in fact, influence the direction in which civil society turns: if not quite whithersoever the governor listeth, then nearly so. In *De L'Influence des Philosophes* Jean Joseph Mounier had insisted the origins of the French Revolution were exclusively political, results of inept policy on the part of the French government and its neighbors rather than the effect of ideas circulated in books and periodicals. Jeffrey thinks this a false choice: "To produce the effects that we have witnessed [in the French Revolution], there must have been a revolutionary spirit fermenting in the minds of the people, which took advantage of those occurrences, and converted them into engines for its own diffusion and increase."[79] He scorns the idea of an intellectual cabal bringing about a new republic, but insists that the philosophers "contributed in some degree to its [the revolution's] production, by the influence of their writings."[80] The essay was, as Neil Berry has written, "a declaration of faith that there exists an intimate connection between intellectual activity and social progress, between printed argument and political action."[81] It was also a conspicuous bid for influence on the part of the reviewer and the *Review*. That bid becomes increasingly obvious as the reviewer, trying to dispose of the objection that the Revolution produced a great deal of violence and injustice, and had now yielded military dictatorship, employs positive or otherwise apologetic phrases to describe the effects of the philosophers' ideas—and by rather obvious extension the effects of the *Edinburgh Review*'s ideas: "advances . . . in opulence and information"; "the diffusion of information, and the prevalence of political discussion"; "spirit of discontent and innovation"; "this love of liberty had been inculcated with much zeal and little prudence."[82]

Jeffrey's other contribution in the first number, equally sensational, was a review of Southey's long poem *Thalaba*. Here was another assertion of authority, even more startling in its brashness than the first. The reviewer alleges the existence of a "Lake School" of poetry and, assuming the vestments of a judge, proposes to "discharge [his] inquisitorial office" by "premising a few words upon the nature and tendency of the tenets he [Southey] has helped to promulgate."[83] Students of the Lake School, he warns, are spreading aberrant ideologies—they adhere to the "antisocial principles . . . of Rousseau." They encourage "false taste": they "have, among them, unquestionably, a very considerable portion of poetical talent, and have, consequently, been enabled to seduce many into an admiration of the false taste (as it appears to us) in which most of their productions are composed."[84] They constitute "the most formidable conspiracy that has lately been formed against sound judgment in matters poetical."

Whereas in its first essay the new journal spoke of "the diffusion of information, and the prevalence of political discussion" in distinctly auspicious terms, here, about fifty pages later, one finds that that openness has allowed frauds to "promulgate" antisocial principles and poor taste. Both reviews address the same sphere. Jerome Christensen has recently noted the contrast between the review of Mounier, which "seem[s] to signal the re-emergence of a civil sphere in which views could be exchanged, claims made and disputed, without danger of state intervention," and the review of *Thalaba*, in which Jeffrey employs the kind of hyperbolic language of conspiracy-denunciation commonly used a few years before by paranoid Francophobes.[85] Christensen adds to these reviews a third, Horner's of a book about governmental banking policy, and argues that each of these implies the truth of two contradictory claims: that society need no longer fear conspiracies, but that society necessarily operates by the uncontrollable and untraceable movements of collusive groups and individuals. Christensen's analysis helps to elucidate the sophistication with which Jeffrey as writer and editor established the *Edinburgh Review*'s authority from its inception: as an engine of social and political progress presiding over a nascent public sphere which, apart from the good husbandry of this journal, might at any time fall victim to the forces of regression and reaction.

Jeffrey, as these two reviews make plain, refused to distinguish the political sphere from the literary sphere; thus Scott's comment about the disagreeable "strain of politics so artfully mingled with topics of information & amusement." True enough, it is generally the case that when Jeffrey expresses optimism with regard to public's intellectual capabilities he does so in reviews of political or historical books, whereas he is at his most pessimistic about the reading public when addressing poetry. Yet some of his early reviews of poetry speak highly of the public's discernment, and anyhow his "literary" reviews always take subjects of public concerns into their purview, quite distinct from formal considerations (the Lakers, e.g., "Instead of contemplating the wonders . . . [of] civilization . . . are perpetually brooding over the disorders by which its progress has been attended").[86] Jeffrey always insisted that political and literary subjects could not be entirely separated.

The *Edinburgh Review,* he wrote with self-congratulation in the preface to his 1844 selection of reviews, had ever refused "to confine itself to . . . the mere literary merits of the works that came before it," and insisted on going "deeply into *the Principles* on which its judgements were to be rested"; and again, "I have, more uniformly and earnestly than any preceding critic, made the Moral tendencies of the works under consideration a leading subject of discussion."[87] The sphere over which Jeffrey intended his journal to exercise influence was that of civil society itself, irrespective of its sundry departments and divisions.

The social and political significance in such ostensibly "literary" reviews as "Thelwall's Poems," in the April 1803 number, is therefore easy to see. John Thelwall was a notoriously radical reformer (in 1794 he had been tried for treason, unsuccessfully, with John Horne Tooke and Thomas Hardy), and for that reason—here was someone whose standing in public estimation was already questionable—provided Jeffrey with an excellent subject on which to bemoan the overcrowded state of the public sphere. "Ploughboys and carpenters are first drawn into the shops of mercers and perfumers, and into the service of esquires, baronets, and peers: the runaway apprentice next goes upon the state; hairdressers and valets write amatory verses; coffeehouse waiters publish political pamphlets; and shoemakers and tailors astonish the world with plans for reforming the constitution, and with *effusions of relative and social feeling.*[88] All of this, he says, is a result of "increasing luxury," by which he refers to the economic liberalization that, by increasing the availability of printed material, had made hairdressers and valets believe they could write amatory verses. But the argument that the accretion of wealth in society has contributed to a cheapening of literary taste and high-cultural values is only one of two lines of argument. The expansion of "opulence" and "luxury" is depicted just as frequently by Jeffrey—as in the passage quoted earlier from the Mounier review ("advances . . . in opulence and information")—as an essential and salutary part of "diffusion" and the development of the public sphere. These two lines of argument coexist in Jeffrey's reviews. One or the other was used according to whether Jeffrey wished to emphasize past and present advancement through informed public interchange, or whether it served his purpose better to emphasize the decadence in which that same process had resulted. As long as both were in some substantial sense true, the *Edinburgh Review* could justify its centrality and authority.

The more optimistic line appears boldly in the October 1803 issue, two numbers after "Thelwall's Poems." In his review of John Millar's reprinted *Historical View of the English Government,* Jeffrey contends that the effects of the division of labor on the lower classes (it "stupif[ies] the faculties, by circumscribing the range of observation and exertion") are more than counterbalanced by an enhanced ability to acquire refinement brought about by widespread prosperity. "The ease and affluence which is diffused in this way through all the middling classes of the community, naturally gives them leisure and inclination for the cultivation of their faculties, and creates a great demand for all the productions of literature and the arts . . . The example of the middle classes descends by degrees to the ranks immediately below them; and the general prevalence of just and liberal sentiments which are thus spread by contagion through every order of society, serves in some degree to correct the debasing influence of mechanical drudgery on the labourers."[89] This passage is straight out of the lectures of Dugald Stewart, who attempted to formulate satisfactory solutions to the social problems arising from the division of labor, problems on which Adam Smith had remained mostly silent in *The Wealth of Nations.*[90] Here opulence and luxury, or in this case "ease and affluence," are, like knowledge and learning themselves, "diffused through all the middling classes." "[L]eisure" produces "a great demand for literature and the arts," which demand "descends by degrees" and thus a "general prevalence of just and liberal sentiments" spreads "by contagion through every order of society." The implication is barely hidden: most of the *Edinburgh*'s readers were of the "middle classes," and in any case would have been pleased to learn that the "ranks immediately below them" were thus recipients of "just and liberal sentiments" and that their "demand for all the productions of literature and the arts"—that is, their readiness to pay five shillings for a copy of the *Edinburgh Review*—contributed to this grand movement of societal progress.

   The contradiction in Jeffrey's writing on the public sphere between optimism and nay-saying is in some measure a part of the larger "paradox," as John Clive terms it, in the thinking of the *Edinburgh* reviewers as a group on the subjects of "civilization and progress. On the one hand, refinement and politeness are desirable, for . . . without them no distinguished achievements in the arts are possible. . . . On the other hand, there can be no progress towards refinement without commercial wealth and division of labour," developments which have exacted the price of "dissipation for the upper, misery for the lower classes, and in a general lowering of standards."[91] Clive is wise to designate the contradiction as a paradox rather than, as is the tendency of some older studies of periodical literature, succumbing to the urge to unify. Jeffrey himself, though, put the paradox to work by oscillating between the two depictions of British culture and by implication installing the *Edinburgh Review* into a position of authority in each one. Thus for several numbers after the Millar essay, Jeffrey continues to underscore the progressive trends of modern civil society and public discourse, always subtly pointing out that these things have come about largely through means which bear some resemblance to the periodical in which those subjects are raised. Responding, for example, to a passage in which Jeremy Bentham supposes modern society to be easily misled by metaphorical language, Jeffrey contends that "expedience," which is to say utility or wise policies, "may be readily and certainly discovered by those who are interested in finding it": "in a certain stage of civilization there is generated such a quantity of intelligence and good sense, as to disarm absurd institutions of their power to do mischief, and to administer defective laws into a system of perfect equity. This indeed [i.e. that "quantity of intelligence and good sense"] is the grand corrective which remedies all the errors of lawmakers, and retrenches all that is pernicious in prejudice . . . and he who could increase its quantity, or confirm its power, would do more service to mankind than all the philosophers that ever speculated on the means of their reformation."[92] That last sentence, once its personal pronoun is put aside, emerges as another claim to authority. The contrast is between individual "philosophers" like Bentham, on the one hand, who inevitably represent only one voice uttering their own idiosyncratic "speculations" on how to correct the errors of lawmakers and retrench prejudice, and on the other hand that entity capable of increasing the "quantity" and confirming the "power" of society's "intelligence and good sense." However perceptive a writer Bentham might be, Jeffrey suggests, he is after all just another "philosopher" speculating on the great question of how to base civil society more squarely on sound reason and humaneness. But such an effort requires the aggregated work of a periodical. Thus, again, "expedience . . . may be readily and certainly discovered by those who are interested in finding it"—not in the complicated works of Jeremy Bentham, or in Cobbett's vociferous newsletter, but in the *Edinburgh Review*.

In this way Jeffrey manages to champion the benefits of collaboration, the essence of the liberal public sphere, while implicitly arrogating to his journal the right to speak with authority—which in practice means without fear of contradiction, outside and above the discussion. He does so again in the April 1805 number, in which Jean Sylvain Bailly's memoir of the French Revolution comes under review. The Revolution, Jeffrey says, mixing a measure of pessimism into his argument this time, "has thrown us back half a century in the course of political improvement; and driven us to cling once more, with superstitious terror, at the feet of those idols from which we had been nearly reclaimed by the lessons of a milder philosophy."[93] He alludes (with a footnote) to the Mounier review of three years before and builds on that essay's argument by distinguishing between the culpability of those, on the one hand, who urge ideas in print, and those on the other who attempt actually to impose or implement their ideas. "What is written may be corrected; but what is done cannot be recalled": thus again he asserts the necessity of written argument and deprecates the exercise of power in its absence. But the specific sort of written arguments he means are, as in the Bentham review, those which interact with other arguments, which participate with different minds and are hence capable of revision and improvement. "[A] rash and injudicious publication naturally calls forth an host of answers," and so "a paradox [i.e. a logical flaw] which might have been maintained by an author, without any other loss than that of a little leisure, and ink and paper, can only be supported by a minister at the expense of the lives and liberties of a nation."[94]

Whether Jeffrey actually believed that the cost of bad arguments in the public sphere amounted to no more "loss than that of a little leisure, and ink and paper" begins to seem doubtful, however, in reviews published later that year. In the October 1805 he chastens the philosopher William Drummond for writing an energetic and hostile critique of the ideas of major European philosophers in an attractive and approachable style, thus inviting the less well-read and otherwise uninitiated to reject or ignore major parts of European philosophy without understanding what they reject. If Drummond intended "to engage the attention of polite readers, by a certain vivacity and polish in the turn of expression," he succeeded too well; but "it is proper that he should settle his creed with the initiated votaries of the science, before he exerts himself to make converts among the multitude; . . . we would exhort him . . . to think less of the style in which he is to promulgate his discoveries."[95] One discerns here a distinct uneasiness with the idea that "polite readers" are capable of handling serious philosophical discussion; those "just and liberal sentiments . . . spread by contagion through every order of society" seem distant now. Still, Jeffrey's comment appears at the end of a long and extremely abstruse discussion of philosophical problems, and he may have felt that such problems have minimal bearing on questions of public moment. He may also have guessed that most of his "polite readers" would not reach the end of the review anyhow.

That, however, cannot have been true of his July 1806 review of

Benjamin Franklin's writings, a short essay on a popular subject. Speculating on how Franklin would have fared had he been brought up in refined and civilized Europe instead of in America, Jeffrey seems almost to reject the liberal public sphere as inherently hostile to individual ability.

> The consequences of living in a refined and literary community, are nearly of the same kind with those of a regular [as opposed to formal] education. There are so many critics to be satisfied—so many qualifications to be established—so many rivals to encounter, and so much derision to be hazarded, that a young man is apt to be deterred from such an enterprise, and led to seek for distinction in some safer line of exertion. He is discouraged by the fame and the perfection of certain models and favourites, who are always in the mouths of his judges . . . and his originality [is] repressed, till he sinks into a paltry copyist, or aims at distinction by extravagance and affectation . . . In his attention to the manner, the matter is apt to be neglected; and, in his solicitude to please those who require elegance of diction, brilliancy of wit, or harmony of periods, he is in some danger of forgetting that strength of reason, and accuracy of observation, by which he first proposed to recommend himself. . . . he becomes an unsuccessful pretender to fine writing, and is satisfied with the frivolous praises of elegance or vivacity.[96]

Thus Jeffrey revisits the pessimism of the Thelwall review; the initial reference to the "consequences of living in a refined and literary community" may not mention "opulence" and "luxury" explicitly, but the complexity and multifarious nature of the situation he describes ("so many . . . so many . . . so many . . . so much") must refer primarily to modern prosperous metropolitan environments. Yet instead of generating reasonable debate and producing liberal principles on which society may be profitably governed, this public sphere is productive mainly of superficially elegant works of a wholly derivative character. And not only so: it also lays itself open, as Jeffrey avers in the same number, to the contagion of immorality. It is unfortunate, he writes, that so many of the poems in Thomas Moore's *Epistles, Odes, and Other Poems*, suggestive as many of them are of debauchery, "are dedicated to persons of the first consideration in the country, both for rank and accomplishments," persons whom the poet speaks of in the most familiar terms.[97] This, to Jeffrey, is alarming.

> By these channels, the book will easily pass into circulation in those classes of society, which it is of the most consequence to keep free of contamination; and from which its reputation and its influence will descend with the great-

est effect to the great body of the community. In this reading and opulent country, there are no fashions which diffuse themselves so fast, as those of literature and immortality: there is no palpable boundary between the *noblesse* and the *bourgeoisie,* as in old France, by which the corruption and intelligence of the former can be prevented from spreading to the latter. All the parts of the mass, act and react upon each other with a powerful and unintermitted agency; and if the head be once infected, the corruption will spread irresistibly through the whole body.[98]

As with the Franklin review, this passage, in which the rigidity of Old Regime France is recalled almost with admiration, represents the inverse of what Jeffrey had written elsewhere in the *Review.* In previous essays the openness and wealth of modern civil society, by bringing minds of various dispositions into an arena of educated debate, necessarily encouraged the circulation of liberal principles of governance and the production of original and praiseworthy works of art and literature; but here those very characteristics—the refinement of a highly developed civilization, the openness and energy of a "reading and opulent country"—generate little more than moral "corruption" and the fakery of "fine writing."

Jeffrey's reviews continue to fluctuate between these two points of view over the following year's work. In one essay, to take examples almost at random, he writes with utmost confidence that through public discourse on questions of high moral importance "perseverance is sure to be rewarded with success, and . . . reason will certainly be triumphant, provided she return with sufficient patience to the charge, and resolutely repeats the argument which has originally failed of effect," and that this is true "in all cases in which expediency and justice are on one side, and established prejudice or habit on the other"; while in another he speaks of the reading public as consisting "chiefly of young, half-educated women, sickly tradesmen, and enamoured apprentices" who "create a demand for nonsense, which the improved ingenuity of the times [i.e. technological advancements, the effects of "luxury"] can with difficulty supply."[99] In the issues of 1807 and 1808 he even begins to give expression to both views in the same reviews, though rather less convincingly. Thus in his first review of Wordsworth (*Poems* of 1807) he begins by complaining that the *Lyrical Ballads* had contained "occasional vulgarity, affectation, and silliness," and that those very flaws had "recommend[ed] themselves to the indulgence of many judicious readers" and had produced "among a pretty numerous class of persons, a sort of admiration of the very defects by which they were attended."[100] But a moment later he announces that "it belongs to the public, not to us, to decide upon their merit, and . . . we are willing for once to take the judgment of the present generation of readers . . . as conclusive on this occasion."[101] In a specific sense, of course, Jeffrey is confronting in this review the problem faced by literary critics throughout the second half the eighteenth century: the recognition that "taste" and therefore public reception rather than some courtly value system determined the merit of a work, but also that many of the people who made up "the public" had poor taste.[102] Over time Jeffrey did come down on the side of the public's authority, combining an associationist aesthetic with, to use William Christie's phrase, a "semi-legalistic *consensus genitum.*"[103] But in his earliest reviews this ambivalence, though it does appear strikingly in his literary criticism, is part of a broader rhetorical approach that encompasses his political and historical reviews as well.

As long as these divergent accounts of modern British culture could be simultaneously maintained with some level of plausibility, and as long as each account contained some element of truth discernible to the reader, it made perfect sense for that reader to continue regarding the opinions of the *Edinburgh Review* as authoritative. Taken together, the foregoing passages from Jeffrey's contributions convey an image of the liberal public sphere as a thing incessantly expanding and pushing back prejudice and corruption, but which is somehow also under constant threat of implosion from those same forces and which therefore must not be allowed to develop without close supervision — supervision so close, in fact, that the liberal public sphere ceases sometimes to seem very liberal. Like a benevolent dictator whose commitment to the idea of an open society is sincere but who is never quite ready to allow free elections, Jeffrey constantly ascribes great ameliorating powers and, indeed, historical inevitability to the public sphere, but intermittently re-asserts authority over it by, in effect, undermining it as an ideal. But Jeffrey's tergiversations themselves only reinforced the impression many readers would have had that the journal entertained many and diverse opinions, even including the opinion that the co-existence of too many opinions was likely to produce unreason and tawdriness rather than wisdom and discernment.

EXCURSUS: JEFFREY AND WORDSWORTH

The comparison of Jeffrey with a benevolent dictator should not be taken too far. No account of him would be complete without an ac-

knowledgment that the authority of public opinion always retained centrality in his thought, and accordingly that the public was capable of
assuming greater responsibilities in the processes of decision-making.[104]
In light of Jeffrey's writing as a whole, and in light of "philosophic
Whiggism" as an outlook with which he was so closely associated, one
is almost bound to conclude that the more optimistic assertions of public-sphere liberalism comprise the dominant strain in Jeffrey's critical
discourse. It is evident, in other words, that the skeptical line of argument served mainly as a device rather than as something that held for
Jeffrey substantial explanatory power. Put still otherwise: Jeffrey's periodic disavowal of the wider implications of public-sphere liberalism
should be understood, not as a rejection of it as an ideal, but as an un-
systematic method of checking its logic, like the minority opinion in a
court decision. Thus on at least one occasion Jeffrey conceded that in
one of his disconsolate passages (the review of Franklin's works) he
had overstated the case: "We ventured, on a former occasion, to say
something of the effects of regular education, and of the general diffusion of literature, in repressing the vigour and originality of all kinds of
mental exertion. That speculation was carried perhaps somewhat too
far."[105]

For Jeffrey the public sphere held out real promise, quite apart from
his "speculations" on the subject. That belief appears with obvious sin-
cerity in his friendship with Carlyle. In the 1820s and early '30s, when
Carlyle had little to recommend himself to someone in Jeffrey's position
apart from high intelligence (no family connections, poor manners, no
Oxbridge education or literary reputation), Jeffrey urged him continually not to isolate himself from society, which of course Carlyle was
prone to do. For instance: "I am startled at the notion of your Nithsdale
retreat—and my impressions . . . are certainly ag[ains]t it—I think it
has been your misfortune not to have mixed sufficiently with intelligent
men of various opinions, and open and intrepid minds—and that such
a retirement as you meditate would aggravate all the peculiarities which
in my humble opinion (you'll forgive the freedom) now fetter your understanding—and obstruct your career both of usefulness and distinction."[106] By remaining aloof from other minds, Jeffrey thought, Carlyle
risked squandering his intelligence on some obscurantist philosophy:
failure to "mix sufficiently with intelligent men of various opinions," or
to engage in the defining dynamic of the public sphere, could deprive
Carlyle of the balance and moderation essential to a humane philosophy. Jeffrey therefore urged the Carlyles to reside in Edinburgh, even
allowing them to stay in his flat in Moray Place.

To repeat then: the liberal public sphere and conceptually overlapping notions of the benefits of "diffusion" and "dissemination" stand at the center of Jeffrey's thought, early and late. It is true that, as with J. S. Mill and Tocqueville in Habermas's reading, Jeffrey stopped well short of advocating that political society replace civil society, or in other words that the public sphere itself should exercise direct political power: such a position would necessitate allowing those with little or no education—the "lower orders"—to exercise power, which was clearly out of the question. And yet, despite the misguided assumptions of many scholarly discussions of Jeffrey's reviews of Wordsworth, the former's philosophical commitment did not lie with entrenched aristocracy. Granted: he addressed the question of the lower classes with all the assumptions of early-nineteenth-century "improving" optimism. In that, he often sounded like any number of Scottish educationists of the era, whose answer to the problem was not to give the poor the franchise but to give them enough education and economic liberty to improve their lot. His review of Elizabeth Hamilton's *Cottagers of Glenburnie,* in which he suggests that the book should be re-published in cheaper form, is typical in this respect:

> a strong current of improvement runs at present through all Scotland, and a much smaller impulse than would once have been necessary, will now throw the peasantry within the sphere of its action. Besides *our* cottagers [meaning Scotland's poor: like Brougham, Millar, Mill, et al., Jeffrey relied on the supposition that Scotland's lower classes were on the whole literate and educated] are reading and reasoning animals; and are more likely perhaps to be moved from their old habits by hints and suggestions which they themselves may glean from a book, than by the more officious and insulting inference of a living reformer.[107]

The component of Jeffrey's reformist outlook asserted here is merely part of his liberal philosophy. The public sphere was, ultimately, open to the lower classes, albeit with all the restrictions attaching to a political approach that placed high value on stability and refinement.

Jeffrey's views on electoral reform, education, public opinion, and the benefits of cultural engagement and interchange—these have until recently been either ignored or, when briefly referred to, misconstrued by scholars treating the Jeffrey-Wordsworth conflict. Aesthetic concerns were certainly a major part of that conflict. However, Jeffrey's own insistence that "literary" considerations could not be wholly distinguished from moral and social considerations should have, but by and large has not, prompted scholars concerned with this material to examine the political aspect of the conflict between Jeffrey and Wordsworth in a serious and nuanced way—which is especially odd in light of the fact that many nineteenth-century writers, Scott and Lockhart among them, routinely alleged ill-defined "party politics" to have motivated Jeffrey's attacks on the Lake poets.[108] James Greig's characterization of Jeffrey's literary criticism as a "system" containing "no serious inconsistenc[ies]" but which contained an "Augustan fallacy" that led him to misjudge the Romantic poets is therefore clearly insufficient.[109] One wonders why a scholarly community attuned to historical contexts has done so little to rectify this conception, which has now solidified around the common belief that Jeffrey's "views on poetry were conventional and scarcely advanced beyond what he had learned to like as a young man."[110] Part of the problem may well be that the most obvious political interpretation of Jeffrey's reviews is now, or would seem to be, old news. It is an interpretation that incorrectly assumes that, as Leslie Stephen put it with unfortunate finality, "Jeffrey's politics were but slightly in advance of the true old Whigs, who worshipped according to the tradition of their fathers in Holland House."[111] If that were the extent of the truth, it would be pretty apparent that Jeffrey objected to Wordsworth's presentation of the poor in a favorable light because it suggested an unsettling of class distinctions. Typical among contemporary critics' remarks are these: "In so far as romanticism . . . meant that pedlars and leech-gatherers were of a sudden endowed with the tongues of philosophers . . . he felt that it had to be condemned as childish and absurd. For then it played havoc with accepted social gradations."[112] "The danger was obvious. Quite simply, in the post-1789 world, to endow a rustic with philosophic ideas undermined the arguments on which he was denied a vote. The preservation of the idioms peculiar to each order in society was of crucial importance."[113] "Jeffrey of the *Edinburgh*, self-appointed guardian of public taste, denounced the Lake poets as . . . a threat to traditional social rank."[114]

The problem with this interpretation is not only that it relies entirely on the facile characterization of Jeffrey's political creed as roughly equal to that of (say) Lord Grenville, but also that it ignores what could fairly be called the governing concept of his writing: the promise of the diffusion of knowledge. On the matter of Wordsworth's portrayal of the poor, Jeffrey attacks him more as a Whig would attack a Tory than as a Tory would attack a radical. In a limited but real sense, Jeffrey attacks Wordsworth from the left rather than the right. By making the poor more intelligent and well-spoken than in truth they were, Wordsworth had obviated the need to educate the real poor, and in that way renders the call for diffusion superfluous. True, in the 1802 review of *Thalaba*, Jeffrey inveighed against the Lake school's use of the language of the poor (he even quotes from the "Advertisement" to *Lyrical Ballads*) by claiming that "The language of the higher and more elevated orders may fairly be presumed to be better than that of their inferiors," and that "The language of the vulgar . . . has all the opposite associations to contend with; and must seem unfit for poetry . . . merely because it has scarcely been employed in it."[115] But this passage (frequently quoted by Romanticists as though it were representative) is best understood as an attempt by an unknown start-up reviewer to shock his audience and increase its size.[116] In any case, although the review asserts snobbery for effect, its criticism of the Lake poets' use of language is just as much a product of Jeffrey's progressive political outlook as of his poetic elitism: the Lake poets, by rendering their poetry in the language of the poor, were glorifying the status of the poor and thus implicitly advocating that they be kept that way.

But the issue of the poor in Wordsworth's poetry was, in Jeffrey's criticism, only a part of the larger issue of knowledge-expansion and participation in public interchange. The poet's glorification of solitude defied Jeffrey's entire political outlook, nullifying his contention that political wisdom and humaneness are arrived at principally through public engagement and discussion. In the 1800 preface Wordsworth contends that "a multitude of causes . . . are now acting with a combined force to blunt the discriminating powers of the mind"; "The most effective of these causes are the great national events which are daily taking place, and the increasing accumulation of men in cities, where the uniformity of their occupations produced a craving for extraordinary incident, which the rapid communication of intelligence hourly gratifies."[117] Jeffrey believed the opposite: the "accumulation of men in cities" was part of the process of enlightenment, and if the "uniformity of their occupations" produced by the division of labor gave rise to some unhappy consequences, the wealth produced by that process would convey to the middle and, eventually, the lower classes the ability to improve their knowledge and station. But Jeffrey's stake in countering Wordsworth's system was yet higher than that: as an inhabitant of a provincial town with a hybrid accent seeking to assert his validity as a major participant in Britain's public sphere, and as the editor of a journal that sought to assert authority over the whole of that sphere, he could not endure

Wordsworth's attempt to invalidate that endeavor. Which is why Jeffrey objected to Wordsworth's tendency, and that of the Lake poets generally, to make poetry a thing accessible only through intense study and scrutiny. "By resorting to what Jeffrey called 'a sort of cypher' that 'can only be learned by pains and study,' the Lake poets threatened the broad, inclusive . . . cultural coherence for which the *Edinburgh* struggled."[118] Thus the critic's constant complaint that the Lake poets refused to accept any obligation to public taste.[119]

Again, though, as with the issue of the poor, Jeffrey's complaint about the recondite qualities of Wordsworth's poetry was only part of a more general assault on its rejection of the public sphere—a rejection especially pronounced in *The Excursion,* the review of which began with the infamous words "This will never do." Time and again in *The Excursion* (as also in "Tintern Abbey" and, ultimately, in *The Prelude,*) Wordsworth attributes an enlightening capacity to the natural world that exceeds in scope and importance whatever instruction may be found in civil society—formal education, interaction with books and ideas, conversation with an assortment of informed people. The poem's narrator, whom Jeffrey understandably takes to be Wordsworth, extols the benefits of seclusion at every opportunity, and even his conversation with the Wanderer, which by definition requires something other than isolation, pleases him because by it he learns the virtues of solitude.

> We sate—we walked; he pleased me with report
> Of things which he had seen; and often touched
> Abstrusest matter, reasonings of the mind
> Turned inward . . .
>
> (1:63–66)[120]

To Jeffrey such a disposition would have seemed hostile to the ideal of the diffusion of knowledge, and indeed the poem seemed even to cast doubt on the institutions through which that diffusion took place:

> What wonder, then, if I, whose favourite school
> Hath been the fields, the roads, and rural lanes,
> Looked on this guide with reverential love?
>
> (2:28–29)

Again, "Thus informed, / He had small need of books" (1:162–63). Or still again, when in Book 6 the Pastor describes a debonair young man who came from his parish, he explains the figure's improbability with the remarks,

If ye enquire
How such consummate elegance was bred
Amid these wilds, this answer may suffice;
'Twas Nature's will; who sometimes undertakes,
For the reproof of human vanity,
Art to outstrip in her peculiar walk

(6:298–303)

This young man, the Solitary agrees, "must have found / Abundant exercise for thought and speech, / In his dividual being, self-reviewed" (6:384–86). Or, still again, the Pastor tells the story of two fiercely antagonistic political opponents who, having both retired and settled in this rural parish, experienced (in the words of Book 6's "Argument") "the harmonising influence of solitude" and thus left off their former "desperate strife" and unethical political maneuvering (6:376–521). From Jeffrey's point of view, the author of *The Excursion* believed that political culture breeds conflict rather than resolving it, and that the public sphere is largely counterproductive.

Wordsworth's "peculiar system" would, if valid, nullify Jeffrey's entire social-political philosophy—and indeed the *Edinburgh* project itself. Unable to make this point directly, he implies that the poet himself practices what he preaches too well: a "sincere convert to his own system," Wordsworth has failed to "mingle" with "men of literature and ordinary judgment of poetry," and so his "settled perversity of . . . understanding" must be quite unfeigned.[121] It is inconceivable that Jeffrey was unaware of *The Excursion*'s social significance in relation to his own political philosophy. In this light his oft-repeated point that poor and uneducated people do not speak as though they were otherwise begins to seem less like snobbery and more like a logical outworking of his politics. In the *Excursion* review he ridicules Wordsworth's making his Wanderer, the poem's most fluent character, an elderly peddler—who, Jeffrey is careful to point out, stopped attending school at age six.[122] "A man who went about selling flannel and pocket-handkerchiefs in this lofty diction, would soon frighten away all his customers."[123] Though notoriously wrong about Wordsworth's poetry in general, here Jeffrey does have a point: the Wanderer is an extremely improbable character. But the fact that he made the point so often has led a number of critics, understandably but mistakenly, to suspect him of having been uneasy with the egalitarian ideology of Wordsworth's poetry. It would make far better sense of Jeffrey's political interests to interpret his ridicule of pedlars and leech-gatherers being "endowed with the tongues of philosophers" (as Clive puts it) as an attack on Tory-oriented nativism and sentimentalizing of the poor: If the peddler were already a genius, what need had he of improvement and the enlightening benefits of diffusion? Again, Jeffrey has a point. As Dan Jacobson has recently observed in an insightful essay on the poet's quasi-physiological relationship with the natural world, Wordsworth had no wish for the world he relayed in his poetry to be altered in any way—even when it came to the world's weak outcasts like old men travelers and leech-gatherers. "Precisely because he cannot take his eyes off them, he wants them to remain just as they are, and he finds various specious reasons why busybodies and do-gooders should leave them alone in their weakness and incomprehension."[124]

Indeed, much of Wordsworth's poetry from 1798 forward, as James Chandler has argued, intimates a profoundly conservative conception of societal order. When, for instance, the Wanderer speaks of a "true equality" existing between rich and poor, he echoes Burke's dismissal of the notion that true equality is material equality.[125] Whether and to what degree Jeffrey recognized Burkean overtones in Wordsworth's poetry is hard to know—Jeffrey's own view of Burke was (as one might imagine) characterized by ambivalence, and in any case Wordsworth's conservative ideology, even in Chandler's interpretation, was anything but foursquare.[126] As for the Pastor's advocacy in *The Excursion* of a national system of education for the poor, Jeffrey merely quotes it with high praise as "a very animated exhortation to the more general diffusion of education among the lower orders; and a glowing and eloquent assertion of their capacity for all virtues and enjoyments."[127] He speaks of their "capacity" rather than their "possession" of these things, suggesting that at some level he recognized a contradiction in Wordsworth's poem and philosophy, a contradiction that, however, he was not prepared to discuss explicitly in the review. Perhaps it would have been too obviously motivated by "party politics," a transgression at this time routinely imputed to the *Edinburgh Review* by Tory irredentists. One suspects, at the very least, that Jeffrey was not surprised to learn (if he did learn) that Wordsworth opposed the Reform Bill of 1832. "A Whig in politics, Mr. Jeffrey was a Tory in poetry," quipped John Wilson.[128] The truth was otherwise—Jeffrey was a Scottish Whig in both politics and poetry.

SCOTCH REVIEWERS AND THE IDEA OF A PUBLIC SPHERE

The fact that the Wanderer was Scottish may have contributed to Jeffrey's indignation as well; Wordsworth may have seemed to the critic to be suggesting that the Scottish tradition of educating the poor was immaterial—that the Wanderer himself, whose having had almost no formal education exposed that tradition as a myth, had no need of it in the first place. Certainly Jeffrey did relate the Scottish educational system with public-sphere openness: when the Scottish Universities Commission visited Edinburgh, Jeffrey defended that system as conducive to the wide dispersal of knowledge in Scotland. "The possession of knowledge is a pleasure to every individual, and however slight his smattering of it may be, it is a means of liberating his mind, and elevating his condition beyond what it would otherwise have been; I should be sorry, therefore, to have anything so rigorous in any prescribed scheme of instruction, as at all to deter people from getting—not indeed profound learning, for that is not to be spoken of—but that knowledge which tends to liberalize and make intelligent the mass of our population, more than anything else."[129]

Jeffrey spoke these words in 1826, but he might have said them at any point in his career; the concept was part of his intellectual framework, part of what it meant to be Scottish at that time. Indeed, the cultural and philosophical origins of his public-sphere liberalism— maximizing its philosophical appeal, promoting it as an eminently attainable ideal—lay in early-nineteenth-century Scotland's understanding of itself as a country of widely dispersed education where any man, social and financial limitations notwithstanding, had the capacity to contribute to the society in which he lived. And, what is equally important, that concept aided Scottish writers generally as a conceptual tool by which the "provincial" intellectual might introduce himself into the literary and political culture of Great Britain.

This helps to explain why Edinburgh introduced London to the power of the periodical review rather than, by and large, the other way around. Periodicals, after all, "are best adapted to the needs of a mass audience. They can be produced and sold much more cheaply than books. They appeal to millions of men and women who consider the reading of a whole book too formidable a task even to be attempted."[130] And a "mass audience" is precisely what Scots believed their country to be: a society in which literacy and intellectual capability were spread widely, largely irrespective of class differences, and in which, therefore, periodicals would likely succeed and bring notoriety and distinction. Lowlands metropolitan Scotland had long been the scene of a great deal of publishing activity for "the masses" and "the lower orders," activity that itself signified a uniquely Scottish approach to publishing, and that prepared the way for the great periodical upsurge of the early-nineteenth century. The case of *Donaldson* v. *Becket*, 1774, which ended publishers' claim to "perpetual copyright," illustrates this development well, for it was a Scottish bookseller, Alexander Donaldson, who had upset the London booksellers by selling cheaply reprinted "classics" to lower-income book-buyers.[131] Throughout the second half of the eighteenth century, in fact, Scottish publishers insisted on (and in 1774 attained) their right to issue cheap reprints, and in contesting for that right frequently employed the universalist and quasi-egalitarian language of diffusion.[132] The same phenomenon occurred in periodical publishing: from 1764 to 1794 countless inexpensive magazines had been published in Edinburgh explicitly for poorer readers, and ceased between 1794 and the 1800s only because the government in London viewed such projects with suspicion.[133] The *Edinburgh Review* itself, though erudite and pitched to the middle class, was undertaken with largely the same intention of civilizing the masses—a truth understood (and gently deprecated) by Carlyle, who in an early attempt at fiction wrote, "The men were mostly poor, and all uncultivated; no Mechanics' Institute, no Edin, no Quarterly, or even British Review had yet reached them."[134]

Simply put, Scottish writers of the early-nineteenth century were at ease with the idea of a public sphere, or at least with the broad outlines of such a concept, in a way that many if not most English writers, apart from the radicals and Dissenters mentioned earlier, were not. The Scottish writer understood that the "reading public" in Britain consisted of rapidly increasing number of middle-class readers who were not "learned" in any Renaissance sense, but basically literate, capable of handling an essay or review on a topic of importance. And that instinctive cultural understanding, coupled with desire to establish their presence in Britain's literary and political culture, begins—if only begins—to account for the Scots' dominance over nineteenth-century periodical literature.

The next chapter treats another vital element in the development of the public sphere in Europe, an element that for reasons I shall discuss proved especially potent in late-eighteenth-century Scotland: the conversation. One of the most evident dynamics in the *Edinburgh* reviewers' promotion of public-sphere interchange was, in fact, personal spoken interchange. In conversations among well-groomed and educated Edinburgh residents of this period, the public sphere probably came as close to realizing itself as it ever did, and reviews in the *Edinburgh* sometimes emerged from these conversations in the most literal way. In 1806, when Jeffrey found a submission by Henry Hallam unsatisfactory, he urged Horner to rewrite it, but first to speak to Lord Webb Seymour, who "will give you in a morning's conversation materials for an admirable article."[135] Conversation-to-review would become conversation-as-review in the writings of John Wilson, but these were both manifestations of the same development in Scottish culture, a development in which Scots, having "improved" their conversation during the latter part of the eighteenth century, now asserted their speaking abilities almost as a national pastime. That Francis Jeffrey should have been simultaneously the city's most famous reviewer and its most famous conversationalist is no coincidence.

2

"Edinburgh is a talking town": Christopher North and the Review Essay as Conversational Exhibition

FROM RECIPROCITY TO COMPETITION

"THE CONVERSATION OF THE SCOTS GROWS EVERY DAY LESS unpleasing to the English," wrote Samuel Johnson at the conclusion of his *Journey to the Western Islands of Scotland.*[1] Johnson was right: polite Scots were indeed energetically cultivating the English phrase and pronunciation, as literary and historical scholars over the last fifty years have documented. Speaking "proper" as opposed to "provincial" English was a great enthusiasm in eighteenth-century Edinburgh. The playwright John Home described the thinking behind this enthusiasm when, in 1761, he wrote in a letter, "Eloquence in the Art of Speaking is more necessary for a Scotchman than anybody else as he lies under some disadvantages which Art must remove."[2] Among many others, the actor Thomas Sheridan (father of the playwright and Member of Parliament) offered well-attended lectures on elocution; his first course, also in 1761, dealt with articulation, pronunciation, accent, emphasis, pauses or stops, pitch and management of the voice, tones, and gestures.[3] Debating, literary, and otherwise "improving" societies and clubs sprouted up throughout Scotland, especially in Edinburgh, as part of an upsurge in voluntary associations throughout Britain in the eighteenth century. But while clubs and societies in England embraced all manner of interests, from political and agricultural issues to food and philanthropy and sports, most of the prominent Scottish clubs were interested primarily in improving members' ability to speak well, to improve their "conversation."[4] The best known of these were the Easy Club, founded in 1721 "in order that by a Mutual improvement in Conversation" members "may become more adapted for fellowship with the politer part of mankind"; the Select Society, founded in 1754 for the purpose of "Promoting the Reading and Speaking of the English Language in Scotland"; the Robinhood Society (later the Pantheon), begun in 1773 for the purpose of "improvement in public speaking"; and the Speculative Society (of which Scott, Jeffrey, Brougham, and Horner were members), begun in 1764 for the "Improvement in Literary Composition, and Public Speaking."[5] In fact, as Richard Sher has recently shown in great detail, the Scottish Enlightenment itself was made possible in large part by the custom of sociability among Scottish authors of the second half the eighteenth century.[6]

In order to participate in and contribute to polite British culture, many North Britains felt they would have to learn proper pronunciation, rid themselves of "Scoticisms," and cultivate an ability to "shine" in conversation. Interest in conversing well became more and more self-conscious, almost obsessively so. Scottish periodicals of the day are full of advice for those wishing to improve their conversational skills, and censures against those who need improvement but won't go to the trouble. Typical is "On Conversation," an article in the *North-British Intelligencer* belittling "those pests of society, who act in repeated violation" of the rules of polite conversation.[7] Also common are poems such as this one, from the *Scots Magazine:*

> What books we read, though read with critic zeal,
> 'Tis Conversation stamps the final seal;
> Marks what's original, and what is known,
> And adds another's strictures to our own.

Conversation, says the poet, is so essential to the human condition that even heaven will be one grand discussion among the saints:

> Where man, "made perfect," feels celestial fires
> Glows in discourse, or hymns in heavenly choirs;
> Where, blest communion! Every joy is thine
> Eternal truth, and harmony divine.[8]

Zeal for polite conversation was a middle-class preoccupation, to be sure, but it appealed to the intellectual coteries of Edinburgh and Glasgow as well, manifesting itself most obviously in the writings of the Scottish or New Rhetoricians such as Hugh Blair. In his immensely popular *Lectures on Rhetoric and Belles Lettres,* Blair goes against the tendency in the eighteenth century to disregard the oral aspects of "rhetoric" by including lectures on "Eloquence, or Public Speaking," "Eloquence of the Bar," "Eloquence of the Pulpit," "Pronunciation," and "Means of Improving Eloquence"—many of which read like conversational instruction manuals.[9] (Blair's obsession with the oral doubtless contributed to his taking up the case of Ossian with such enthusiasm.) Especially during the 1780s and 1790s, books instructing Scottish readers in speech and pronunciation were much in demand; even their titles give a sense of the degree to which their readers were willing obediently to submit to rules laid down by seeming Anglophiles.[10] The most famous of these was James Beattie's collection entitled *Scoticisms,* which listed incorrect Scottish words and phrases alphabetically, with large spaces left throughout for the purpose of adding more.[11]

Something happens in Scottish writing of the early-nineteenth century, however, suggesting that the craze for conversation had been more than an Age of Improvement phenomenon; there was a more profoundly cultural impetus behind the interest. After all, by far the most prestigious professions in Scotland were the law and the ministry, which, together with the universities, had after 1707 become the only properly national institutions. To excel in either the law or the ministry required a proficiency in speaking: the minister made his mark by moving churchgoers to repentance and urging them to good works, the advocate by persuading a judge of a defendant's guilt or innocence. The Scottish legal profession was well known for the excessive emphasis it placed on oratorical skill. "Dr. Johnson," recorded Boswell on their tour, "one day visited the Court of Session. He thought the mode of pleading there too vehement, and too much addressed to the passions of the judges. 'This,' said he, 'is not the Areopagus.'"[12] Even the universities in Scotland required students to exhibit a degree of skill in impromptu speaking not expected of their southern counterparts, the classroom itself serving as a forum for the demonstration of skill in dialogue.[13]

In the early-nineteenth century one discerns a shift in emphasis in the way Scottish writers treat the idea of conversation, proficiency in which becomes a distinctly Scottish characteristic, a national trait. Some of the treatments of conversation continue to draw on the tradition of politeness as it had developed in eighteenth-century England after the Restoration and in the Scottish Enlightenment. Although historians now generally avoid portraying the eighteenth century as one in which religion declined in Britain, notions associated with politeness did in some respects take the place of religion as a system of governing societal manners and behavior.[14] And there was nothing more important in polite society than the ability to converse well, a fact that Lawrence Klein has documented comprehensively in his description of the different ways in which conversation was used by English intellectuals in the early part of the eighteenth century. The Third Earl of Shaftesbury had undertaken in his political-philosophical writings to replace the authority of the Church and of the Court with the concept of politeness as a body of principles that would, as he thought, govern social and political behavior by ensuring individual autonomy and, to use Klein's term, "discursive liberty" or freedom of debate and expression. These ideas had a profound effect on the most important political and literary writers of the eighteenth century, and, as Nicholas Phillipson has argued, did a great deal to define the intellectual character of the Scottish Enlightenment.[15] In particular the idea of "polite conversation" was used throughout this era as the ideal activity by which free men might settle their differences and arrive at truth. Summarizing the sundry uses of these concepts, Klein writes:

> Conversational "politeness" was the art of pleasing in conversation, the pursuit of verbal agreeableness. Polite conversation assumed the equality of participants and insisted on a reciprocity in which participants were sometimes talkers and sometimes listeners. It provided an opportunity for self-display at the same time that its norms disciplined self-expression for the sake of domestic peace. It was described as a zone of freedom, ease, and naturalness.
>   . . . writers on conversation were uniformly generous with their recommendations and proscriptions. Conversants were warned against taciturnity, stiffness, self-effacement, and withdrawal, which starved conversation. They were also warned against excesses of assertiveness and sociability . . . It was wrong to dominate discussion or push one's opinions too relentlessly. . . . Finally, affectation, the striving for effect, was noxious to conversation.[16]

The rules of politeness, existing as they did as an alternative to actual political power, were vigorously adhered to; the ideal realm of conversational exchange gave the middle-class conversant an opportunity to influence cultural and political realms from which he would otherwise be cut off. The ability to converse according to established rules thus became a kind of passport to a realm of seemingly more important things. To put it in terms of the Scottish middle class, the public sphere in its manifestation as verbal interchange—in coffeehouses, debating societies, and the like—allowed the northern provincial citizen to introduce himself into the wider world of polite Britain.

In Scotland at the turn of the century, however, introducing begins to look more and more like overpowering. In the 1770s, '80s, and '90s Scottish writers had spoken of English conversation as a general set of rules, or even as an abstract ideal that the civilized person must imitate or to which he must aspire; as late as 1799 Francis Horner expresses delight at the prospect of "two English friends" coming to Edinburgh: "I promise myself much pleasure and much instruction from their conversation. . . . I cannot but learn candour, liberality, and a thirst for accurate opinions and general information from men who possess in so remarkable degree these valuable dispositions."[17] But that must be one of the last published expressions of Scottish inferiority in speaking; for with the turn of the century the treatments of conversation begin to lose that manner of self-deprecation so prominent in the Scottish writing of the previous fifty years. Thus Henry Cockburn recalls the contrast between Scott and Jeffrey by noting the former's "Scotch accent and stories and sayings, all graced by gaiety, simplicity, and kindness, made a combination most worthy of being enjoyed. Jeffrey, his twin star, made a good contrast. He was sharp English; with few anecdotes, and no stories, delighting in the interchange of minds, bright in moral speculation, wit, and colloquial eloquence, and always beloved for the constant transpiration of an affectionate and cheerful heart."[18] Scott's conversation was simply Scottish without being the worse for it: that such an observation could have appeared in, say, the 1770s is extremely unlikely. Many Scottish writers, however, begin attributing conversational supremacy to Scotland. Ann Grant of Laggan in a letter of 1812 propounds her view that "One high pre-eminence . . . that Edinburgh holds above other towns, and more particularly above London, is the liberal style of conversation." In Edinburgh, she writes, people realize the need to "elevate the tone of their general conduct and discourse," while in England people in "middle life" spend their time talking about petty things. "This style of conversation is, of all the styles I have met with, the most contemptible."[19] Henry Mackenzie makes similar remarks in his 1812 biographical sketch of John Home. Recalling the playwright's brilliant circle of friends, and having assessed the "talk" of each, he concludes: "Such was the free and cordial communication of sentiments, the natural play of fancy and good humour, which prevailed among the circle of men I have described. It was very different from that display of learning—that prize-fighting of wit, which distinguished a literary circle of our sister country, of which we have some authentic and curious records. There all ease of intercourse was changed for the pride of victory; and the victors, like some combatants gave no quarter to the vanquished."[20]

The reference is to Boswell: "a literary circle of our sister country, of which we have some authentic records" refers to the one portrayed in the *Life of Samuel Johnson* in which Johnson, Boswell, Garrick, Goldsmith, and others had participated—and over which Mackenzie, despite having only read about it in "authentic records," claims superiority for his countrymen. One senses a hint of the same kind of national feeling of superiority in an 1812 letter from Charles Kirkpatrick Sharpe (born 1781) in which he remarks of an acquaintance, "She certainly was a very amiable person as far as public conversation went," but "she was somewhat spiritless—somewhat English."[21] Similarly, in her distinctly Scottish novel *Marriage*, Susan Ferrier makes the conversational bores to be, not the novel's simple Highland spinsters, but London bluestockings, one of whom is said to have had "great conversational powers, &c. and, to use her own phrase, nothing but conversation was spoke in her house."[22] Again, Thomas Hamilton in his novel *Cyril Thornton* relays a conversation among young Glaswegians, among them one young lady who had spent a year at a "seminary for young ladies" in England (which sounds very much like the one Horner attended for young men). She considers the conversation of Glaswegians "quite shocking," but is herself an intolerable bore.[23] Still again, John Galt satires the tendency (perhaps by 1821 a former tendency) among Scots to think their own manner of dialogue lacking in comparison to that of the English. Andrew Pringle, the young son of the Reverend Zechariah Pringle in *The Ayrshire Legatees*, resembles James Boswell in several ways, not least in his deeply self-conscious desire to converse well with his English companions; on his first visit to London Andrew is disappointed to discover that the Englishman's conversation outshines the Scot's. "A raw Scotchman, contrasted with a sharp Londoner," he writes in another letter about his experience in a London coffee-house, "is very inadroit and awkward, be his talents what they may."[24]

For Scots, it seems, the conversational sphere was no longer a thing to approach with deference and a desire to improve. The governing attitude seems to be that, while the rules of politeness may or may not be applicable, they are not to be slavishly followed merely because their provenance is England. Accordingly by the 1820s the conversational sphere has become something defined almost solely by competition and self-display; reciprocity disappears altogether, and only the "brilliant talk" of individuals remains. There are many accounts of Jeffrey's free-flowing conversation; here for example is a 27-year-old Jane Welsh Carlyle describing Jeffrey on his visit to the Carlyles' home in the coun-

try: "And how on earth did Mr Jeffrey get himself amused in Craigen-
puttoch? Why, in the simplest manner: he talked—talked from morning
till night, nay till morning again—I never assisted at such a talking since
I came into the world; either in respect of quantity or quality."[25] Joseph
Farington records in his diary some comments made by his friend Sir
William Calcott after the latter had returned from Scotland. Having
dined with Jeffrey and some other *Edinburgh* reviewers at Craigcrook,
"Calcott remarked the difference of the Scotch from English society.
He said the '*Scotch are all points and needles,* each striving to exhibit the
brilliancy of his thoughts.' Calcott thought this kind of wit might have prevailed in England abt. the reign of Queen Anne, but in England the
ablest men now meet without any such attempts at sparring."[26] Similarly, when Edward Irving counsels Thomas Carlyle on his mode of
conversation, gone is any trace of politeness: "Your utterance is not the
most favourable. It convinces, but does not persuade; and it is only a
very few (I can claim place for myself) that it fascinates. Your audience
is worse. They are, generally (I exclude myself), unphilosophical, un-
thinking drivellers, who lie in wait to catch you in your words, and who
give you little justice in the recital, because you give their vanity or self-
esteem little justice, or even mercy, in the encounter."[27]

Conversation has become an arena for self-promotion. Irving con-
gratulates his friend for refusing to make allowances for the vanity and
self-esteem of his "audience." Lockhart's *Peter's Letters to His Kinsfolk*,
which purports to describe the "styles of conversation" of nearly every
prominent person in Edinburgh and Glasgow, does so in similarly non-
polite, individualistic, almost theatrical terms. On Scott, "Every remark
gains, as it passes from his lips, the precision of a visible fact, and every
incident flashes upon your imagination, as if your bodily eye, by some
new gift of nature, had acquired the power of seeing the past as vividly
as the present."[28] On Jeffrey, "His conversation acted upon me like the
first delightful hour after taking opium . . . his thoughts, I say, were at
once so striking, and so just, that they took in succession entire possession of my imagination."[29] Lockhart even describes himself, although he
is less than impressed, since "one meets with an abundance of individuals every day who shew in conversation a greater facility of expression,
and a more constant activity of speculative acuteness."[30]

This new attitude to conversation seems to have corresponded to a
change in middle-class manners in metropolitan Scotland, or in other
words in actual conversational conventions. In her 1832 autobiography
Elizabeth Fletcher remarks upon the differences between polite society
of 1790s Edinburgh and 1811 Edinburgh. In the former, dinner parties

in which "hot meals" were served were typical, but in the latter tea and coffee parties became the fashion; in 1811 "card-playing generally gave place to music or conversation. . . . people did not in these parties meet to eat, but to talk and listen. There you would see a group . . . listening to the brilliant talk of Mr. Jeffrey."[31] By the mid-1820s Hazlitt—no great admirer of Scottish society, it has to be said—could credibly represent conversational bullying as a generally Scottish characteristic. "In Scotland generally . . . every one . . . is looked upon in the light of a machine or a collection of topics. They turn you round like a cylinder to see what use they can make of you, and drag you into a dispute with as little ceremony as they would drag out an article from an Encyclopedia. They criticise every thing, analyse every thing, argue upon every thing, dogmatise upon every thing."[32] Just such an abrasive and unilateral manner of spoken discourse was promoted in the pages of *Blackwood's Magazine* in its famous "Noctes Ambrosianæ," that series of fictional conversations about culture and politics that were supposed to have taken place in Ambrose's tavern in Edinburgh. Initially the products of collaboration among Lockhart, Wilson, and William Maginn, the episodes appeared in *Blackwood's* from 1822 to 1835.[33] These conversations represent the inverse of everything Addison and Steele had advocated. The characters try to outshine each other as if competing for a prize; their displays of intelligence are often gratuitous, in no sense intended to contribute or augment; they ridicule each other, their jokes sometimes verging on ribaldry. If the enormous popularity of the "Noctes" is anything to go by, the criteria of politeness had now become, if not obsolete in Scotland, then at least something other than conventional. Some among the older generation seem to have disapproved of the new impoliteness, as they thought of it. Scott remarked late in life that "The art of quiet and entertaining conversation which is always easy as well as entertaining is I think chiefly known in England. In Scotland we are pedantic and wrangle or we run away with the harrows on some topic we chance to be discursive upon."[34] In a similar vein Cockburn seems to express regret when, recalling in 1852 the charm and good humor of the Friday Club, he sniffs: "The professional art of show conversation was held in no esteem."[35]

Even as "conversation" became a more popular topic than ever in Scotland, the way it was thought of—and, it would seem, the manner in which many high-profile people actually engaged in it—ceased to reflect eighteenth-century ideals of reciprocal dialogue and polite rational debate. It was in this cultural moment that John Wilson, "Christopher North," achieved fame as both a conversationalist and an essayist, two appellations which, during the first decades of the nineteenth century in Scotland, seem almost to amalgamate.

JOHN WILSON

Blackwood's Edinburgh Magazine, or Maga as it was known, has accurately been said to have intentionally exhibited conversation-like qualities. The magazine's tone imitated a discussion among friends, full of light-hearted banter and sarcasm and occasional bursts of anger, rather than a classroom lecture or a sermon. It aped conversations most directly, of course, in the "Noctes Ambrosianæ." But the "Noctes" did not begin until March of 1822, and the intermingling of learned conversations and magazine articles appeared before then. In 1819 a review appeared entitled "Two Reviews of a Military Work" in which two reviewers ("O'Doherty" and "Timothy Tickler"—pseudonyms for, in this case, Thomas Hamilton and Lockhart) review the same book from opposite perspectives, the review imitating the interchange of a friendly if argumentative conversation. "It is quite impossible," the editors write, "to find any where a finer specimen of independence, than may be met with in the monthly meetings of the Contributors of this Magazine."[36] This style of presentation led naturally to a surprising level of inconsistency in literary judgments (as distinct from political judgements, on which *Blackwood's* maintained some level of coherence). J. H. Alexander has demonstrated cogently that the magazine's unpredictability, however intentional, amounts to a style of Romantic criticism, implying as it does a consciousness of the fundamentally subjective nature of aesthetic appreciation.[37] As Jeffrey had achieved authority for the *Edinburgh Review* by fostering political inconsistency, the Blackwoodians established some degree of legitimacy for their magazine by displaying a less serious and more "literary" version of the *Edinburgh's* unpredictability, but with the helter-skelter of intoxicated conversation. A number of tactics were used by the Blackwoodians to give the impression of heterogeneity: for instance John Wilson's use in the "Noctes" of James Hogg's persona as the "Ettrick Shepherd" in tandem with his own as "Christopher North," thus expressing two cultural identities simultaneously, one raucous and rough-hewn, the other genteel and sophisticated.[38]

It was Wilson, in fact, who was most responsible for imparting to the new magazine its capricious character. His own character was nothing if not capricious, and his literary personality reveled in inconsistency.

In the first "Noctes" composed exclusively by him, Christopher North responds to the understandable objection that he had just contradicted one of his earlier pronouncements: "With Fahrenheit at 80 in the shade," says North, "I praise the poetry of no man."[39] The most notorious instance of this cultivated impetuousness occurred in 1818, when he responded to Wordsworth's *Letter to a Friend of Burns* with three of his own letters, published in subsequent issues, one by "a Friend of Robert Burns" attacking Wordsworth's poetry and his *Letter*, one by "N" praising both, and another by "D" attacking "N."[40] Such volatility was an early manifestation of Wilson's project during the 1820s of presenting his reviews and essays as exercises in the new, more exhibitionist style of conversation—a cultural phenomenon he exploited for his own purposes and in the process helped to propagate.

The impetus, or a large part of the impetus, behind Wilson's project was the simple fact that he was emotionally volatile and drank too much. He could not concentrate for very long. For years he badgered his friend Alexander Blair to write his lectures for him—this although he was entirely capable of writing them himself, if he could only have put his mind to it. "I lose many more hours and days," he complained in a typical letter to his editor William Blackwood, "in trying to fix on what to write, and to bring my mind into capacity to write, than in writing. . . . For three days have I sat like an idiot with slips before me, and scribbling childish nonsense without success or hope of reward, and ended in disappointing you."[41] This inability to concentrate, coupled with a remarkable capacity (as his contemporaries report) to talk for hours in succession, enticed Wilson to transfer his talk to his writing.[42] Incapable of writing an intellectually serious book (even if he could compose a disjointed novel, a collection of stories, and a long poem), he often celebrated the periodical as an institution that would replace the book-length treatise as the principal medium of intellectual discussion—a medium in which he was well-equipped to dominate. The following passage, from a "Noctes" episode written by Wilson in 1829, illustrates his enterprise well:

> *North.* . . . Formerly, when such disquisitions were confined to quarto or octavo volumes, in which there was nothing else, the author made one great effort, and died in book-birth—his offspring sharing often the doom of its unhappy parent. If it lived, it was forthwith immured in a prison called a library—an uncirculating library—and was heard no more of in this world, but by certain worms.
>
> *Shepherd.* A' the world's hotchin wi' authors noo, like a pond wi' powheads

[tadpoles]. Out sallies Christopher North frae amang the reeds, like a pike, and crunches them in thousands.

North. Our current periodical literature teems with thought and feeling, James, — with passion and imagination. There was Gifford, and there are Jeffrey, and Southey, and Campbell, and Moore, and Bowles, and Sir Walter, and Lockhart, and Lamb, and Wilson, and De Quincey, and the four Coleridges, S.T.C., John, Hartley, and Derwent, and Croly, and Maginn, and Mackintosh, and Cunningham, and Kennedy, and Stebbings, and St Ledger, and Knight, and Praed, and Lord Dudley and Ward, and Lord L. Gower, and Charles Grant, and Hobhouse, and Blunt, and Milman, and Carlyle, and Macaulay, and the two Moirs, and Jerdan, and Talfourd, and Bowring, and North, and Hogg, and Tickler, and twenty—forty—fifty—other crack contributors to the Reviews, Magazines, and Gazettes, who have said more tender, and true, and fine, and deep things in the way of criticism, than ever was said before since the reign of Cadmus, ten thousand times over, — not in long, dull heavy, formal, prosy theories — a coinage of the purest ore — and stamped with the ineffaceable impress of genius. Who so elevated in the intellectual rank as to be entitled to despise such a Periodical Literature?[43]

Wilson invokes a discursive sphere in which all sorts of capable writers are permitted to make valuable contributions who, a generation before, would not have been given the chance — William Gifford, the first-named in the list, was widely known to have come from a poor family. But although North is only one among many, he is manifestly the star "crack contributor" of the lot: "Out sallies Christopher North frae amang the reeds" to crunch book-authors by the thousand. He can do this, he means to imply, because he is the best talker, as witness this long paragraph spouted out impromptu. Likewise in his reviews and essays for *Blackwood's*, Wilson constantly invokes the images and dynamics of conversation, but it is only he who does the talking, and so the supposedly reciprocal sphere of rational discourse — or at least one literal manifestation of that abstraction, the conversation — is arrogated and dominated by one personality. In the eighteenth-century public sphere, as Terry Eagleton has written, "exchange without domination [is] possible; for to persuade is not to dominate, and to carry one's opinion is more an act of collaboration than of competition."[44] In the 1820s, by contrast, Wilson employs the ideals of discussion and collaboration for his own aim of achieving centrality and authority. Indeed, by capitalizing on the widespread interest among the Scottish reading middle-class in conversational "brilliance," and by projecting his own well-established reputation as a great talker, Wilson creates authority for himself: a certain kind of authority, to be sure, one defined more by his status as a celebrity than intellectual profundity, but authority nonetheless. In short, Wilson uses his celebrity to popularize his journalism and his journalism to widen his celebrity. Moreover, throughout the 1820s he attempts to out-shine Jeffrey and the *Edinburgh* by attributing his talking abilities to his national origin: the competitive and exhibitionist conversation is, he implies, intrinsically Scottish, and the *Edinburgh* reviewers, anchored as they are in eighteenth-century improving ideals, are therefore insufficiently Scottish; or, in C. K. Sharpe's words, "somewhat spiritless—somewhat English."

CHRISTOPHER NORTH'S "SCOTTISH" CONVERSATIONS

Among the most immediately evident characteristics of John Wilson's contributions to *Blackwood's Magazine* is the supremacy it claims, implicitly and explicitly, for Scotland—the worship of Burns, the derisive use of "Cockney" to describe young English literary men of any origin, the exaltation of Scottish religion and natural landscape, the romanticization of the literate Scottish peasant. "Christopher North," the nom de plume Wilson adopted not long after its introduction in the magazine, itself represents an assertion of Scottish supremacy: "North" refers to Athens of the North, and that character, whether in the "Noctes Ambrosianæ" or in the magazine generally, always appears the most sophisticated member of the company, always makes the insightful remarks, and always wins the argument.

Wilson's earliest contributions are, however, devoid of any nascent nationalism—and indeed of anything interesting at all. His productions for the first volume of *Blackwood's* publication (April to September of 1817, when it was edited by James Cleghorn and Thomas Pringle) are intolerably boring, containing little more than long extracts and plot summaries and dry, predictable literary analysis. In October of 1817, the first issue to appear after Blackwood sacked the original editors, the famous "Chaldee Manuscript" appeared, as well as Lockhart's first Cockney School essay and Wilson's equally infamous review of Coleridge's *Biographia Literaria*. After the success of the October issue, Blackwood settled on the formula on which he would rely until his death in 1834, namely to give contributors as much imaginative freedom as possible, provided they stayed within the parameters of Tory politics and more or less orthodox Protestantism. "Write *con amore*" was his customary counsel to his contributors: dozens of manuscript submissions intended for the magazine, evidently returned to the authors for revision, bear this open-ended advice from Blackwood's pen.[45]

Wilson's writing transforms after Pringle and Cleghorn's departure. Under Maga's first editors he had written reviews of poetry consisting of long, monotonous, almost verse-by-verse commentary, never looking up from the work under review (*Lalla Rookh*, *Manfred*) till it had been gone over ad nauseam. But now, encouraged by Blackwood himself to write whatever and however he wished, Wilson begins using his contributions to project an image of himself as the brash, overpowering, and above all eloquent chief of the *Blackwood's* circle. He begins, in 1819 and '20, by merely flirting with the idea of rendering his contributions more like speech, as though trying to find a way to communicate a sense of what he was like at the tavern or over postprandial claret. Some of his early satirical and comic pieces appear as though they had been speeches to some club or society; in a "Speech Delivered by an Eminent Barrister," for instance, he satires the grandiloquence of some unnamed parliamentarian ("But this Alaric—this Attila—this Atrides—of atrocity, questions my acquaintance with the long labyrinths of law, with the jargon of judgments," etc.).[46] In 1818 a strange "letter" to the editor appears, "Account of Some Curious Clubs in London, About the Beginning of the 18th Century," in which he reflects on a book entitled *The Secret History of Clubs in London*, published, according to the letter, in 1709. The author of the probably fictional *Secret History* disparages club after club as asinine and frivolous, but the letter-writer defends those who have taken the time to record their proceedings: "It is undeniable," he says, "that much truth evaporates in conversation, and is lost—but it is equally so, that much truth is compressed in written documents, and is never found"; in other words, conversations are, as vehicles for truth, quite as useful as written documents.[47] Again, he prefaces one of his early fictional pieces, "Pilgrimage to the Kirk of Shotts," by noting that its supposed author, Mordecai Mullion, "handed over to us the following letter from his brother Hugh . . . ; with his permission, we read it *aloud*."[48] Still again, in one of Wilson's earliest reviews, this one of Isaac D'Israeli's *The Literary Character*, he compares the author's discussion to "the conversation of a well informed and intelligent friend." "If we have formed a just estimate of the value of this volume, an abstract of some of its most interesting chapters cannot fail to afford pleasure . . . And in our abstract we shall imitate the desultory manner of Mr. D'Israeli himself."[49]

Oftener during these first two years of Maga's publication, however, Wilson's articles consisted primarily of semi-slanderous imputations and fatuousness; and that method of image-creation, he found, proved troublesome — lawsuits were brought against Blackwood by, among others, William Hazlitt and Leigh Hunt. And in 1820, when Wilson lobbied to get himself appointed as Professor of Moral Philosophy at Edinburgh University, his *Blackwood's* articles were held against him, nearly preventing his appointment despite the support of a host of Tory luminaries. Beginning in about 1820, therefore, Wilson changed strategy and began writing his pieces in ways that made them seem like riotous, largely one-sided conversations: the subject raised at the outset of the essay or the book listed at the head of the review would now serve as a point of departure for a wide-ranging and apparently impromptu discussion of matters relevant, or somehow related, to the subject or book. An especially good instance of this is an 1823 essay entitled "The General Question," a monologue on the general loathsomeness of "Liberals" and Whigs and, finally, ecclesiastical innovators. Midway through he interrupts himself: "if I were writing an article for Blackwood's Magazine, I could not indulge in a more digressive, excursive, and occasionally rotatory style, than that along whose involutions and gyrations I have for half an hour past been carried."[50] The writer/speaker concludes his address:

> . . . and being now somewhat thirsty with my oration, I beg leave to sit down, with the most perfect contempt for the Reverend Edward Irving, and admiration of Patrick Robertson.
>
> *Mr. Ambrose, a pot of porter — From the fresh tap, sir — "swifter than meditation on the wings of love."*

By the midtwenties Christopher North was making straightforward arguments that good prose, or at any rate good criticism, ought to exhibit the qualities of verbal exchange. Vapid prose, as well as lifeless criticism, were exemplified in the *Edinburgh Review:* time and again he scourges the *Edinburgh's* "dull prosing," often singling out for special ridicule a long article on Bacon by Macvey Napier (which the latter had written for the *Encyclopaedia Britanica*).[51] The "Preface" of the August 1826 issue, on *Blackwood's'* ten year anniversary, makes this self-serving point in scathing terms. As the other collaborators on this "Preface" laud *Blackwood's* for its contribution to political questions of the day, Wilson lauds it for breathing life back into literary criticism by returning to the putatively old but undefined tradition of what he calls "conversational criticism." The true critic, he observes, must approach the work criticized with some degree of spontaneity. "Without enthusi-asm—without something of the same transport that seizes the poet's soul—what signify the imperfect sympathies of the critic? . . . That de-light does not speak in short, measured, precise, analytical sentences, nor yet in the long winded ambulatory parade of paragraphs circu-itously approaching, against all nature and all art, to a catastrophical climax. But thoughts that breathe, and words that burn, break forth from the critic's lips who is worthy of his bard."[52]

Criticism, North says, is an intrinsically spoken activity; the critic "speak[s]," not as the *Edinburgh* reviewer does, in an "ambulatory pa-rade of paragraphs," but in words that "break forth from the critic's lips." Whereas the *Edinburgh* dispenses "evaporated soda-water," *Black-wood's,* which is to say Christopher North, had tried to "speak" to the magazine's readers, to carry on an intelligent and enlightening conver-sation with them. By making conversational ability the principal issue separating the *Edinburgh* from *Blackwood's,* Wilson was able to do his part in portraying Scottish Whigs as foreign imports or even sellouts: as those who wished above all to purchase intellectual respectability in England and who, in a lamentable attempt to ape the style and manners of the polite and cultured English, had become obsolete and irrelevant. In the King's Jaunt of 1822, the Tories, coordinated by Scott, had been able to present themselves as both good Tories, expressing allegiance to the monarch, and good Scottish patriots, championing Scottish history and custom. Meanwhile Wilson was doing precisely the same by por-traying his party as intellectually astute and high-spirited conversation-alists, as against the tiresome, dull, and intellectually anachronistic Whigs, throwbacks to a "polite" age when English norms determined the boundaries of respectability. In a sense Wilson was trying to put to rest the whole ideal of "improvement," an ideal with which the *Edin-burgh Review* was closely associated, its inner circle having been taught and influenced by Dugald Stewart and John Millar, in many ways con-summators of the Scottish Enlightenment. Scotland, Wilson argues, had now got past all that "improvement" business, and those who had not yet realized it were little better than bores peddling an outdated ideology. Rejecting the era of politeness, Wilson attempts to hold up coarse but intelligent, wild but cultured, alcoholic orating as authenti-cally Scottish, and himself, his magazine, and his party as the true rep-resentatives of that authenticity. Jon Klancher's observation that "there is a strong stylistic tendency in this most influential of middle-class jour-nals [*Blackwood's*] to experiment with turning the form of a discourse into a layer of its content" is especially true in the case of Wilson's conversational pieces: at every turn the style insinuates that the high spirit evident *here* is now absent among the Whigs, who have grown pedantic and unimaginative.[53]

It was a difficult case to make, not least because Jeffrey and Henry Brougham were by this time legendary conversationalists. Moreover, as Fiona Stafford has shown, Jeffrey as editor was striving to achieve a "balance between an obvious personal interest in Scottish subjects and his desire to project an air of editorial detachment and urban sophistication."[54] Still, the *Edinburgh* had often struck certain readers as unduly Anglophilic. In 1824 J. S. Mill, complaining of what he considered the review's reflexive hostility to France, remarked that "English and excellent it employs as synonymous terms; that a foreigner admires England, is a sure passport to its praise; that he does not, is of itself sufficient to draw down its censure."[55] Mill does not mention the irony that the allegedly Anglophilic *Edinburgh* was a Scottish publication, but it is safe to assume that he and his readers were aware of it. His language is hyperbolic, but the criticism is a fair one: the *Edinburgh*'s writers—Jeffrey very much included—often used "England" and "English" when clearly "Britain" and "British" would have been correct; and it did, as Colin Kidd has argued, tend to Anglicize Scottish history by portraying Scotland's pre-1707 political institutions as having failed by their dissimilarity to England's.[56] (An 1832 broadside promoting Jeffrey's election to Parliament referred with disapproval to the feeling among some that Jeffrey was other than altogether Scottish: "Some fo'k hae dared to speak o' you, / They said to Scotland you was not true; / May they be d——d the silly crew, / Wha wou'd despise our Jeffrey." The question of Jeffrey's Scottishness had evidently been a common subject of debate.)[57]

Not only, though, did the *Edinburgh* sometimes leave itself open to the charge Anglophilia; it was known, too, for its occasionally excessive heaviness—it often bored. "The complaint was loud and universal," wrote Sydney Smith to Jeffrey from London in 1819, "of the extreme dulness and *lengthiness* of the Edinburgh Review."[58] Its "dulness and *lengthiness*" had been the complaint probably since the mid-1810s, when the *Edinburgh*'s articles had become fewer per issue and therefore longer. Trying in 1828 to convince Carlyle that his article was simply too long to print, Jeffrey groaned that "it is distressingly long—you do not know how much I am abused, and by my best friends and coadjutors, about these long articles."[59] And the following year, when Macvey Napier became the journal's editor, he referred to the many complaints in recent years "of the too great length of articles generally, instead of that variety which the present state of knowledge and speculation and the tastes of the reading world require."[60] Wilson capitalized on these impressions of the great Whig periodical by asserting conversational fluency and hilarity as distinctly Scottish characteristics, characteristics abandoned by the *Edinburgh* reviewers but epitomized in Maga and Maga's Christopher North.

Thus are Wilson's "conversational" essays expressed, with few exceptions, in the language of Scottish nationality. Typically outspoken in national pride is "Meg Dods's Cookery"—one of the few early *Blackwood's* pieces worth reading for its own sake. Using various recipes and observations in *The Cook and Housewife's Manual* as points of departure, Wilson composes a series of satires on modern prandial gentility. These satires range as far from the book's subject-matter as an intoxicated conversation might from any comment made along the way. As with many of the books Wilson "reviewed," this one, a straightforwardly "Scottish" cookbook with recipes for haggis and sheep's-head broth, allows the reviewer to discourse on the putatively unsung wonders of Scottish history and culture—in this case cookery. (The author of the book was Christian Isobel Johnstone, then editor of *Johnstone's Magazine;* Meg Dods is the name of the colorful Scots-speaking cook in Scott's *St. Ronan's Well.*) "A Scotchman in London is perpetually pestered with the question, 'What is a Haggis?' Now, no man can reasonably be expected to have the definition at his fingertips . . . A blind man cannot by any effort of the imagination conceive colour—nor can any man alive, no, not the greatest poet on earth, not Barry Cornwall himself, conceive a haggis, without having had it submitted to the senses," and so on.[61] What follows is an essay on the vagueries of Edinburgh table manners, not anything like a review in the usual sense.

Another such piece bears the title "Cruickshank on Time," ostensibly a review of *Illustrations of Time,* a book of engravings by George Cruickshank (later one of Dickens' illustrators). Wilson uses several of the plates to raise some idea or subject, and rhapsodizes on it until, sensing boredom in his readers or listeners, he turns the page to another plate, which at one point he claims to have done accidentally. "We have inadvertently turned over three pages, and got to Plate VI.," he says, moving to another topic.[62] The conversation takes in a fantastic array of topics: whether *Macbeth*'s witches are sufficiently supernatural, fishing in the Borders, whether one ought to show hospitality to intruders. The tacit assumption throughout this "review" is that Scotland, or perhaps Edinburgh, is the center of civilization; references to London, here and elsewhere in the essays of Christopher North, are few and usually cutting.

One of the most readable, formally inventive, and overtly "Scottish" review-essays Wilson contributed falls under the heading "Preface to a Review of Chronicles of the Canongate." The subject with which it begins is the value of literature that addresses themes and presents characters and places of a commonplace nature. This overarching idea allows Wilson to range over a host of ideas related to the commonplace in literature: the abundance of reviewers in contemporary British society and the reasons for that abundance, the nobility and bitterness of Crabbe's poetry, the earthbound qualities of Burns' poetry, Jeffrey's idealization of Augustan poetry and condemnation of Wordsworth's, the condescension of English "Cockneys" regarding Scottish religion, and, finally, the use of historical "fact" (Wilson's quotation marks) in Scott's poetry and novels. As if to remind the reader that this is not a "philosophical" essay of the kind they are likely to encounter in the *Edinburgh* but a conversation on literature in general, Wilson twice switches from monologue to dialogue.

"But, dear Mr. North, did you not always think that Sir Walter had some assistance in his works?"

"My sweet young friend, I never did think so—although coming from your lips, the supposition sounds very natural . . . Beaumont, had he never seen Fletcher, had probably been no poet at all. Fletcher's finest plays are entirely his own. But where were we, dearest?"

"Conversing, sir, about the Great Unknown."

"Ay, there is an absurd expression for you."[63]

But of course this is not a conversation, but a periodical essay. Even so, by evoking the imagery or the feeling of a conversation Wilson is able to invoke the legitimacy of the (as it then was) new public sphere of mass-circulated print; and by seeming to dominate that sphere with his legendary conversational adeptness he is able, in turn, to assert his own authority over it. And, in the midst of all this conversational flourish, North imposes a subtle but definitely intentional Scottish bias; Scotland itself is censured for only one thing, namely for allowing itself to be unduly influenced by the *Edinburgh Review*.

Or take another passage from the same essay. It illustrates not only the manner in which Wilson advances conversationlike from topic to topic, but also his predilection for portraying Scottish Whigs as having prostituted themselves to foreign-born philosophies and ideologies that had since—according to Wilson—become passé. He is discussing the abstract question of why some writers only produce one great work while others, who seem also to possess "genius," are able to produce scores of them.

> . . . And this brings us to say a few words about Scotland, and about Sir Walter Scott.
>
> With respect to Scotland, it is, in some parts of England, a popular topic of such sneer as may be extorted from the lip and nostril of a Cockney. It needs that you see such sneer, to know the intensity of the meaning of the word—*small.* But take a Tims, and put him—in perfect safety—under the arch of a Highland cataract, and he sneers no more at Scotland. Yet it must be confessed, that we people of Scotland have done, or rather written, or rather said, a good deal, within these last thirty years, to place us occasionally in a ludicrous light before the eyes even of the wise men of England. For rich as is our Scotland in treasures of scenery yet unexplored in her dim interior, and along the rock-bound bays of her sounding seas . . . and above all, in the virtues, and manners, and customs, and habits of her peasantry . . . —from this our own native land our men of genius turned away their eyes and their hearts, and sought in shallow, and worse than shallow, metaphysics, to extinguish all national feeling and national thought, and having first half-Frenchified themselves with the philosophy of deists and the literature of demireps, to become at last, as the consummation of their wisdom, Citizens of the World.[64]

Wilson goes on to suggest that Jeffrey's hankering after purveyors of "half-Frenchified" philosophy of the eighteenth century caused him to underrate Burns and Scott, to insult Wordsworth, and generally to humiliate himself. The typically Wilsonian conversational flavor of the piece further serves his purpose by implicitly contrasting Christopher North's fluency and uproarious humor with the tiresome and vaguely un-Scottish characteristics of his political opponents. This, in effect, is the strategy employed by the Blackwoodians in the "Noctes Ambrosianæ." The image intentionally conveyed by the series is that of good-natured, intelligent, witty Tories whose eloquent urbanity is never allowed to compromise their essential Scottishness.

In his *Reminiscences,* Carlyle recalls having dinner at Wilson's house in the same year this "Preface" appeared, 1827. Several others were present, but the host talked "nine-tenths" of the time. Wilson, Carlyle recalled, was not "one of those *soliloquy* talkers" (he specifies Coleridge as an example) "who *pump* their talk into you as if you were a bucket: on the contrary he rather seemed to wait for your inquiry, for your suggestion of a subject; and never failed to pause at once when his quick glance told him you nearly had enough."[65] Whether Carlyle realized it or not, and it seems likely he did, he has captured Wilson's style and method perfectly. Wilson goes out of his way in these pieces to keep his readers entertained by moving from topic to topic, taking his reviews in unpredictable directions, and in the process creating the image of Christopher North, the larger-than-life conversationalist. Maintaining an atmosphere of politeness and discursive exchange by constant references to conversation, he nonetheless controls—as Coleridge might have put it—"nine-tenths" of the discussion. That image also served the political ends of *Blackwood's Magazine* and Scottish Toryism, although what Wilson might have been trying to achieve in real political terms is unclear; "Whig" and "Tory" rarely appear to be anything but designations of certain people. In truth, Wilson seems to have known and cared little for politics in any serious sense (his final political act was to vote for Macaulay to be MP for Edinburgh), and his aim in ridiculing Whigs was as much an attempt to enhance the popularity of his own social circle as anything to do with political principle.

Wilson's "conversational criticism" may therefore be best understood as a reaction, not merely against the *Edinburgh Review*'s Whig politics or its alleged Englishness or foreignness, but more generally against Scotland's endeavor in the latter eighteenth century to conform to English notions of social propriety. His practice of turning his reviews and essays into conversations—his belief that the true critic does not "speak in short, measured, precise, analytical sentences" or in a "long winded ambulatory parade of paragraphs"—generates the stylistic equivalent of that conversational competitiveness that other Scottish writers at this time were proposing as a new convention of conversation. Wilson's periodical writing actually becomes more speechlike. Hence his reviews and essays often assume, as one does in speech, the bodily presence of the reader. Typical examples: "Reader! lay your hand upon your heart and say, have you ever more than thrice, during the course of a long and well-spent life, eaten . . . a boiled mealy or waxy? We hear your answer in the negative."[66] "But enough—too much perhaps—of blows and blood—so cast your eye, fair reader, down to the left-hand corner of Plate I."[67] North fumbles over wording much as one does in speech: "Yet it must be confessed, that we people of Scotland have done, or rather written, or rather said, a good deal, within these last thirty years."[68] The writer might simply have erased "done" and substituted "written," then erased "written" and substituted "said," but the effect

Wilson wants is that of a verbal exchange. Again, "Must I — *We* we mean — sicken over our dinner . . . ?"[69]

At the time Wilson was writing, these sorts of stylistic mannerisms stood out. By the late-eighteenth century prose had become, as Carey McIntosh has scrupulously documented, excessively "written" rather than "oral." Prose from the early part of the century had often manifested the characteristics of speech, in particular structural and grammatical looseness; whereas the writings of the later period tend to exhibit awkward though correct grammatical structures, highly abstract language, and analytical directness.[70] There were, of course, practitioners of what Ian Gordon has called "Romantic prose," as typified in the emotionally torrid style of Elia (at times) or *Sartor Resartus*.[71] But there was nothing like Wilson's analytic but grammatically loose and self-interrupting style, a style generated by his attempt, increasingly apparent during the 1820s, to ape the sound and structure of raucous conversations. As a stylist, Wilson could not have spurned the improving ideals of the Scottish Enlightenment more forcefully. Adam Potkay, in his study of the ideas of eloquence and politeness in the mid-eighteenth century, has shown that many writers of this period, especially Hume and others associated with the Scottish "new rhetoric" such as Adam Smith and Hugh Blair, equated language in which frequent use is made of tropes, as well as highly passionate or "vivacious" language, with earlier stages of human development. They believed that children and barbarians may speak in this way, but polite and refined adults did not. For these Scots, "The proof of enlightened maturity" was "an accurate and cool style of expression." By the middle of the century, "even the mild floridity and splendour of a Shaftesbury could not be brooked."[72] Wilson represents precisely the opposite view: for him, an accurate and cool style of expression was little more than "dull prosing" (although without such "dull prosing" he would not have been able to set himself up as the exciting alternative).

What is most revealing about Wilson's style, however, is that it is merely the most extreme instance of a much wider phenomenon in Scottish periodical writing of the early-nineteenth century. Wilson put into practice the new individualistic and competitive conception of conversation more directly and forcefully than did any other writer of his day, but many other Scottish writers of the period — indeed most of those who generated the periodical culture that was Scotland from 1802 to the mid 1830s — were in a sense giving textual expression to this new mode of "conversing."

PERIODICAL-WRITING AS CONVERSATION

In 1817 *Blackwood's Edinburgh Magazine* made its debut in a society in which sophisticated conversation represented not only a social and intellectual ideal but also, increasingly, an activity educated middle-class Scots were eager to engage in—a society, in short, full of people keen to show themselves adept conversationalists. Various venues offered themselves for satisfying that eagerness: the small parties given by Elizabeth Fletcher, the debating and conversational clubs, the drawing rooms of publishing houses (assuming residency in the city). If, however, the popular interest in conversation may be defined more broadly as an interest in expressing oneself engagingly and persuasively, the periodical suggests itself as another, perhaps a superior, conversational medium.[73] There had certainly been eighteenth-century precedent for this notion; the impulse among Scottish writers of the eighteenth century to engage in polite conversation was intimately related to the impulse to write competent periodical essays: both were genteel demonstrations of fluency, intelligence, wit, or insight in response to a book, speech, social trend, or some such thing. As is well known, conversational clubs of one kind or another (coffeehouses, public houses, debating societies) and periodicals (literary and political) had been essential components in the rise of the public sphere in eighteenth-century Europe. In continental Europe, the salons, coffeehouses, societies, and *amateurs éclairés* gave rise, eventually, to institutionalized art critics, who of course practised their criticism in periodicals.[74] But in Scotland, where the desire to converse with fluency had long been the goal of the educated classes, but where speech had been a source of awkwardness and even embarrassment for those same classes, the relationship between conversation and periodical publication was even stronger. Conversations tended as it were to transmogrify into periodical essays.

This almost organic relationship between the two is apparent, for example, in the popularity in mid-eighteenth-century Scotland of the *Tatler* and *Spectator,* periodicals whose authors had made it their business to promote polite conversation among the English middle class.[75] In fact, the *Tatler* and *Spectator* themselves—reprinted in Edinburgh many times throughout the eighteenth century—played an important role in generating the ideas and ideals of the Scottish Enlightenment.[76] For many Scots these periodicals served chiefly as expressions of the idea that polite society was no longer the exclusive province of the upper classes; thus as early as 1742 David Hume had stated his intention to promote his own essays as a link between the "learned" and "conversable" worlds, in other words between those with more formal education (men) and those with less (women).[77] Hence the practice, among several of Edinburgh's conversational clubs during the eighteenth century, of initiating discussions by having *Tatler*s and *Spectator*s read aloud.[78] Hence also the circulation of Scottish imitations of these periodical essays with such titles as the *Tatler of the North*—all written and published, as Lord Woodhouselee remarks in his 1807 biography of Kames, "by a few young men of good education belonging probably both to the church and bar who had formed societies or clubs for literary learning and improvement in conversation."[79] Later in the century, periodicals were still springing from coteries of young literary men; the first issue of Henry Mackenzie's weekly magazine *The Mirror* (yet another imitation of Addison and Steele, this one begun in 1779 by members of the Mirror Club) announces that "the idea of publishing a periodical paper in Edinburgh took its rise in a company of gentlemen whom particular circumstances of connection [they were all lawyers] brought frequently together. Their discourses often turned upon subjects of manners, and of taste, and of literature. By one of those accidental resolutions of which the origin cannot easily be traced, it was determined to put their thoughts into writing, and to read them for the entertainment of each other. Their essays assumed the form, and soon after someone gave them the name of a periodical publication."[80]

The founding of the second *Edinburgh Review* took much the same course, beginning as it did among a group of friends whose mature acquaintance had begun at the Speculative Society, a kind of conversational club for intellectually ambitious university students.

But in the *Edinburgh* these "conversations" took a very different form: here the new attitude among Scots towards conversation made itself felt. The *Edinburgh* reviewers allowed themselves, and indeed were encouraged by editor and publisher, to go far beyond merely relaying a book's contents and offering brief critical comments. And although the *Edinburgh* did occasionally offer straightforward synopses and long extracts, what made it so dramatically different from any periodical-writing of the time was the exhibitionist form many of its reviews took. "[T]he important feature of most articles," Derek Roper explains, making largely the same point, "was opinion, usually aggressively and often voluminously stated, and sometimes only slenderly connected with the work in hand."[81] Suddenly, in 1802, the periodical review became a forum for the display of the reviewer's eloquence, a medium in which the "literary man" might demonstrate his ability to discuss various topics in a fluent and intellectually sophisticated way. Literal conversation and reviewing transformed in parallel: from reciprocity to exhibition-ism, from exchange to domination. Several Scottish observers recognized the exhibitionist nature of the *Edinburgh* when it first appeared. Scott remarked that it "savours more of a wish to display than to instruct."[82] Lawrence Dundas Campbell commented that the reviewers had "render[ed] their publication a convenient vehicle for the display of their powers in elaborate disquisition."[83] In his momentarily popular satirical poem *Epistle to the Edinburgh Reviewers*, Alexander Boswell touched upon this point several times:

> A knack at words you have, some fancy too;
> But have you judgment, think you, to review?
>
> .   .   .   .
>
> Why ev'ry trifle to our notice bring,
> Merely that you may say a clever thing?[84]

Everybody seems to have agreed that the *Edinburgh* reviewers were showing off, and that it was precisely that quality that made the new review attractive. The case could hardly have been otherwise. For not only did the idea of literal conversation undergo a conceptual shift about this time, but the first *Edinburgh* reviewers themselves had come of age in a culture of improving societies in which essay-writing and conversing had been thought of as twin talents. Thus in the 1790s Jeffrey wrote essays in order, specifically, to improve his conversation. By writing a series of essays on various topics, he recorded in one of his early notebooks (1789 or 1790), "I thought I should never want something to say upon trivial subjects—something to the purpose on more important ones."[85]

The Blackwoodians sought straightforwardly to take advantage of the review as a forum for conversational display. With its freer form, its propensity to belie expectations, and its general inconsistency, *Blackwood's* presented itself as a collection of brilliant conversations. In an early number Scott and William Laidlaw observed that "a well-supported magazine such as yours [the editor's], is very like a general conversation of well-informed people in a literary society, who have met together freely, for one another's mutual entertainment, without any particular subject being fixed on for the theme of the evening."[86] The magazine continued over the following two decades to project this image of itself, as a venue for the display of spoken brilliance (though the hint of reciprocity here—"for one another's mutual entertainment"—was rarely in evidence). In the same way, the articles and essays throughout Maga's first twenty years or so purport to be textual manifestations of Edinburgh's conversational exhibitions. Lockhart recognized the propensity of this competitive style of conversation to transmute into reviews and essays when, in the *Life* of Scott, he described the conversational style prevalent in the Edinburgh of Scott's day as characterized by a spirit of exhibitionism that made the mild and courteous Scott sometimes seem out of place: "The best table-talk of Edinburgh," says Lockhart, "was, and probably still is, in a very great measure made up of brilliant disquisition—such as might be transferred without alteration to a professor's note-book, or the pages of a critical Review."[87] Sydney Smith recalled Jeffrey's manner of preparing for a review, "reading, searching, inquiring, seeking every source of information, and discussing it with any man of sense or cultivation who crossed his path. . . . he might be seen committing his ideas to paper with the same rapidity that they flowed out in his conversation."[88]

Such remarks reveal an important dynamic at work in this period: periodical-essays and reviews had suddenly become forms of self-expression, ways in which authors could show just how well they could "say a clever thing." The possibility of exhibiting their skill in writing rather than in speaking seemed all the more attractive to Scots who, like Boswell or John Home or Jeffrey, were embarrassed about their improper accents but who wished to assert their ideas persuasively and attractively. The awkward self-consciousness engendered by understanding without being understood, the desire to express oneself without the encumbrance of an improper accent,[89] could be circumvented by conversing through the periodical. Once the periodical became a customary part of the Briton's life in the 1780s and '90s (magazines and reviews were still too expensive for most people, but they were read by many in coffeehouses and taverns), periodical-writing suggested itself as a medium in which the educated Scot could carry on learned and elegant conversations without the usual embarrassments of northern pronunciations and "Scoticisms."[90] If, to repeat Home's remark, "Eloquence in the Art of Speaking is more necessary for a Scotchman than anybody else as he lies under some disadvantages which Art must remove," then the periodical must have seemed an excellent tool for getting around those "disadvantages."

Again as with literal conversation, there was a pronounced element of cultural nationalism implicit in this new conception of the review as self-display. After the turn of the century, and more apparently during the 1820s, cultural nationalism became respectable—an assertion of pride in Scottish cultural achievement albeit within the framework of the Union; a belief in the ascendancy and exportability of Scotland's cultural achievements, using the word "cultural" in it broadest sense to include art, architecture, and literature as well as manners and folk culture. National pride vis-à-vis England had of course existed before and since 1707, but the attitude prevalent after about 1800 was manifestly new, not least because the poetry of Burns and later Scott were then making the old national pride respectable again by combining Scottish patriotism with literary sophistication. Hence the construction, begun in 1821 but never finished, of the National Monument on Calton Hill. In fact the monument's full title was, or was intended to be, the National Monument of Scotland; and although it is sometimes mistakenly named as an example of British patriotism, its originators made clear that it would commemorate the Scots who died in the Napoleonic Wars, not simply the Britons. The monument was intended, though, to honor much more than the valor of Scottish soldiers, which is why the Temple of Minerva in Athens was chosen as the model rather than something thematically related to war, as with the nearby Nelson Monument. The National Monument of Scotland would be a new Parthenon for the Athens of the North. The monument would, in the words of one of its supporters, "be such that, by its symmetry and beauty, our national taste may be improved, and thence our national manners still further dignified and refined."[91] Even Highland culture was now worthy of display, as the tartan-clad reception of George IV in 1822 made clear.

Conceit in Scottish letters was just as pronounced, if harder to exhibit so plainly. The Blackwoodians often gave expression to the literary side of cultural nationalism—as for instance in the mock-biblical "Chaldee Manuscript" of 1817 ("Chaldee" = Aramaic, but here Caledonian) in which Edinburgh is described as "the great city that looketh toward the north and toward the east, and ruleth over every people, and kindred, and tongue, that handle the pen of the writer."[92] With *Peter's Letters*, as Ian Duncan has shown, Lockhart himself helped to generate the new cultural nationalism by promoting a radical distinction between the inauthentic Whiggism of the recent past and an organic and mystical cultural unity.[93]

Not that Scots of the eighteenth century had never betrayed nationalist attitudes; many of Scotland's literary figures had from time to time expressed cultural and at times political nationalism.[94] But it is plain that Scots of the first three decades of the new century, and especially of the 1820s, were vastly more confident in Scotland as a locus of cultural preeminence than their grandparents had been. Carlyle, whose hostility to the eighteenth-century Enlightenment was already plain in his 1828 essay on Burns in the *Edinburgh*, remarked upon this change in national spirit when he noted that, since the death of Burns, "our chief literary men, whatever other faults they may have, no longer live among us like a French Colony, or some knot of Propaganda Missionaries; but like natural-born subjects of the soil, partaking and sympathising in all our attachments, humours and habits."[95] Decades of cultivating conversational ability and shedding Scoticisms had given Scots an overweaning desire to brandish their skills. An increasing number of periodical organs made it possible for the nascent intellectual elite of Scotland to display their facility in discussion, argument, and appraisal by writing reviews for the *Edinburgh* and *Blackwood's*, as well as for lesser publications such as the *Edinburgh Literary Miscellany*, *Tait's Magazine*, and the venerable *Scots Magazine*. Jeffrey reveals the way in which a sense of cultural nationalism had motivated him and his confreres to produce their review when he confesses to Horner, a year into their adventure, that the "main object" of the *Edinburgh* had been not only "amusement and improvement," but also "the gratification of some personal, and some national, vanity."[96] Here then, to use Ernest Gellner's terminology, was a country that, having moved conclusively from an agrarian age to a fully industrial age, had now developed a high culture in need of some kind of political expression—in this case, an acknowledgment of Scotland as its own cultural (though not politically autonomous) entity.[97]

From this perspective, John Wilson appears to be merely an extreme and obvious manifestation of a wider phenomenon: the educated Scot brandishing his (as he thought) peculiarly Scottish aptitude in dazzling and intelligent conversation. The conversational competitiveness apparent by the first years of the nineteenth century revealed itself in a new form of periodical writing, one defined by self-display and discursiveness. The *Edinburgh Review* originated this style of reviewing. That is a large part of what made it famous. Often its contributors wrote their reviews and had the editor attach the title of a book, a practice that became standard by the 1830s and, turning humble book reviews into substantial essays, enhanced the prestige and influence of periodical reviews in early Victorian Britain.[98] *Blackwood's*, founded as an avowed rival to the *Edinburgh*, took the practice to gratuitous and sometimes comical extremes; indeed William Blackwood's advice to contributors or would-be contributors to "write *con amore*" seems to assume that the most important factor in periodical-writing is the urbane and fluent manner in which one expresses oneself rather than the judgments made and arguments asserted.

The wider implications of this shift can hardly be overstated. The notion of a book review as an exhibition of fluency and intelligence assumes a fundamental equality between the review and the thing reviewed. At the beginning of the century, as Ina Ferris notes, literary critics associated with the *Edinburgh* and *Quarterly* occasionally betrayed anxiety about their own membership in the republic of letters. "Despite the university, professional, and club background of many of the reviews, they fit as uneasily into the republic as did the novel that they so often derided as vulgar, commercial, and superficial."[99] Early-nineteenth-century reviewers were faced with the question of what the status of their own form of discourse was or ought to be. One must remember, of course, that "literature" or "letters" was still a fluid concept in the 1790s, encompassing history, science, travel writing, philosophy, as well as aesthetic works of fiction and poetry. The status of the review would ultimately decline (nowadays we think of book reviews as a lower form of writing than the freestanding essay—only people like John Updike can get away with publishing their book reviews between hard covers), but in the 1790s the status of the review seemed to threaten that of the book itself. The term "literature" generally applied to whatever seemed likely to endure in interest past the time of its original appearance; but while the encyclopaedic nature of eighteenth-century Reviews implied that the importance of their contents exceeded, say, that of newspapers, the reviewers' general reluctance to go very far beyond relaying the contents of books effectively presupposed the reviews' importance to be secondary. So although a number of reviewers in the 1790s began to assume the seemingly more elevated roles of judge and public censor, consequently adopting moderately adversarial language, they still defined their function as servants and preservers of the republic of letters.[100] The custodial imagery employed by the late-eighteenth-century reviewers—guardians of the "fortress of Taste," as one *Critical* reviewer put it—implied a conception of the reviewer as unquestionably subordinate and instrumental.[101]

The great innovation of the *Edinburgh* reviewers was to depart from the book under review and "enter at large," as they often put it, on a discussion of the larger issues raised by the book—an innovation itself arising from the new style of (literal) conversation favored by much of the polite middle class in metropolitan Scotland. The effect was to elevate the review-essay as something equal in importance to the book reviewed; the review-essay became a kind of counterpart to the book, a response equally deserving of attention. To the *Edinburgh*'s opponents this seemed little more than gratuitous display of "eloquence" without substance. Josiah Conder, in his 1811 pamphlet *Reviewers Reviewed*, argued that the new exhibitionist style of reviewing had the effect of beguiling people into believing that they were somehow taking in the substance of books when in fact they were reading the mere opinions of those who, however "eloquent," had done none of the preparatory work undertaken by the authors whom reviewers affected to judge. The modern reviewer derives satisfaction, Conder thought, not so much from the subject to which he puts his mind, but from "the exercise of his own faculties in a particular way upon those objects."[102] On the subject of Jeffrey's reviews Conder was slightly less dismissive, but still scathing: "were I to select the distinguishing feature of the articles attributed to his pen it would be in a word, eloquence. It is by the powerful magic of words, into which the breath of genius has infused mysterious life and energy, that the reader is impelled to yield up his opinions and his feelings."[103] What annoyed Conder most, it seems, was that this supposed "mysterious life and energy" was really nothing more than a collection of book reviews; and his observations on this score are far from baseless. The *Edinburgh* reviewer's frequently indulged tendency to depart from the reviewed book's contents and even to compose a largely or wholly independent essay—sometimes without so much as mentioning the book under "review"—did indicate a suddenly elevated conception of the reviewing role. Indeed, to the extent the review took a more independent form, it presented itself as more important than the book, which served merely to raise the topic of discussion.

The more competitive, less reciprocal mode of conversation popular among Scots at the beginning of the nineteenth century had generated this new style of reviewing. It began with the *Edinburgh* in 1802, and reached its rhetorical limits with John Wilson in the 1820s: indeed Wilson and his friends at *Blackwood's* were merely trying to beat the *Edinburgh* at its own game. If, as Mark Parker has argued, literary magazines of the 1820s such as *Blackwood's* and the *London* "themselves aspire[d] to *be* literature" by inventing their own multi-layered discourse, that aspiration had first appeared in the public sphere with the *Edinburgh* reviewers' appetite for rhetorical display, an appetite that had its origins in the cultural vicissitudes of metropolitan Scotland.[104]

In the Edinburgh of this period, then, we witness one literal component of the eighteenth-century public sphere, conversation, transforming into something quite incompatible with the conventions of politeness, without which the public sphere could not exist in the way originally envisioned. That incompatibility gives rise to a print culture characterized by the new conventions: reviewing aspires to greater independence and originality, but also, on the regrettable side, treats works deserving of praise or at least respect as incidental and irrelevant. The new manner is captured by Henry Crabb Robinson in a diary entry from 1811. He accounts for Coleridge's intense dislike of Scots by noting the latter's propensity to talk as much as he did, and in the same solipsistic way. "Edinburgh is a talking town, and whenever in their conversaziones a single spark is elicited, it is instantly caught, preserved, and brought to the Review."[105]

3

"A deal more safe as well as dignified": Lockhart's Modified Amateurism and the Shame of Authorship

POLITE LITERATURE IN SCOTLAND

OVER THE COURSE OF THE EIGHTEENTH CENTURY, EDUCATED SCOTS began to place a higher value on secular literature and, concurrently, less value on narrowly theological literature—all true enough. But although it is obviously true that "polite" literature was written and read in Scotland with increasing frequency and appreciation throughout the second half of that century, it is also true that writing in certain forms of polite letters oneself—poetry and especially fiction—continued to imperil one's reputation well into the nineteenth century. While no suspicion attached to the writing of history or religious poetry, most would-be poets and all would-be novelists were encouraged to keep their writing as inconspicuous as possible.

There were two principal sources of suspicion. The first and in many ways the most deeply ingrained was that long-standing aversion among Calvinist Presbyterians to anything suggesting idleness. This disposition, though prejudicial, was an old and principled position, and so amounted to more than mere prejudice. It is not true, as is sometimes carelessly stated, that Calvinism was an essentially anti-intellectual creed. Calvinists had always revered historical writing—though the Enlightenment ideal of objectivity troubled many—and were generally disposed to favor rigorous scholarship of any kind.[1] Calvinists, however, understood art to be primarily instrumental in nature; they believed that art, if it is to enjoy esteem and patronage, must serve some perceivable function: a function that writing poems, plays, and novels did not have in any obvious way.[2] Furthermore, Calvinists had always placed high value on remunerative labor (as against self-imposed poverty, which some Roman Catholic traditions had idealized).[3] For many of those in Calvinist traditions, therefore, the idea of reading and writing poetry and fiction suggested laziness and aimlessness. The producer of it, so went the reasoning, could hardly be expected to support himself financially, and the reader of it could only divert time and energy away from worldly and spiritual duties. This is why Thomas M'Crie began his angry rebuttal of Scott's treatment of the Covenanters with a largely irrelevant swipe at novel-reading: "The great object of habitual readers of novels is to kill time, and they are not very scrupulous as to the means which they employ to rid themselves of this troublesome companion."[4] Hence the satirical portraits of old-school Presbyterians in Scottish literature: the Cameronian Burley in *Old Mortality* who judges poetry to be "as trifling as it is profane"; the Reverend Balwhidder in *Annals of the Parish* who objects to "poem-making" as "a profane and unprofitable trade."[5] Many Presbyterians had difficulty thinking of poetry and fiction as anything other than low amusement.

Further disposing Scottish Calvinists against legitimizing polite literature—and from the 1750s to the early-nineteenth century the issue was one major point of difference between the established church's Evangelicals and Moderates—was the fact that deistic and otherwise radical philosophical views had long been associated with those who championed "politeness." In English writing, politeness had fully emerged as a category of knowledge or "learning" by the early eighteenth century: as an adjective to describe written works "polite" indicated literature of an aesthetic character that emphasized elements of taste and style, the classics and especially English poetry, which socially aspirant gentlemen ought to have read.[6] The Evangelicals would have been at least vaguely aware that the ideas of politeness had originally been promulgated by such notorious deists as the third Earl of Shaftesbury and his followers, as well as, later, by the more heterodox figures of the Scottish Enlightenment, and that these figures had invoked politeness as a system of cultural organization in which society would be governed, not by the Church or the monarchy, but by gentlemen.[7] Traditionalist Presbyterians objected most energetically, however, to polite literature's associations with desultoriness and laziness. While for their part the Moderates believed that the promotion of polite ideals in manners and literature ought to be among the central efforts of their ministries, the Evangelicals contended that such ideals, harmless as they might be in themselves, were far less important than the traditional endeavors of evangelism and doctrinal instruction.[8] Some had shown outright hostility to the very idea of secular writing of any kind, yet by the latter part of the eighteenth century this position had been reduced to the argument that polite literature was in itself harmless or usually harmless, but was hardly something a respectable adult should spend much time on. Thus the famous Evangelical churchman John Erskine (1721–1803) could criticize Moderates in uncharacteristically pointed terms for, as he thought, dithering in literary subjects at the expense of the duties of flock-tending.[9] In a similar vein, Samuel Charters (1742–1825), Kirk minister in Wilton, defended the plainness of his sermons with these remarks: "Works of taste are composed to please; but the object of religious instruction is more serious and severe; it is to undeceive, to reclaim, to conduct in a steep and thorny path. Taste and imagination revolt, leaving reason and the heart to ponder."[10] Neither Erskine nor Charters held polite literature itself in contempt or considered it an enemy of true Christianity; rather they thought it merely unworthy of much attention. "Works of taste" were intended merely to "please," not to instruct—an attitude adopted by, among many others, James Hogg's parents, who thought "that reading too much would induce to a neglect of business" and so "dissuaded [James] powerfully from the perusal of every book, that was not some religious tract or other."[11] In such an outlook as this, imaginative literature had very little standing; actually writing it would therefore have been less than respectable.[12]

The second source of prejudice against imaginative literature, itself to some degree an effect of the first, was the spirit of mercantilist and professional respectability among the middle class fostered in the newly prosperous Scotland of the latter eighteenth century. The business and professional classes' prejudice against most forms of literary activity is hard to gauge because it was rarely articulated—there are no pamphlets on poets being dodgy characters. Part of the reason must have been the usual one that poetry, art, and so forth offer little in the way of profit or practicality.[13] More specifically, though, these suspicions seem to have arisen from the notion that writing novels and poetry was neither a remunerative nor a stable mode of life and therefore signaled indolence and dandyism. That such a prejudice was pervasive in metropolitan Scotland toward the latter part of the eighteenth century and after appears in the apprehensive dispositions of Scottish writers who felt ill at ease with their literary predilections. Henry Mackenzie contributed poems to the *Scots Magazine*, "but so shy was I of being known as their author, that I used to go to Sand's shop after it was dark and deliver the MSS. in silence to the shop boy."[14] James Mackintosh (1765–1832), later a *Monthly* and *Edinburgh* reviewer, and still later an MP, had written poetry in his youth and adolescence, and at Aberdeen Univer-

sity even became known as "the poet" and "poet Mackintosh"; yet
when a university friend later asked him about these nicknames, "he
disclamed it, pleading not guilty to the extent of a single couplet."[15] Alexander Balfour (1767–1829), a poet but also a successful merchant
who headed his own firm in Arbroath, liked to deprecate his own literary activities—"the 'idle trade' of tagging rhymes," he called it. "I have
often . . . almost sworn to be 'rhyme proof against my last breath.'"[16]
John Galt, aged twenty-five, told a friend that one of his goals in writing poetry had been that of "showing that literary studies were not
incompatible with business"; he wished to "prove that literary propensi-
ties were not disorderly."[17] A decade later Walter Scott decided that it
was not in his professional interests to "plead guilty" to writing *Waverley;* being known as a published poet as well as a published novelist, it
seems, would have been too much.[18] "In truth I am not sure it would be
considered quite decorous for me as Clerk of Session to write novels.
Judges being monks clerks are a sort of lay-brethren from whom some
solemnity of life may be expected."[19] Some young litterateurs were able
to brush these inhibitions aside, with varying degrees of success.
Thomas Campbell simply disregarded the misgivings of his father, the
head of a shipping business in Glasgow who, upon finding his eighteen-
year-old son writing poetry, told him he would do much better "reading
Locke than scribbling so."[20] And R. P. Gillies, founder of the *Foreign
Quarterly Review,* recalled with distaste the contemptuous attitude to
poetry adopted by otherwise literate people at Edinburgh University,
where he began attending in 1804: "I might as well have proposed . . .
reading fortunes in the clouds, as devoting time and strength to such a
pursuit [as poetry]. It '*proved nothing.*'"[21]

Others were more affected by cultural prejudices. Andrew Picken
(1788–1833), a poet from Paisley who had formerly been involved in
various business ventures, persisted as a poet but was never quite at
ease about it; he confessed to another poet that "I can hardly wonder at
Galt's being a little shame-faced about it, and the sort of reputation it
brings even to such as he. I have tried to get out of it, and back to mer-
cantile life, but cannot."[22] Likewise Francis Jeffrey, who as a young
man wrote a great deal of poetry but never published a line of it, de-
sponded in 1794 that his desire to be a poet would get him nowhere in
life; his "romantic temper," he said, would probably keep him from
"success as a man of business."[23] Too many poets were, in his opinion,
undereducated slouches to redeem poetry as an occupation; thus in
1805, a short time after he himself gave up versifying, he wrote of
Southey as having "more learning and industry than commonly fall to

the lot of those who dedicate themselves to the service of the Muses," and a year later he lamented sarcastically the number of people who "labour under the complicated diseases of poverty, poetry, and want of principle."[24]

Of course, the increasing availability of imaginative writing at the end of the century, the expansion of a public sphere in which imaginative works were a central medium of interchange, gave more Scottish people a taste and appreciation for nonreligious poetry and fiction and so helped to mitigate the force of these cultural prejudices. The mercantile-professional spirit of the urban middle class discouraged young men and women from undertaking careers in writing even as it helped to make such careers more attractive by creating wealth and thus the ability to buy books. Still, it would be a mistake to suppose that in 1800 educated Scots were fully at ease with "poem-making" and associated activities. Certainly many in ecclesiastical circles were not, despite the tendency in modern scholarship to concentrate on the Moderates, who had high-profile careers as churchmen and who wrote and published more than their Evangelical counterparts (and whose views on these subjects correspond more closely than those of the Evangelicals to modern scholarly interests). Richard Sher has argued that after the *Douglas* affair of 1758, in which John Home, then a minister, was censured by several presbyteries for writing and staging his play *Douglas*, the Church of Scotland began slowly to reconcile itself to the legitimacy of secular learning and literature.[25] This is true as far as it goes; Home's play was a great hit in Edinburgh, and anyhow Burns, and later Scott and Hogg, could not have become celebrities in a culture pervasively hostile to imaginative writing. Yet the Evangelicals were more influential in middle-class Scotland than were the Moderates, who, despite twentieth-century assumptions to the contrary, never enjoyed anything close to a majority in the Kirk, and among dissenters no influence at all.[26] In any case the Evangelicals' opposition to the playhouse, and by extension their aversion to the idea of reading and writing novels and poems, flowed more from their stridently Calvinist view of labor than from ignorance or philistinism.[27]

The belief, then, that polite literature was little more than a diversion for the idle and frivolous was adopted by intelligent and indeed influential people well into the nineteenth century. Thomas Macaulay's father Zachary, the Scottish-born evangelical reformer and anti-slavery campaigner, was one such moralist; he thought imaginative literature next to worthless, though he suffered his children to indulge in it—in the daytime. Thomas's sister recalled that "Poetry and novels, except during

Tom's holidays, were forbidden in the daytime, and stigmatized as 'drinking drams in the morning.'"[28] That had been a common view for a long time; here for example is a newspaper notice about the Pantheon, a public debating society in Edinburgh where members of the public, frequently lawyers and clergymen, deliberated on a wide variety of issues. "Thursday last the question, 'Does reading Novels tend to promote or injure the cause of Virtue?' underwent a discussion of considerable length. Thirteen gentlemen delivered their sentiments upon it, Ten of whom appeared against novel reading; notwithstanding of which, however, it was determined by a majority of TEN (out of 120), that reading novels tends more to promote than to injure the cause of Virtue."[29] Fifty-five out of 120 held forth against novel-reading. In the same spirit, some Scottish novelists of the period would insert disparaging remarks about novels into their own novels.[30] It is difficult to say why they might have done this, but they seem to have been intimating for the benefit of their readers that they were aware of the moral dubiety involved in writing fiction, but that they were determined to redeem the craft.[31]

Here, then, was a culture in which imaginative literature was written and read, but in which—for many—an aura of misgiving hung about the idea of being a producer of it. What with the gradual secularization of Scottish life and the circulation of an ever-greater variety of published writing, this aura of misgiving was bound to fade—especially when Scottish intellectuals of almost every description were (as I have argued in chapter 1) at home with some form of a public sphere in which all literate people could participate. These Scottish intellectuals knew as well as anybody that imaginative writing was a central component in the sphere of rational interchange increasingly evident around them—a sphere in which they were determined to participate. But how? In the following pages I shall argue that many of these Scots, mostly university-educated middle-class young men, found a way to assuage their apprehensions about imaginative production by directing their creative efforts towards periodical-writing. By writing essays and reviews, which were not imaginative in the way poems and novels were, and by publishing them in the anonymous pages of magazines, whose substantial payment for contributions lent the activity (should they wish to divulge their having engaged in it) at least a hint of professional respectability, these writers managed to avoid the shame of outright authorship while also satisfying the urge to participate in the literary world of modern Britain.

The assumptions about literature underpinning these writers' thinking conflicted violently with the tenets and attitudes summed up by the term Romanticism; and, indeed, the discursive conflict captured by the title of Byron's work *English Bards and Scotch Reviewers* was largely, I would propose, a result of this tension. Still, it must be pointed out that the doubts about imaginative literature entertained by Scottish periodical-writers were part, or part of the result, of a wider phenomenon in British writing: throughout the 1790s many writers had been re-casting their function as authors in terms of professionalism. Thus, as Paul Keen writes, "The image of the Romantic writer as outcast implies a certain haughtiness towards any mundane place within the working world, but . . . the dominant image of the author in the 1790s was more closely tied to . . . the prestige of the professional," which is what precipitated the countercultural disposition of the Romantic writers in the first place.[32] The periodical-writers dealt with in this study, then, were in some ways part of the movement to make writing a professional and therefore respectable and consequential function. What set them apart from other writers discussed by Keen, however, was their reluctance to give *imaginative* works the same kind of boost in importance—or, depending on the mood and context, any importance at all.

LOCKHART AND ROMANTICISM

Writers of the Romantic movement, of course, wished to appropriate for themselves a prestige far higher than that of the professional. Although lofty claims for poetry had been made long before Wordsworth and Coleridge, after their early work these claims would be made with greater openness and frequency. The poet, Wordsworth had written in the 1800 Preface to *Lyrical Ballads*, is "endowed with a more lively sensibility, more enthusiasm and tenderness, . . . a greater knowledge of human nature, and a more comprehensive soul, than are supposed to be common among mankind."[33] As if in response, English poets over the following twenty years assigned more and more importance to themselves as poets and, by extension, to the composition of poetry.[34] Implicitly degrading means to knowledge traditionally thought of as primary, science and theology, the Romantic poets asserted poetry as the highest form of understanding. They were more intensely conscious of themselves as poets, in other words, because they believed that the knowledge imparted by their art transcended other forms of knowledge.[35] These ideas (as Francis Jeffrey had anxiously foreseen) almost necessarily implied the notion that the true poet is alone or, more precisely, that solitude and isolation rather than engagement were essential to the poetic vision.[36]

Such notions would inevitably conflict with the apprehensive attitude toward imaginative literature emanating from the Calvinist and middle-class mercantilist-professional outlooks in Scotland, and that, again, must account for at least part of the varied reception of Romanticism in that country. To say this, however, is not to rely on the facile conception of (as a recent study has put it) "Scotland as the lack, or simulation, or repression of Romanticism": in fact, a number of recent scholarly treatments have done much to recast Scotland as a generator of Romantic ideas.[37] Even so, there is a great deal of truth in Kenneth Simpson's observation that the Scots' evolving sense of national identity, combined with the austerity and self-restraint of traditionalist Presbyterianism, tended to distort certain impulses typically designated as Romantic.[38] To be specific, the prevalent (though of course not exclusive) view in Scotland that writing poetry and fiction was an activity customarily engaged in by indolent dandies or superficial fops was not one likely to absorb the extravagant claims of Romantic poets. It was simply outrageous for the new generation of poets, who could reasonably be expected to conceal, or at least not to flaunt, their activities, to claim power and superiority *as* poets: Many if not most Scottish reviewers had been attracted to reviewing in the first place owing to a vague sense of shame in writing verse and fiction; now, having found a way to be "literary" without the shame, they were confronted with poets who seemed not only unashamed of being poets but actually proud of it. I shall try to illustrate this dynamic by recourse to the writings of Scottish periodical-writers themselves, published and unpublished, in due course. Over the following pages, though, one writer in particular falls under examination whose attempts to resolve this conflict illustrate the dilemma faced by others in his position.

First as one of the original Blackwoodians, then as the editor of the highly respectable *Quarterly Review*, John Gibson Lockhart sought not only to censure the new poets' self-absorption and egotism, but also to explain why it was worthy of censure and to formulate a disposition that could take its place. To do this he found it useful to combine two seemingly antithetical notions of the writer: amateurism and professionalism. For Lockhart, the ideal of the amateur—the "man of the world" who writes in his spare time purely for amusement, never for money—offered itself as a defense against an ideology whose proponents he believed to be circulating the idea that poets are superior beings and ought therefore to sequester themselves from society and to commune with their own inspired thoughts. That ideology, he believed, was corrosive to poetry and poets, and was little more than an excuse for radicals such as Leigh Hunt to promote their ideologies. The problem for Lockhart was that he was not entirely comfortable with amateurism either, and so he amalgamated it with a sturdy Calvinistic belief in the importance of remunerative work.

A fuller definition of amateurism is in order. From the early Renaissance period through to the end of the seventeenth century, the most common, if not always accurate, notion of the author was that of an aristocrat with a considerable allotment of spare time and, commercial motives being vulgar, substantial independent income. Essentially an upper-class dilettante, he published his writings strictly, if at all, for the benefit of his fellow courtiers or his friends. As an ideal, amateurism had begun to deteriorate early in the eighteenth century as printing technology made it possible for greater numbers of people to publish and profit by their work. The difference between Pope and Johnson is often used to illustrate these changes: Pope carefully cultivated the image of himself as an amateur, scorning any serious intentions as a writer, even as he put to use his considerable business acumen to profit handsomely by his books; while Johnson, who in the 1755 preface to his *Dictionary* repudiated Lord Chesterfield's patronage (and thus patronage generally) as insufficient, almost always spoke forthrightly about his commercial motivations.[39] Amateurism was in full decline when in 1774 the House of Lords in *Donaldson* v. *Becket* invalidated "perpetual copyright," thus making it at least possible for writers to earn a significant income from writing, and thus sounding the amateur's death knell.[40] Further contributing to the demise of amateurism and the emergence in its place of authorship as a viable occupation was the rise in the eighteenth century of literary criticism, a practice which assumed the author's work to be a product requiring assessment and valuation and which therefore bolstered the notion that it ought to be paid for.[41] Yet the ideal of amateurism outlasted its reality, surviving well into the nineteenth century: writers continued to present themselves as disinterested amateurs even if in most cases they worked and profited as professionals.[42]

Returning from Balliol in 1814 to begin a career in law, Lockhart failed to make much progress, and so amateurism as a posture must have seemed attractive and convenient. "I have been amusing myself with writing a novel," the twenty-year-old wrote, in high amateur style, to Archibald Constable.[43] Certainly Lockhart played the part, idling around the Court of Session or dawdling in Blackwood's "lounging-shop," as he called the bookshop on Princes Street.[44] But as an ideal,

too—as a defined position on the role of the poet or novelist—
amateurism offered itself as a useful conceptual tool with which to
counter the claims then being made for poetry and art by, first, Wordsworth and Coleridge, and later by Leigh Hunt and late Romantic writers such as Keats, Shelley, and Robert Haydon. During the late 1810s
and early '20s, though, Lockhart seems to have recognized that the use
of this conceptual tool was a more complicated affair than he had
thought. The beginnings of this recognition may have had to do with
the fact that his father, a staid Kirk minister to whom Lockhart was
devoted, disapproved of his son's posturing as a "literary man."[45] In any
case, in his writing he began a few years into his reviewing career to
advocate moneymaking as a legitimate and salutary motivation for the
writer, which implied professionalism. Yet, in one sense at least, Hunt
et al. were quintessentially professional, inasmuch as—in Lockhart's
opinion—all they did was write poetry. This is why as a reviewer he
would often ridicule Romantic writers by recourse to the language of
professionalism: "the profession of authorship," "the occupation of
poetry," and so forth. What he meant by this was not that they took a
favorable view of market values or that they approached their work
with a moneymaking mindset (although they often did, despite all the
pretense about aloofness and solitude).[46] Lockhart might have tried to
champion the market-oriented side of the Romantic poets' motivations
had they themselves not concealed it; as a reviewer he had only their
published work to go by, and so could only see what J. W. Saunders
has called "the Romantic Dilemma" in which poets felt supremely confident in their "special vision of truth which ought not to be socially
corrupted or circumscribed" and therefore were, or at least seemed to
be, unwilling to engage in the grimy business of making a living.[47] What
Lockhart wished to appropriate was not, then, professionalism as ordinarily conceived; rather he wanted the professional *disposition*, its common sense, its realistic view of how life works: that part of it that was
most unlike the inchoate poetics of Romanticism. In short, he wanted
amateurism modified by the Presbyterian and mercantilist-professional
worldview—a worldview exemplified in his mind by Sir Walter Scott,
who preferred to be known as a "man of affairs" rather than as a mere
writer. "[T]he literati of Edinburgh," he had written in 1811 with respect to the *Edinburgh Review*'s severity on new writers, "are generally
engaged in other pursuits in life, and are not . . . apt to feel sore under
the lash of criticism, as probably more indifferent to literary fame than
their brethren of the south."[48] The engaged and realist attitude Scott
boasts of here, Lockhart would attempt over a period of twenty years

to express as an artistic disposition: in his *Blackwood's* and *Quarterly* reviews, and finally in his biography of the man himself.

Now to describe Lockhart's writing as a search for an "artistic disposition" implies a departure from the manner in which some recent scholarship has framed the conflict between Romantic poets and "the Tory press." Jeffrey Cox has argued that the "Cockney School" attacks in *Blackwood's* "were literally reactionary, a conservative response to a pre-existing positive presentation of the group [i.e. the Cockney poets]," and Nicholas Roe has explicitly confined Lockhart's motivations to the political.[49] There is no doubt that the political affiliations avowed by Hunt, Keats, Haydon, and Shelley influenced Lockhart's putatively aesthetic judgment of their published writings, a fact made obvious by the critic's unstated policy of always exempting Wordsworth (whom the *Edinburgh* had never really stopped castigating) from the vices attributed to these "Cockneys." In view of the rest of Lockhart's criticism, however, it seems clear that aesthetic concerns were a major part of the "Cockney School" reviews. Indeed, the particular aesthetic concerns implicit in those reviews are so pervasive elsewhere in Lockhart's criticism, and that criticism is so pronouncedly nonpartisan (at least in the narrow sense of favoring writers according to party affiliation), that one is tempted to believe that the "Cockney School" essays are criticism trying to pass itself off as political hectoring, rather than the other way around. The fact is that Lockhart tried persistently to imitate what he felt to be the unpoliticized outlook of his father-in-law, whose long poems and novels had acknowledged the virtues in both sides of old conflicts, and whose break with the *Edinburgh* had been occasioned, as he claimed and Lockhart believed, by the Whig journal's increasing tendency to allow politics to dominate its views on literature.[50] Although it is certainly true that by the time Lockhart knew Scott, the latter's Toryism had drifted in a reactionary direction, it was well known that he maintained warm personal relations with Whigs, not least Constable and the *Edinburgh* reviewers themselves.[51] Lockhart wished to avoid being known as a crudely political reviewer. When such reviewers take a book in hand, wrote Lockhart in 1818,

> his first question is not, "is this book good or bad?" but it is, "is this writer a ministerialist or an oppositionist?" . . . the author is a person who lives in his province, and eats beef and drinks port, without ever asking who is minister, regent, or king. But he has a nephew, a cousin, or an uncle, who is a member of parliament, and votes. . . . If he votes with Lord Castlereagh, the poetry, or biography, or history . . . of his kinsman, is excellent in the eyes of the Quarterly, and contemptible in those of the Edinburgh Reviewer.[52]

Politics was never absent from Lockhart's criticism, but in order fully to understand his writings on authorship, and equally his biography of Scott, one must look beyond its political aims. In fact he habitually took swipes at the politically polarized world of the 1820s, as when he claimed that at a Burns Banquet the *Edinburgh* reviewers refused to toast Wordsworth and Coleridge for reasons of "party politics"; or as when in his novel *Reginald Dalton* he has a Tory remark, "I believe there was something good about him, after all." "Good about him?" answers her doltish companion, "No, that's too tender by half, Betty. Blount is a Whig."[53]

BLACKWOOD's: 1817–25

Although he admired Wordsworth's poetry, there was one aspect of it that Lockhart believed compromised the poet's work, and that was his egotism, his view of himself as a source and conveyer of higher truth. "Mr. Wordsworth," he wrote in an early pamphlet, "is humbly of opinion that no man in the world ever thought a tree beautiful, or a mountain grand, till he announced his own wonderful perceptions."[54] Lockhart's high regard for Wordsworth's poetry was diminished only (as he would write many times over the years) by the poet's tendency to think and write too often about himself—a tendency for which, according to one of his "Cockney School" essays, Wordsworth at least had an excuse.

"On the Cockney School of Poetry," a series of review essays on Hunt, Keats, and Shelley, has marred Lockhart's reputation, and there is a good argument to be made that he deserves that fate. Still, there is more at work in these reviews than the class-snobbery and political vilification customarily seen in them. In these essays Lockhart is attempting, however crudely at points, to demonstrate that the indulgent introspection so characteristic of post-Wordsworthian poetry is nothing more than self-worship, the sort of shallow and insulated vanity that distorts what would otherwise be praiseworthy verse. The problem with these diatribes is that, instead of dispassionately propounding his view that Hunt's and Keats's fascination with themselves had compromised the avowed merits of their poetry, Lockhart responded to vanity with insult. Leigh Hunt had made extravagant claims for poetry, his own in particular, and Lockhart belittled this self-aggrandizement by depicting it as petty class-aspiration.

The animating idea of the first essay is that while he may believe himself entitled to glory and honor because he is a poet, and may express himself thus in his poetry if he likes, Leigh Hunt has little knowledge of any poetry apart from his own. "He pretends, indeed, to be an admirer of Spenser and Chaucer," but his most heartfelt admiration is for that which "bears some resemblance to the more perfect productions of Mr. Leigh Hunt; . . . the real objects of his admiration are the Coterie of Hampstead and the Editor of the Examiner."[55] Such comments as these indicate that the critic's disgust is with Hunt's high regard for himself as a man; and so in part it may have been. But it is clear, too, as the article continues, that the real target is Hunt's belief that poets, as poets, occupy a higher level of virtue and worth than other people, and that therefore their productions merit some sacred status. Lockhart scorns Hunt for his "want of respect for all the numerous class of plain upright men, and unpretending women, in which the real worth and excellence of human society exists. Every man is, according to Mr. Hunt, a dull potato-eating blockhead—of no greater value to God or man than any ox or drayhorse—who is not an admirer of Voltaire's *romans*, a worshiper of Lord Holland and Mr. Haydon, and a quoter of John Buncle and Chaucer's Flower and Leaf. Every woman is useful only as a breeding machine, unless she is fond of reading Launcelot of the Lake, in an antique summer-house."[56] The critic mocks Hunt for his snobbery; that is, for thinking himself better than "plain upright men" and "unpretending women" because he is a poet. The meanness is in the representation of literary snobbery as class snobbery; or, as Peter Murphy has put it from a slightly different perspective, "poetic 'stretching' is made into an undignified sort of social climbing."[57]

In any case, it is easy to appreciate the difficulty of Lockhart's task here: how to attack Hunt for exalting himself as a creator of poetry without seeming to underestimate the value of poetry? In this instance he ridicules the particular specimens of literature read by its putative worshipers; but this was not really a satisfactory answer because Hunt could as simply claim to admire poets whom it would be boorish to denigrate. More typical of subsequent "Cockney School" reviews, and of Lockhart's criticism in general, is the assertion that the poet who assigns some exalted or high-flown meaning to his task as a poet thereby corrupts his own ability to compose. "Mr. Keats has no hesitation in saying," he writes in the most infamous of these reviews, "that he looked on himself as '*not yet* a glorious denizen of the wide heaven of poetry,' but he had many fine and soothing visions of coming greatness."[58] Accordingly, the critic reproduces those passages from the *Poems*, in particular "Sleep and Poetry," that indicate the poet's fixation on himself as a creator of poetry, and that exhibit the corollary of that fixation (as Lockhart believed it to be), the notion that poets must insulate themselves from everything that is not poetry. For instance,

> O for ten years, that I may overwhelm
> Myself in poesy; so I may do the deed
> That my own soul has to itself decreed.
> Then will I pass the countries that I see
> In long perspective, and continually
> Taste their pure fountains.
>
> (96–101)

Or, again, "And they shall be accounted poet-kings / Who simply tell the most heart-easing things" (267–68). M. C. Hildyard long ago suggested that Lockhart resented Keats for having written poems on Greek mythology without any knowledge of Greek.[59] There may be some truth in that, but he objected most strenuously to Keats's propensity to write too much about himself, his art, his own faculties of perception and insight. What Lockhart could tolerate in the poetry of Wordsworth could not be endured in that of a misguided young apothecary under the influence of Leigh Hunt, the belief that as a poet he was on a plane above the rest of mankind. Hence the reviewer's notorious counsel to the poet at the review's conclusion: "so back to the shop, Mr. John Keats, back to 'plasters, pills and ointment-boxes,' &c." A mean gibe, certainly, but a gibe meant to ridicule what Lockhart took to be the poet's own sanctimoniousness, his belief that the "shop" was below him now that he had become a poet-king.

This becomes clearer still in the fifth Cockney School review, again on Hunt. Lockhart begins by proclaiming the superiority of Wordsworth's and Coleridge's poetry to anything yet produced by Hunt, Keats, or Shelley. There is, however, one characteristic shared by all these, in the critic's opinion: their self-serving poetics, or more simply their egotism. Yet "egotism is pardonable in him [Wordsworth], which would infallibly expose any other man of his genius to the just derision even of his inferiors."[60] After all Wordsworth, Lockhart reasons, has an excuse for his self-absorption, namely that the British reading public under the influence of the *Edinburgh Review* had spurned him and effectively driven him into contemplative isolation. (In fact, the *Edinburgh* had spurned Wordsworth in large part for his having gone into contemplative isolation.) Hunt, on the other hand, "sits at Hampstead with his pen in his hand, from year's end to year's end, and . . . he never yet published a single Number of the Examiner . . . of which one half at least was not in some shape or other, dedicated to himself."[61] The reviewer goes on to quote lines from "Sonnet on Myself," an anonymous poem satiring Hunt which Lockhart seems to have thought genuine (its author is given as "Editor of the Ex-m-n-r").

Apart from the vituperation, these essays foreshadow what would mark Lockhart's criticism of the next eighteen years: the interpretation of introspection as conceit and narcissism. They are Lockhart's early protests against Romanticism's tendency to make the occupation of poetry not just respectable but godlike. To write beautiful verse, he insists, is not necessarily to surpass in merit those "upright men, and unpretending women" in whom "the real worth and excellence of human society exists." The argument he produces here, and the one he would repeat and modify in the future, is that nothing so vitiates a young writer's work as self-importance, isolated contemplation, and excessive self-examination. While Keats overwhelms himself in poesy for ten years, and Hunt "sits at Hampstead with his pen in his hand," they deprive themselves of profitable experience, and their poetry comes increasingly to look more like deranged blustering.

Lockhart met Walter Scott in May of 1818. About this time the belittling gives way to calmer and more measured, if not always gentle, criticism. Rather than prompting him to look more sympathetically on the Cockney School, however, his acquaintance with Scott reenforced the suspicion with which he viewed self-absorption in writers. Lockhart adulated those aspects of Sir Walter's persona—the open and outgoing demeanor, the varied and multifaceted interests, and the reluctance to put himself forward as a Writer of Great Literature—that seemed to him the very inverse of the disengaged and "unmanly" poet-kings whom he had been reviling for two years. Whether Scott actually possessed these characteristics is another question: but it is likely, as will become clear shortly, that Lockhart himself helped to propagate that tradition in his 1837 biography.

It is foreshadowed as early as 1819 in *Peter's Letters to His Kinsfolk*. Lockhart was writing it when he met Scott, and their first meeting he records in Letter LI. Though Scott is the object of the world's admiration, writes Peter, his humility is genuine: "There is no kind of rank, which I should suppose it so difficult to bear with perfect ease, as the universally-honoured nobility of universally-honoured genius." The contrast with Leigh Hunt was too good to pass up. "Good heavens! what a difference between the pompous Apollo of some Cockney coterie, and the plain, manly, thorough-bred courtesy of a W— — S— —!"[62]

In *Peter's Letters* Lockhart, now a mediocre advocate with ample spare time, begins to evoke amateurism as an ideal over against what he saw as the narcissism of the new poets. Here is his account of meeting Henry Mackenzie.

> They [Mackenzie and a lawyer called Adam Roland] are both perfectly men of the world, so that there was not the least tinge of professional pedantry in their conversation. As for Mackenzie, indeed, literature was never anything more than an amusement to him, however great the figure he has made in it, and the species of literature in which he excelled was, in its very essence, connected with any ideas rather than those of secluded and artist-like abstraction. There was nothing to be seen which could have enabled a stranger to tell which was the great lawyer, and which the great novelist. I confess, indeed, I was a little astonished to find, from Mr. Mackenzie's mode of conversation, how very little his habits had ever been those of a mere literary man. He talked for at least half an hour, and, I promise you, knowingly, about flies for fishing; and told me, with great good humour, that he still mounts his pony in autumn, and takes the field against the grouse with a long fowling-piece slung from his back.[63]

As a tribute to amateurism, this could hardly be bettered: the writer to whom "literature [is] never anything more than an amusement" and who spends most of his time doing things other than writing or contemplating himself as a writer—as over against the newly famous Hampstead set who advocate "secluded and artist-like abstraction." Now, it is dangerous to assume that everything uttered by "Peter Morris" represents the sentiment of his creator, but in this case Lockhart seems to have expressed his own opinions about the practice of authorship. All the qualities here attributed to Mackenzie—humble about his own abilities, competent in disparate departments of life, averse to taking himself and his art too seriously—would be attributed to Sir Walter Scott in Lockhart's biography, then almost twenty years from publication.

In 1825 (he had married Scott's daughter Sophia in 1820), Lockhart wrote a review of a book by Sir Egerton Brydges, *Recollections of Foreign Travel, on Life, Literature, and Self-Knowledge*. Here he begins to place the ideal of amateurism under more scrutiny. Henry Mackenzie, after all, had been independently wealthy; what about financially disadvantaged but equally talented writers? He is provoked by Sir Egerton's counsel to young writers, that if they possess true genius they ought to withdraw from worldly affairs altogether, put away their books, and converse with their own thoughts—advice that may be well and good for Sir Egerton, who, having been born into wealth, could always afford to spend his days "writing and publishing works, not one of which ever paid . . . the paper maker and the printer." The idea that poets ought to quarantine themselves, he says, "is a doctrine exceedingly acceptable, no doubt, to many young persons who prefer lounging in a green lane over a Coleridge or a Collins, to the ignoble fatigue of copying briefs or pounding medicines" (Keats again). "But this is not the situation of many of those who, in opening manhood, feel the movements of literary ambition in the absence of that sort of power of mind and talent which alone can enable any man to gain anything like Fortune, or anything like Fame, worthy of the name, by devoting himself to the pursuits of literature *as his occupation*. We are sickened when we think of the multitudes of naturally amiable tempers that have been for ever soured and embittered by the indulgence in such dreams."[64] The writer who possesses anything less than sheer genius, he argues, is tempted to withdraw from society, thus depriving himself of the experience without which his writing will always seem artificial and truncated, and ensuring that he will give up poor and exasperated. He denotes Brydges's disengaged ideal by the phrase "literature *as his occupation*," hence equating professionalism, which we would normally associate with a down-to-earth and businesslike attitude, with the "artist-like abstraction" of the Romantic poets.

In this Lockhart was perceptive. The Romantic-era notions of "genius" and "inspiration" as things inside the poet's soul or mind (as opposed to outside, e.g., the muse), had arisen largely in tandem with the rise of professionalization of writing in the eighteenth century: desperately wanting financial independence, many European writers in the late-eighteenth century had begun more emphatically to locate the source of poetry inside the poet, thus wresting ownership of their works (copyright) from printers and publishers.[65] Thus when Lockhart characterizes Brydges' advocacy of inwardness and isolationism as an attempt to professionalize writing, he refers to the shift away from the Renaissance conception of writing as external and instrumental (the writer merely fashioning words according to long-established rules), toward the Romantic conception of writing as the result of internal genius and inspiration—a shift that helped to create the concept of "authorship," which in turn implied professionalization. At the same time, Lockhart always held to the Johnsonian dictum that writing for money was the only sane reason to write at all. Hence his problem: how to separate writing for money from the inwardness and self-indulgence of Romanticism? In the present instance he lists the great writers of the past who engaged with the world rather than withdrawing from it.

Homer—does any one read him and believe that he was a man only fitted for, and accustomed to, a quiet fireside, and a stroll among the daffodillies? Æschylus—was he not a stirring politician and valiant soldier throughout his life? . . . Was Dante a moper?—Was Bacon nothing but a man of contemplative *genius?* Was not Milton a schoolmaster and afterwards a Secretary to Cromwell?—Was not Shakespeare himself a merry good-natured player, who framed the very greatest works of human genius in the mere intervals of his professional labours?—Was not Swift a busy churchman and politician all through life? . . . What was Burns himself, (of whom Sir Egerton Brydges is so fond of speaking)—a ploughman, a farmer, an exciseman!—What is Scott?—has he not been all his life a lawyer, and is he not at this moment both a law-officer, occupied in that capacity the best part of the day, during the greater part of the year, and a great farmer and planter to boot, to say nothing of living eternally in company?[66]

Egerton Brydges (a well-known Tory, incidentally) was urbane and independently wealthy and thus was in some respects the perfect amateur. The problem was that he was circulating among a younger generation the highflown and overwrought ideas of Leigh Hunt. But all this affected talk of artistic genius persuades young poets that they need only look inward for inspiration, when in fact the most valuable sources of inspiration lay everywhere else; "that one word *genius* has done more harm than anything in the vocabulary."

This was not the kind of amateurism Lockhart had in mind when he praised Mackenzie's easygoing attitude to writing. Such a doctrine was poison for the young aspiring writer who lacked Brydges's sizeable income (a lack which Lockhart, despite an Oxford education and pretensions to good breeding, was then realizing himself). And so, in this latest expression of his ideal, he makes room for those of little or no income. In effect he strips amateurism of its assumption of independent wealth and its idealization of idleness; he democratizes it, updates it for nineteenth-century middle-class Britain. Or, to view it in theoretical terms, he professionalizes and Calvinizes amateurism by making the writer someone who, if he writes at all, must write between stretches of respectable, moneymaking labor. Lockhart does not repudiate amateurism; he transforms it. The ideal writer is no longer an idling, scribbling aristocrat, but a working man, a "ploughman, a farmer, an exciseman," as he calls Burns. Only two poets who followed such advice as Sir Egerton offers ever succeeded, he concludes: Wordsworth, for whom Lockhart always made exceptions, and William Collins, whom he designates as the only talented members of the "Moping School of Poetry" (a more clever name than the other, though it never caught on).

Lockhart was observant enough to see that the vast majority of poets and novelists did not make enough money to live on; the writer who "devot[es] himself to the pursuits of literature *as his occupation*" will almost certainly, he believed, come to nothing. The aspiring writer ought, he holds, to do as much as possible outside of writing. Lockhart's rhetorical question about Scott—"has he not been all his life a lawyer, and is he not at this moment both a law-officer . . . and a great farmer and planter to boot, to say nothing of living eternally in company?"—looks forward to the 1837 biography, which is in one major sense a massive expression of his ideas on authorship. The intervening years, during which he moved to London to begin his long career as editor of the *Quarterly Review*, were, to judge from his published criticism, spent contemplating the difficulties inherent in his ideas.

The *Quarterly Review:* 1825–1837

In his literary reviews written before the publication of the *Life* of Scott in 1837, Lockhart attempts with partial, but only partial, success to express his ideal of moneymaking amateurism—that is, a mode of life engaged primarily in nonliterary, moneymaking endeavors such as law or medicine or business, and secondarily in writing. He does this by chiding various poets and critics for inflating the value and importance of imaginative literature; such inflation, he argues, leads the poet or novelist into despair and poverty, and furthermore leads readers to underestimate and undervalue other, equally vital sources of instruction and enlightenment. His problem, obviously, was that he did believe imaginative literature to be a genuine source of enlightenment and instruction. He occasionally said so, as for instance when he responded to an observation by Scott in his collection of biographical prefaces, *Lives of the Novelists,* in which Sir Walter doubts whether literature that glorifies immorality presents any real threat to the morals of its readers. "It may seem strange to find masters of literature thus undervaluing its influence; but our wonder will be diminished when we reflect how strongly such persons are tempted to overlook . . . the extent to which the creations of genius affect every-day natures, incapable of tracing how or for what purposes these are formed."[67] Again, on the value of literary biography, he asserts that the poet, "by his single pen, exercises perhaps wider and more lasting sway over the tone of thought and feeling throughout whole nations, than a regiment of kings and ministers put together."[68]

More common in his *Quarterly* essays, however, are fulminations against those who in his view were exalting the composition of imaginative literature to unwarrantably high social and moral levels—those, in other words, who applied his own intermittently expressed views to the real world of writing. In order to deflect such claims, Lockhart continued to formulate his own idea of moneymaking amateurism. The subject is explored at some length in his review of Thomas Moore's biography of Byron. Moore believed, in Lockhart's words, that "poets of the highest order are essentially unfit for the most precious relations and duties of domestic life"; or, as Moore himself had put it, "It is, indeed, in the very nature and essence of genius, to be forever occupied intensely with Self, as the great centre and the source of its strength."[69] Moore's understanding of poetic genius, Lockhart shows, had allowed him to absolve Byron of the guilt that would necessarily attach to anybody else who had neglected his family (and so on) in the same way. The critic quotes the biographer: "To this power of self-concentration, there is, of course, no such disturbing and fatal enemy as those sympathies and affections that draw the mind out actively towards others." On the contrary, says Lockhart, repeating his view that great artists look outward rather than inward, "these 'sympathies and affections that draw the mind out actively towards others' are, we venture to suspect, even more essential to the formation of a Homer or a Shakespeare, than the 'power of self-concentration.'" It is, the reviewer goes on to say, precisely Byron's self-absorption that led him into such gross errors and rendered him indolent, capricious, incapable of producing the poetry that God had equipped him to produce. "Self had become, to a miserable extent, not only 'the centre and source' of his poetry, but the centre of his feelings, and the source of his actions as a man." So, rather than excuse Byron's misdeeds by invoking his allegedly great poetry, it would have served the poet and those who admire his poetry better if he had been treated as every other person of his station and rank is—or should be—treated.

> Laying the obligations of religion aside, we think the time is come, that those whose fortune it is to possess land and rank in this country cannot be too often, or too earnestly reminded of the fact, that the possession of such advantages constitutes, in every case whatever, a retaining fee on the part of the nation . . . The country gentleman, the peer, and the prince, have their professions fixed on them—let them surrender the fee, if they mean to shrink from the work—let the sinecure be a sine-salary . . . Nor will it deceive any one, to say that Lord Byron's poetry was an equivalent for all that

he neglected [i.e. that he shirked his duties in order to write poetry]. Poetry never occupied the whole, or even the greater part of any man's time: his poetry did not occupy more of his time than Lord A.'s merino sheep do of Lord A.'s, or Lord D.'s larch plantations of Lord D.'s. He had plenty of time for other things than poetry; if he had not, his poetry would never have been worth the cost of printing.[70]

Lockhart makes two important points here. First, whatever Byron's poetic abilities were, they should never have exempted him from the moral strictures governing everybody else. Again Lockhart insists that high-flown and pretentious talk about the "nature and essence of genius" and "the power of self-concentration" does nothing for poets and nothing for literature. Second, he turns Moore's argument on its head by saying that Byron's poetry was as good as it was because he spent very little time writing it and thinking about it, and that it would have been better had he been less, not more, fixated on himself. In all this, Lockhart subtly blends the concepts of amateurism and professionalism: poetry should be one pursuit among many, as in the former; but it ought to be undertaken diligently and resourcefully, as in the latter.

Byron, though, was an aristocrat and possessed independent wealth, and he was thus a difficult case from which Lockhart could comfortably theorize—rather as Egerton Brydges had been. He returned to the subject three years later, this time in a review of the *Life and Poetical Works* of George Crabbe, whom Lockhart was able fully to admire both as a man and as a poet. In that review he expresses irritation at those who bemoan the twenty-two years during which Crabbe, whose duties as parish priest demanded all his time and effort, wrote little and published nothing. "[W]e have never been much disposed to marvel at the abstinence from publication of any man, however gifted, however diligent, who has not the stimulus of want behind him." Again he is inveighing against those who think poetry ought to occupy all the poet's time, that anything less is compromise. "But suppose," he continues, "Mr. Crabbe had never, after he became a parish priest, written one page except of a sermon."

What then? He was, from first to last, a most devout, holy, indefatigable parish priest. He never allowed any call, either of pleasure or worldly business, to interfere with the discharge of his professional duties. If a peasant was sick, and wanted him at his bedside, that was always a sufficient reason for suspending any journey or engagement. . . . Moreover, although he had slender success as a medical practitioner on his own account, he, during the nine-and-twenty years that he was a *country* clergyman, continued to practice as the medical attendant, *gratis,* of all of his own parish poor, supplying them too with medicines at his own sole cost, and not shrinking, when the occasion pressed, even from the most painful and anxious duties of the accoucheur.[71]

Lockhart then states his point as a question: "Had this story been all that was to be told, who would have been entitled to wonder at the poetical *inactivity* of the rector of Muston?" In other words, contemporary poetic theories tacitly accepted by those who regret Crabbe's "poetic *inactivity,*" based as they must be on the assumption that art represents some nobler or morally superior calling, look grotesque and depraved when considered in the context of the real world of sick peasants and women too poor to hire a midwife. Yet the obvious correlative to this point, that Crabbe's later poetry is better than it would have been owing to the experiences of this "silent" period, Lockhart fails to state explicitly—though it seems he was by this time stating it in his biography of Scott.

In the following year, 1835, Coleridge having recently died, Lockhart reviewed a book called *Specimens of the Table-Talk of S. T. Coleridge.* That poet presented Lockhart with another opportunity to clarify what he believed to be the proper disposition of the artist towards art, money, and the world of "affairs" outside art. The reviewer singles out for special attention "one of the most interesting passages" in the *Biographia Literaria:* "NEVER," Lockhart quotes Coleridge as writing, "PURSUE LITERATURE AS A TRADE . . . Woefully will that man find himself mistaken, who imagines that the profession of literature, or (to speak more plainly) the *trade* of authorship, besets its members with fewer or with less insidious temptations than the church, the law, or the different branches of commerce."[72] Here, however, as if afraid to pursue the idea (note the ambiguity of that word "interesting"), Lockhart changes the subject. Then, several pages later, he returns to the question of the author's self-understanding by citing some observations by Coleridge in his lectures on Shakespeare concerning the degree to which Shakespeare was conscious of his own greatness, a subject that had obvious bearing on Coleridge's life. Granted, says Lockhart, Shakespeare must have been aware at some level of his genius; yet he retired after *Othello* (believed by Coleridge and Lockhart to be his last and greatest play), "never once dreaming even of an edition of his works . . . We can only account for this by the presumption that, great as Shakespeare was, and felt himself to be, he had in his mind an ideal of art far above what he supposed himself ever to have approached in his own best dreams. How surely is Modesty the twin grace of Daring in the structure and development of every truly great mind and character!"[73]

The reviewer goes on to lament, in the gentlest of terms, the manner in which Coleridge spent his final, self-absorbed years. Coleridge had died the year before, and Lockhart's forerunner as editor of the *Quarterly*, J. T. Coleridge, the poet's nephew, was still closely associated with the journal. Lockhart therefore expresses his view with caution. Still the point is clear enough: beginning with the *Biographia* quotation in which Coleridge had warned against pursuing "the *trade* of authorship" and then raising the issue of Shakespeare's putatively self-deprecating attitude, Lockhart proposes that Coleridge, by making poetry his "profession"—that is, writing poetry and doing nothing else—isolated himself and thereby squandered whatever genius he had. Lockhart proposes that the professionalization of imaginative literature vitiates it by drawing the writer's attention away from the world he ought to write about and into himself. He has again implicitly invoked the ideal of amateurism: had Coleridge been more like Shakespeare, had he taken the business of writing rather less seriously, he might have made more of his manifestly superior gifts.

Thus does the critic grope toward a satisfactory expression of his position. His problem, still, was that the old notion of amateurism, which had assumed independent wealth and had eschewed openly commercial motives, had serious difficulties in an age in which a moderately wealthy middle-class was becoming common. How was Coleridge supposed to sustain himself if he did not devote most or all of his time to composing poetry? Writing for money might actually lend itself to the "isolation and artist-like abstraction" advocated by Leigh Hunt and Egerton Brydges—that is, using Coleridge's formulation, into LITERATURE AS A TRADE. Given what he believed to be the alternatives, then, Lockhart never reconciled himself to literature as a profession. But a satisfactory articulation of his idea, as he must have realized, can hardly have been achieved in reviews alone; it was a book-length project. And so, even as he wrote his reviews of Crabbe and Coleridge, he was at work on the *Memoirs of the Life of Sir Walter Scott*.

THE LIFE OF SCOTT

Scott had died in September of 1832, aged sixty-one. Even before Scott's death Lockhart was fully expected to write the *Life*, on which he began working within a month. The above-mentioned *Quarterly* reviews were written while their author fixed his attention on his father-in-law's life and art: the essay on Moore's biography of Byron appeared in January 1831; the essay on Crabbe appeared in January 1834; and the piece on Coleridge ran in February 1835. In some ways, then, Lockhart's greatest work can be understood as a delineation of his own views on the nature and function of imaginative literature, and the proper view the writer ought to entertain of his own function. Indeed, the biography is in large part an expression of the biographer's ideal: engaged, moneymaking amateurism. Its central thesis is that the greatness of Scott's poetry and fiction arose, first, from his natural facility, but second from the fact that he actively undertook to be everything but a writer, owing to his belief that imaginative literature represented a merely peripheral aspect of life, that it was of limited importance compared to other (rarely specified) issues. Scott was a mere amateur, a dilettante in the best sense of the word, but one who put his extraliterary endeavors to good use, not only by using them to inform his writing, but also, especially, by making money from them.

This leitmotif is sounded near the beginning of the work, as it happens not by Lockhart or Scott, but by a friend of Scott's, Charles Kerr. In 1799 Scott had only published three works, all of them translations of German poetry. Kerr's letter contains advice on whether and to what extent Walter should pursue a career in writing:

> go on; and with your strong sense and hourly ripening knowledge, that you must rise to the top of the Parliament House in due season, I hold as certain as that Murray died Lord Mansfield. But don't let many an Ovid, or rather many a Burns (which is better), be lost in you. I rather think men of business have produced as good poetry in their by-hours as the professed regulars; and I don't see any sufficient reason why Lord President Scott should not be a famous poet (in the vacation time) . . . I suspect Dryden would have been a happier man had he had your profession. The reasoning talents visible in his verses assure me that he would have ruled in Westminster Hall as easily as he did at Button's, and he might have found time enough besides for everything that one really honours his memory for.[74]

"This friend," comments Lockhart, "appears to have entertained, in October 1799, the very opinion as to the *profession of literature* on which Scott acted through life."

Throughout the work Lockhart makes clear, almost too clear, that Scott himself believed—whatever the biographer's opinions might be—that imaginative literature was essentially a peripheral aspect of life, something of limited importance, a pastime. "Keenly enjoying literature as he did," writes Scott's friend John Morritt, "he always maintained the same estimate of it as subordinate and auxiliary to the purposes of life, and rather talked of men and events than of books and criticism."[75] He quotes Scott's letter (referred to earlier) about not pleading guilty to writing *Waverley*, since clerks of session are expected to exhibit "some solemnity of walk and conduct."[76] Accordingly Lockhart recalls Scott's gentle but impatient response to his son-in-law's remark that "Poets and Novelists [tend to] look at life and the world only as materials for art": "are you not too apt to measure things by some reference to literature — to disbelieve that anybody can be worth much care, who has no knowledge of that sort of thing, or taste for it? God help us!"[77] Indeed, according to Lockhart's rendering Scott believed imaginative writing to be a vaguely suspect enterprise; he was a little embarrassed about his association with it.[78] When Lockhart had suggested to Scott that he exchange his position as Clerk of Session for a seat on the Bench of the Court of Exchequer, "he appeared to have made up his mind that the rank of Clerk of Session was more compatible than that of a Supreme Judge with the habits of a literary man . . . whose writings were generally of the imaginative order."[79] To such a man as Lockhart's Scott, therefore, the notion that artistic genius sets its possessor apart from plain upright men and unpretending women was abhorrent; he disapproved, in Lockhart's words, of "those who, gifted with pre-eminent talents" in literature, "fancy themselves entitled to neglect those everyday duties and charities of life, from the mere shadowing of which in imaginary pictures the genius of poetry and romance has always reaped its highest and purest, perhaps its only true and immortal honours."[80]

Disputable as his interpretation no doubt is at points, Lockhart portrays Scott's understanding of imaginative literature and of himself as a writer as ideal — as, indeed, in large part the source of his work's greatness. It was, he contends, precisely Scott's apologetic and self-deprecatory attitude about writing and the "profession" of writing that propelled him into the worlds of business, farming, law, politics, antiquarianism, investing, and so on, thus enabling him to infuse that world into his writing. This approach had the added advantage of supplying Scott with sufficient funds during the period before the publication of *The Lay of the Last Minstrel;* thus Lockhart is careful to point out that Scott, though never hugely successful in law, resisted the temptation to withdraw from his profession as a barrister until it became clear that he could live comfortably off his writing.[81] And even then he maintained all his professional connections: "On the whole, it forms one of the most remarkable features of his history, that, throughout the most active period of his literary career, he must have devoted a large proportion of his hours . . . to the conscientious discharge of professional duties."[82] In Edinburgh Scott continued to practice law, while at Abbotsford he took up farming. "The truth no doubt was, that when at his desk he did little more, as far as regarded *poetry,* than write down the lines which he had fashioned in his mind while pursuing his vocation as a planter."[83] Lockhart's Scott's energy and the range of his activities were especially remarkable when compared to other poets and novelists of his age. "I have known other literary men of energy perhaps as restless as his," observes Lockhart;

> but all such have been entitled to the designation of *busy-bodies* — busy almost exclusively about trifles, and above all, supremely and constantly conscious of their own remarkable activity, and rejoicing and glorying in it. Whereas Scott, neither in literary labour nor in continual contact with the affairs of the world, ever did seem aware that he was making any very extraordinary exertion. . . . Compared to him, all the rest of the *poet* species that I have chanced to observe nearly—with but one glorious exception [Wordsworth was always Lockhart's exception]—have seemed to me to do little more than sleep through their lives—and at best to fill the sum with dreams; and I am persuaded that, taking all the ages and countries together, the rare examples of indefatigable energy, in union with serene self-possession of mind and character, such as Scott's, must be sought for in the roll of great sovereigns or great captains, rather than in that of literary genius.[84]

Again, the biographer can imagine a "student of statistics" in some future age reading an Edinburgh newspaper and concluding that "there must be at least two Sir Walter Scotts . . . one miraculously fertile author . . . another some retired magistrate or senator of easy fortune and indefatigable philanthropy."[85] Even his personal habits were opposite those of the stereotypical writer—he deplored "those 'bed and slipper tricks,' as he called them, in which literary men are so apt to indulge."[86]

All this emphasis on Scott's activities outside writing raises the awkward question, How was it that he so foolishly permitted his assets to remain tied up in precarious interests? It would seem to suggest that Scott was less a "man of affairs" than the biography has made out. Lockhart is aware of the problem, but can only designate it "the enigma of his personal history."[87] Yet the larger aesthetic question he is able to answer. If the poet or novelist truly does exercise such influence as Lockhart alleges—and in the biography he credits Scott's writings with helping to restore social and political stability in Europe after Waterloo[88]—why, then, is the self-absorption of Keats or Hunt not considered

conscientiousness and responsibility? Put simply, to what extent should
the poet or novelist be aware of the dignity of his work and the extent
of its power? The answer is hinted at in almost every chapter: Scott
himself was in one sense completely unmindful of his own genius, but
in another sense all of his life—that is, his wide-ranging interests, activities, and duties—was put into his art. Thus he observes in the biography's reflective final chapter: "In one of the last obscure and faltering
pages of his Diary, he says, that if any one asked him how much of his
thought was occupied by the novel then in hand, the answer would have
been, that in one sense it never occupied him except when the amanuen-
sis sat before him, but that in another it was never five minutes out of
his head. Such, I have no doubt, the case had always been."[89] By applying his concentration to everything *but* his writing, the biographer says,
Scott created art of the highest order.

In the biography of Scott, then, Sir Walter becomes Lockhart's poetic theory incarnate: the literary artist of immense talent who nevertheless harbors no exalted notions regarding his craft; who therefore makes
his living in spheres outside that craft; who, in consequence, is capable
of imaginatively representing life in its fullness and complexity; and
who, finally, remains an amateur even after he achieves notoriety and
financial success. Among the first reviewers, Carlyle understood this
point better than most; but his earnest, even morose personality generated in him a loathing of amateurs and "literary men." "Literature," he
wrote in his alternately admiring and dismissive review, "*has* other aims
than that of harmlessly amusing indolent languid men: or if literature
have them not, literature is a very poor affair."[90] Nonetheless Lockhart's point of view was unique and, immensely popular as the biography once was, influential: the original edition and 1839 expansion were
widely reviewed and sold extremely well, and were read by an array of
well-known writers.[91] It must therefore have been one of the earliest
and most potent sources of the legend of Scott as the genial and self-
effacing man of affairs who wrote mostly in his spare time. Further,
Lockhart's Scott seems likely to have contributed to the ambivalence
on the part of many early-Victorian writers with regard to the status
and worth of imaginative writing—what Alba Warren called the "eminent practicality . . . of the Early Victorians": "one finds in their criticism, often in the criticism of a single man, a curiously ambivalent
attitude towards art: a certain impatience and hostility towards the
works of imagination because they are less than 'reality,' and an equally
one-sided faith in art as a revelation of reality itself."[92]

AMATEUR REVIEWERS

The largely contrary disposition among many professionals, businessmen, and conservative clergymen towards imaginative literature in late-eighteenth-century Scotland has usually been ascribed to "narrowness." Fair enough perhaps, but that narrowness exercised an influence over the development of Scottish and British writing in more ways than simply as a hindrance to it. Many of Edinburgh's "literary men" of this period were affected by, indeed were the products of, this cultural prejudice against imaginative production: it would in fact be easy to lift some passages out of Lockhart's essays and pass them off as the words of some Evangelical Kirk minister from the 1760s. "How overweening is the vanity of many literary men as to the relative importance of their own pursuit! . . . any one such able and honest labourer in any of those walks of practical usefulness on which crowds of literati think themselves entitled to look down, is worth a whole regiment of authorlings; is by the universal sense of society more estimable living, and has, moreover, fully a better chance of being honourably remembered when dead!"[93] The words recall Lockhart's diatribe seventeen years earlier against Leigh Hunt's "want of respect for all the numerous class of plain upright men, and unpretending women, in which the real worth and excellence of human society exists"; and although in context Lockhart assumes some dignity and consequence to inhere in the writings of "authorlings," it is evident from the demotic language he employs here that he remained deeply apprehensive about exempting imaginative literature from the strictures applied to it by the middle-class merchants, professionals, and clergymen of the north.

The fact that, as in all other literary periodicals of the time, articles in *Blackwood's* and the *Quarterly* were unsigned permitted Lockhart, as it had permitted Jeffrey before him, greater freedom in working out his own conflicting views. It also permitted him to practice in the literary sphere without having to become known as an "authorling"—that is, as a producer of poetry and fiction. And provided him with a latitudinarian rhetoric immanently suitable to the medium. Lockhart spent much more time and energy addressing this problem than other Scottish reviewers of this period, but the same pattern is discernible in their work.

Now, both within and without Scotland literary reviews often provided an expedient way to circumvent full-fledged authorship for those writers who for reasons of their own felt that being known principally as imaginative writers would compromise their reputations. Women such as Caroline Bowles Southey and, later, Margaret Oliphant (the former English, the latter Scottish) found that the anonymous "we" of *Blackwood's* allowed them more freedom than they would have had using their own names.[94] For the original "Scotch reviewers" this motivation was a powerful one. Henry Cockburn, narrating the founding the *Edinburgh Review* in his biography of Jeffrey, discusses the attraction of anonymity among the first contributors.

> Jeffrey, Smith, Brougham, and Horner . . . were all eager for distinction, and for the dissemination of what they, in their various walks, thought important truth. . . . A review combined all the recommendations that could tempt such persons into print. Of all the forms of addressing the public, it is the one which presents the strongest allurements to those who long for the honours, without the hazards, of authorship. It invites every variety of intellect; it does not chain its contributors to long courses of labour; it binds no one to do more than he pleases; it shrouds each in the anonymous mystery; . . . it exalts each into an invisible chair of public censorship, and pleases his self-importance or his love of safety, by showing him, unseen, the effect of his periodical lightning.[95]

Cockburn does not define the "hazards of authorship" or explain why some authors might have valued the "safety" of invisibility. Similarly ambiguous is a passage in *Peter's Letters* in which Lockhart, himself enjoying the pleasures of anonymity as "Peter Morris," confesses that he is tempted by the idea of writing for the reviews, for in them he can enjoy "the privileges of writing *incognito*" and so avoid being drawn into the web of resentments and allegiances necessarily involved in writing books with one's name on them.[96] (All four of Lockhart's novels were published anonymously.) Whether this was the extent of Lockhart's need for anonymity is unclear, but in a letter to J. W. Croker, albeit written eighteen years later, Lockhart was more forthright on the subject. "I have sent off the last of my proofs long ago to Edinburgh," he wrote upon finishing the *Life* of Scott, "and am now enjoying quiet idleness—preparatory to resuming the role of reviewer which is an easier one than that of Author & a deal more safe as well as dignified."[97] The words "safe" and "dignified" are the important terms here: there was something about outright authorship that suggested the unseemliness of the full-time writer, the deviance of the artiste. The author could, of course, publish books anonymously (Lockhart's *Life*, too, appeared anonymously, though in that case everyone knew his identity), but appearing in magazines was much easier to keep secret than appearing between hard covers. The poet David Macbeth Moir, for instance, many of whose poems and squibs appeared in early issues of *Black-wood's*, was able to keep his identity from Blackwood himself.[98]

Writing long after the fact, Brougham in his autobiography hints at the same attraction to periodical-writing when he observes of the *Edinburgh* that "Men who would not think of publishing a book had a place ready to receive their writings, and a place of respectability, in which their works appeared in decent company."[99] The syntax here strongly suggests that many men "would not think of writing a book" because to do so was to miss the mark of "respectability"; which, one gathers, is why Brougham goes on to say in the following paragraph that many of those contributors demanded, and were granted by the editor, strict anonymity. Jeffrey himself made similar observations, though he did so before he began reviewing, not in retrospect as Brougham did. The episode early in his life in which he submitted a collection of his own poetry for publication, then withdrew it at the last minute, never again to try, has often been attributed to a lack of confidence in his own abilities as a poet; and that must have been part of it. But it is clear that Jeffrey's own professional ambitions were not compatible with being known as a poet. In 1791 he could record that "I feel I shall never be a great man, unless it be as a poet"; but by 1798 he had decided to give up his poetry and put his effort into law.[100] Still he found it difficult to forego "my poesies and sentimentalities": "This at least I am sure of, that these poetic visions bestowed a much purer and more tranquil happiness than can be found in any of the tumultuous and pedantic triumphs that seem now within my reach; and that I was more amiable, *and quite as respectable*, before this change took place in my character."[101]

By lamenting that he had been "quite as respectable" writing poetry, Jeffrey betrays the fact that he had left it off in the first place for reasons of social approval or propriety (as James Mackintosh, probably for the same reason, had done a few years earlier). His solution was to review; and although he confided to Horner in mid-1803 his misgivings about journalism—"not perhaps the most respectable" calling—it still worked as a way to remain immersed in "poesies and sentimentalities" without the disadvantages of being known as a litterateur.[102] And in any case, the kind of reviewing these writers were undertaking was pretty far removed from journalism in the sense meant in Jeffrey's day, and indeed (as in the previous chapter I tried to show) pretty far removed from any kind of writing published theretofore. Horner himself referred to the *Edinburgh* project as "our attempt at reputation": not the language of embarrassment and apprehension.[103] Other Scottish periodical-writers reveal in their letters and autobiographical writings the same sense of having been able to avoid the stigma of "book-making" through periodicals. John Galt, a Presbyterian with business ambitions, confessed to being ashamed of his connection to literary authorship; and although he persisted in novel-writing, he insisted that his novels were not novels, and preferred to think of himself as a man of affairs rather than an author. "At no time, as I frankly confess," he writes in the *Autobiography*, "have I been a great admirer of the literary character; to tell the truth, I have sometimes felt a little shame-faced in thinking myself so much an author, in consequence of the estimation in which I view the professors of book-making in general. A mere literary man—an author by profession—stands but low in my opinion, and the reader will, perhaps, laughingly say, 'it is a pity I should think so little of myself.' But though, as the means of attaining ascendancy and recreation in my sphere, I have written too much, it is some consolation to reflect, 'I left no calling for the idle trade.'"[104]

Similarly Hugh Miller, the stonemason turned poet and journalist from Cromarty, confessed more or less explicitly that, although he regretted not pursuing poetry more enthusiastically, he was relieved at having chosen journalism over poetry. He even resolved to write no more verse: "Let it be my business, I said, to know what is not generally known;—let me qualify myself to stand as an interpreter between nature and the public: while I strive to narrate as pleasingly and describe as vividly as I can, let truth, not fiction [i.e. poetry], be my walk . . . I shall succeed also in establishing myself in a position which, if not lofty, will yield me at least more solid footing than that to which I might attain as a mere *litterateur* who, mayhap, pleased for a little, but added nothing to the general fund. The resolution was, I think, a good one; would that it had been better kept!"[105]

Thus did his underlying doubts about the value of imaginative writing ("pleased for a little, but added nothing to the general fund") motivate Miller's decision to pursue a career in newspapers and magazines, for which he could write "truth."

Not only, though, did cultural prejudice affect the choice of medium in which many Scottish writers chose to write; it altered the way in which they viewed and registered their views on the new writing of Romanticism. The foregoing pages have cataloged Lockhart's complicated response to the poetics of this movement: he found it necessary to deploy a kind of trumped-up latitudinarianism against the increasingly extravagant claims made in behalf of imaginative literature. What made his response unique was his endeavor to exhume the tradition of amateurism; but on the larger issue of the possibilities implicit in imaginative writing—the power of imaginative literature, the status of those who purport to produce it—Lockhart's disposition was not at all unique among Scottish writers. The evolving role of the poet in British culture consistently drew from Jeffrey critical responses defined by egalitarian rhetoric. In an 1808 review of Crabbe's poetry, for example, Jeffrey argues that Wordsworth's poetry, unlike Crabbe's, is too enigmatic for "the ordinary run of sensible, kind people who fill the world"; and Keats, whose work Jeffrey lauded on other points, nevertheless seemed to him "too constantly rapt into an extramundane Elysium, to command a lasting interest with ordinary mortals."[106] The very review that provoked *English Bards and Scotch Reviewers*, Brougham's of *Hours of Idleness*, made use of the same accusation. "It is," Brougham wrote, "a sort of privilege of poets to be egotists"; but one who thinks of himself as "an infant bard . . . should either not know, or should seem not to know, so much about his own ancestry."[107] Wilson, too, made use of this rhetoric copiously, usually adding a great deal of bombast about the egotism and self-worth of the writer in question. Typical is his early and notorious review of Coleridge's *Biographia* in which he attacks the poet for believing himself superior to ordinary people: "there seems to him something more than human in his very shadow. He will read no books that other people read . . . and instead of his mind reflecting the beauty and glory of nature, he seems to consider the mighty universe itself as nothing better than a mirror in which . . . he may contemplate the Physiognomy of Samuel Taylor Coleridge."[108] Wilson's review of Tennyson fourteen years later shows the reviewer still employing this device: "What all the human race see and feel, he seems to think cannot be poetical."[109] Now it is certainly the case, as Philip Harling has recently shown, that during the early part of the century the Tory press (English and Scottish) made much of the "egotism" of those associated with the French Revolution and its intellectual progenitors.[110] Yet the fact that the *Edinburgh* reviewers were just as fond of imputing self-worship to Romantic poets as their Scottish Tory counterparts suggests that more was at issue here than politics in the narrow sense: the Scottish men of letters were responding to an aesthetic disposition *as Scots* rather than as conservatives or liberals, Tories, or Whigs.

To be sure, other factors were at work. As for Jeffrey, the Whig mindset was generally ill at ease with mystical talk about genius and inspiration; it sounded like nativism, whereas what counted for "philosophic Whigs" was quantifiable progress. Part of the reason Jeffrey could so easily use egalitarian rhetoric is his abiding interest in the possibilities of a public sphere—a sphere whose potential to maintain political stability through rational interchange seemed to be threatened by the weirdly hierarchical discourse of Romanticism. Lockhart, as mentioned already, began his critical career when the poetry of Romanticism was most closely associated with radical politics. And an intermittently irresponsible Wilson would have been happy with any weapon to use against writers whom, for his own reasons, he wished to deny success. Yet it is still the case that each of these vastly different writers could use egalitarian language when responding to literary writing that seemed to elevate its creators to a higher grade or function or being than those who did not create works of art. The consistent use of this sort of language was a predictable outworking of the cultural prejudices against imaginative writing inherited to one degree or another by these writers; both the apprehensive disposition and the critical maneuver were outgrowths of the same cultural milieu. Even so anomalous a character as Carlyle (whose father disdained poetry) fell into this pattern.[111] In 1820s and early '30s, when he was busy ascribing lofty powers to imaginative writing, he always framed the relationship between writer and reader in terms that assumed the importance of "ordinary" or "common" people—the poet is a "priest of Literature and Philosophy" who must "interpret their mysteries to the common man."[112]

The discursive conflict between Romantic poetry and Scottish criticism proved so infamously volatile in large measure for these reasons. At the height of Romantic writing in Britain, many, if not most, Scottish reviewers were in some real sense would-be poets and novelists; and although some, such as Lockhart and Wilson, did produce imaginative works of their own, while others such as Scott and Galt were best known as poets and novelists rather than periodical critics, yet each approached the task of reviewing literary works with a discernible sense that the writers under review ought—as they did—to exhibit misgivings about their art. Those who did not were required to pay a price. And it is this interaction that gives the title of Byron's 1807 volume its immediate suggestiveness.

4

"Our own Periodical Pulpit": The Presbyterian Sermon, Carlyle's Homiletic Essays, and Scottish Periodical Writing

SERMONS, ESSAYS, AND SERMONIC ESSAYS

IN THE PREVIOUS TWO CHAPTERS I HAVE TRIED TO ILLUMINATE TWO separate, and in some ways contrasting, modes of discourse taken up by Scottish periodical writers of the early-nineteenth century: both the *Edinburgh* reviewers and the Blackwoodians asserted their own reviews as having an importance equal to any other production circulated in the public sphere; and yet the same writers frequently deployed latitudinarian rhetoric against those writers, typically Romantic poets, whom they alleged to be too convinced of their own importance. Over the following pages a similar contrast will appear between, on the one hand, the Scots' use of the discourse of public-sphere liberalism, in which these same Scottish writers invoked that conceptual ideal to establish their own legitimacy in the republic of letters (and in Jeffrey's case to maintain authority for his own journal), and on the other their refusal to adopt the *posture* of public-sphere liberalism—a posture defined by a recognition of equality between writer and reader, writer and writer—and instead to adopt the posture of preaching, in which some fundamental parity exists between preacher and congregation but in which authority clearly lies with the former.

The nineteenth-century man of letters, as Terry Eagleton has written, "is contradictorily located between the authoritarianism of the sage and the consensualism of the eighteenth-century periodicalists, and strains of this dual stance are obvious enough."[1] In the case of the Scottish writers dealt with in this study—so I shall argue with particular reference to Carlyle—the "authoritarianism of the sage" was the result of a long process of formal evolution in which sermons, once the preeminent literary form in metropolitan Scottish culture, came to look more and more like literary essays, whereupon literary essays themselves at last became the dominant form: essays which, however, stubbornly retained the aggressive and peremptory bearing of their forerunners. Printed sermons are rarely dealt with in academic criticism nowadays, but it should be remembered that at the end of the eighteenth century single and collected sermons accounted for more of the British book trade than any other type of publication save political pamphlets—eight percent in the 1780s, sixteen percent in the 1790s.[2] And while more sermons may have been printed and sold in England than in Scotland (though per capita the case may have been otherwise), printed sermons almost certainly occupied a higher level of prestige in the latter.[3] At the same time, essays and essay-collections were extremely popular in Scotland throughout the century; the *Spectator* and *Guardian* themselves, as noted already, were reprinted in scores of editions by Scottish booksellers and spawned many northern imitations. That Kirk ministers of the nascent Moderate party used such polite essays as models for writing sermons is evident not only from the sermons themselves but from the reactions of their disapproving conservative counterparts. As early as 1730 Robert Wodrow grumbled that a sermon he heard at General Assembly seemed to be "borrowed from the Spectators, and ill put together."[4] By the early nineteenth century the word "essay" was routinely applied pejoratively by Evangelicals to the sermons of Moderates. One dismissed a collection of sermons as "cold and phlegmatic essays, unhallowed by the unction of scripture"; another characterized Hugh Blair's sermons as "cold, dull, laboured essays, much better fitted for appearing in the sleepy pages of Johnson's Rambler, than for stirring up and animating the glow of religious feeling."[5]

For others, of course, this change was salutary. As a literary form, and as a form of public address, the traditional sermon was ill-suited to the polite culture of late-eighteenth-century Britain: it implied hierarchy and authority, whereas the polite republic of letters in which many Scots wished to attain validity and distinction demanded that basic equality and consensus should govern discourse. James Anderson, whose sympathies were with the Moderate viewpoint, puts this point straightforwardly in his periodical *The Bee* in 1791. He champions the periodical essay as an arena in which "literary men" may meet together "on a footing of perfect equality," and suggests that ministers are not ideally suited to grasp the advantages of this arena:

It has been remarked, that clergymen, who have confined their literary efforts to discoveries delivered from the pulpit, are more apt to assume that dictatorial air, and dogmatic self-sufficiency of manner, than other classes of literary men. Nor can anything be more natural: Such pulpit discourses, from the reverence due to the place where delivered, are never criticized: The pastor therefore has no opportunity of being convinced of the weakness or the futility of the reasoning. He of course concludes that his arguments are strong and unanswerable; and delivers them with the tone and manner that so long prevailed among mankind with respect to theological controversies and literary disputes managed by divines. Fortunately it has now happened that periodical publications have now become so common in Britain, as to have afforded young divines more frequent opportunities of trying their powers fairly, than formerly. The consequence has been, that gentleness of manner, and liberality of sentiment in disputed subjects, begin to prevail even among this class.[6]

Anderson's hope, as Jon Klancher has explained at length, was already a lost cause when he expressed it; the public sphere, such as it was, was fast becoming "a representation instead of a practice," owing primarily to the cultural fragmentation brought about by the French Revolution.[7] But the notion of periodicals as a space in which writers could meet "on a footing of perfect equality," though it was habitually invoked by Scottish writers of the early-nineteenth century, nonetheless frequently failed to constrain the discursive form in which many of those same writers expressed their views: and for precisely the reason that Anderson touches upon. Although by the time of Anderson's writing, some sermons were sounding more like periodical essays—"young divines" were now adopting "that gentleness of manner, and liberality of sentiment in disputed subjects"—the form of the sermon itself, even the polite sermons of Moderate ministers, was intrinsically incompatible with the ideal of discursive equality. So although Jeffrey or Brougham or James Mackintosh, for example, appealed frequently to the egalitarian and consensual ideals of public-sphere liberalism, their reviews just as frequently presupposed a privileged standing in which the right of definitive interpretation lay on the side of the reviewer; practice belied rhetoric.

Scottish periodicals of the 1790s had tended to adopt one approach or the other, but not both. On the one hand there were a few "literary" periodicals such as *The Bee* (1791–94), *The Trifler* (1795), and *The Gleaner* (1795), generally short-lived miscellanies that presented themselves in the language of reasonableness and consensus. On the other were the more numerous sectarian and otherwise religiously oriented periodicals such as the *Missionary Magazine* (1796–1898), the *Christian Magazine* (1797–1821), and the *Edinburgh Quarterly Magazine* (1798–

1800), which consisted largely of vehement diatribes against societal trends—often enough in the form of actual sermons, though more commonly as "exegetical" or "critical" articles that had rather too obviously begun as sermons and been reworked into slightly more erudite form.[8] Similarly, many individual sermons were circulated as intellectually demanding essays in pamphlet form, for example Charles Findlater's anti-Godwin work *Liberty and Equality: a Sermon, or Essay.*[9] The early 1800s proved an especially fertile decade for religious periodicals of vigorously adversarial dispositions, as witness the *Evangelical Magazine*'s typical promise in its first issue to offer "occasional strictures . . . on many things, long sanctioned indeed by common opinion and custom, but which appear to us as wanting the sanction of Divine authority."[10] Thus at the end of the eighteenth century in Scotland, the polite, egalitarian, consensual periodical existed alongside the adversarial, authoritative, sermon-centred periodical. Over the following three decades, however, beginning with the *Edinburgh Review* and culminating in Carlyle's essays of the 1820s and early '30s, Scottish periodical-writers tended increasingly to combine these two approaches, presenting their essays in an ostensibly polite and consensual frame of reference but adopting a fiercely homiletic disposition towards their readers. Jeffrey's first review of poetry in the *Edinburgh*, recall, began with the words, "Poetry has this much, at least, in common with religion, that its standards were fixed long ago, by certain inspired writers, whose authority it is no longer lawful to question," thus combining an energetic consensualism (*All intelligent people agree*) with a homiletic peremptoriness (*I direct your attention to the Scriptures*).[11] This admixture characterized much of the *Edinburgh*'s and *Blackwood's*' critical discourse over the next thirty years, but did not reach its most overt and abrasive form until Carlyle began "preaching," as he often put it, from the "pulpits" of the *Edinburgh, Fraser's,* and the *Foreign Review*. There were other attempts of this sort, notably James Hogg's *Lay Sermons* of 1834 in which the essay-periodical and sermon were almost explicitly combined.[12] But Carlyle's project spanned a decade or more, and so over the following pages I shall explore the cultural-historical circumstances that made the Presbyterian sermon attractive as a model for Carlyle's early essays, as well as those essays themselves. By examining Carlyle's early work, and by showing it to be the result of his interaction with a specific set of cultural and historical circumstances—circumstances that a majority of aspiring Scottish writers like Carlyle shared to one degree or another—I hope to show that the Presbyterian sermon played an important role in generating the assertive periodical culture that was early-nineteenth-century Scotland.

CARLYLE, CALVINISM, AND THE PRESBYTERIAN SERMON

Nearly every scholarly work on Thomas Carlyle's life and thought contains at least one remark on the degree to which he was influenced by the Calvinist outlook of his parents and of the Ecclefechan community in which he was raised. Even cursory examination, however, reveals many of these observations to be empty of content, relying on reference-work summarization at best, stereotype at worst. This is part of a larger tendency to ignore the relationship between Carlyle's thought and the philosophical, theological, and political debates circulating in Scotland during the first third of the nineteenth century, when Carlyle lived there, however discontentedly at times. "What do we know," Ralph Jessop has recently asked, "about Carlyle's views or reliance upon Knoxian Calvinism, contemporaneous theological debates in Scotland, or Scottish philosophical discourse?"[13] The answer is, Not so much.

This is unfortunate, for Carlyle maintained all his life a genuine if qualified admiration for the religious austerity and moral rigidity in which he was raised. His need to adhere in some fashion to the faith of his parents has generally been appreciated; a recent analysis suggests that he used the notion of metaphor as a means of believing the biblical stories, enabling him to speak to his parents of his belief, and that he invented his own notion, "sacred silence," as a way of disbelieving in a pious and God-fearing manner.[14] There is truth in this, but these ideas only enabled him to sidestep the issue of belief, and Carlyle's personality and intense loyalty to his family and cultural origins demanded more than sidestepping. His letters to his mother, in particular, suggest that Carlyle wished not so much to present himself as an orthodox Christian, as to identify himself with the religious and cultural world of Burgher Presbyterianism—to be what his parents wanted him to be. He assured his mother in 1826 that he and Jane were not only attending church "pretty regularly," but also that they continued to have family worship in the Scottish Presbyterian manner: "every Sabbath-night (last night, for example) we fail to not read some sermon or other piece of that kind to the assembled household."[15] Accordingly he often referred to himself as a Presbyterian, as when he wrote to his brother Alick that Leigh Hunt had been avoiding him because Hunt "felt shocked at my rigorous Presbyterian principles"; or, again, as when he wrote to his mother on the contrast between Count D'Orsay and himself, "with my grim Presbyterian look."[16] Such remarks as these suggest a deep-seated need to maintain in some sense his identity as, not only a Christian, but a Scottish Presbyterian, a Calvinist.

The considerable extent to which Carlyle was influenced by Calvinism has always been recognized, but (to repeat) substantive assessments of the ways in which that outlook might have affected his thinking have been few. In fact, on the matter of Carlyle and Calvinism, many have been content to quote Froude's remark that Carlyle was a "Calvinist without the theology" and define Calvinism with a set of adjectives—dour, authoritarian, humorless—in which there may be elements of truth, but hardly enough to provide insight into the subjects at issue. One element of Carlyle's "theology" that has been frequently and accurately noted, however, is the Calvinist doctrine of work.[17] As with Lockhart's, much of Carlyle's writing may be understood as an attempt to reconcile his own belief in the dignity of labor with a livelihood widely thought to be characterized by idleness; but instead of modifying amateurism to cohere with his Calvinist disposition, as Lockhart did, Carlyle spent his life fulminating against "dilettantism" as poison to the writing profession.[18]

Less successful have been attempts to find in Carlyle's writings elements of the "fatalistic" doctrine of predestination. It is true that Carlyle held to a kind of historical teleology, and that in one passage in *Frederick the Great* he even claims to believe in the doctrine, presumably to evoke the idea of Frederick's destiny.[19] Yet the doctrine of predestination, at least as expressed by those who espoused it, cannot be equated with fatalism; and in any case Carlyle was far from a fatalist: the Carlylean hero brings his *will* to bear on his time and place. And while there is some merit in crediting Scottish Calvinism with Carlyle's concept of God or the Divine as aloof and transcendent, even there one must exercise caution, for Calvinists of continental and British traditions alike emphasized both the immanent and transcendent aspects of God's character; indeed they considered this balance a mark of their theology's superiority.

It is strange, given this shortage in substantive discussions of Carlyle and Scottish Calvinism, that he should have been so often spoken of as a "prophet," a "sage," and a "preacher."

These epithets refer, of course, to that prophetic or sermonlike tone of Carlyle's major works: the authoritative commands, the wholesale denunciations, the exhortations to understand "the times," the emphatic language and syntax of one "crying out in the wilderness," to use one of his preferred biblical allusions, from the prophet Isaiah. Biographers and critics began using the tropes of preaching and prophecy in the late 1840s early '50s (John Sterling used the term "prophetic" to describe Carlyle's writings as early as 1839). This is hardly surprising, since his earliest essays, from the 1820s and '30s, explicitly evoke the imagery of prophesying and preaching to describe what he, the reviewer, is doing.

That imagery can be traced directly back to Ecclefechan. In the Burgher Presbyterian home in which Carlyle was raised the weekly sermon dominated the experience of everyday life. Going to Sermon, to use a phrase recalled in the *Reminiscences*, consummated the week. Preaching and prophecy are related concepts in Christian theology, and to the Covenanters, whom the Seceders strongly believed to be their theological predecessors, preaching and prophecy were uniquely bound together. Yet, facile references to Carlyle "preaching the word" or "sermonizing" aside, scholars of Carlyle's work have rarely paid due attention to the meaning and significance of the sermon in eighteenth-century Presbyterian thinking. In part this is because the idea of prophecy, in its prognosticatory sense, is a common theme in poetry of the early-nineteenth century, and the tendency has been to see Carlyle's prophecy as an outworking of Romanticism—despite the fact that Carlyle himself had little regard for the English Romantic poets.[20] In part, too, the sheer abundance of preaching metaphors and images in Carlyle's work has kept scholars from asking whether it might have any significance beyond the immediately obvious.[21] But to understand fully what Carlyle intended his earliest essays to be, and furthermore to understand their significance for Scottish periodical-writing of the previous three decades, these essays must be examined in light of the Scottish Calvinists' ideas on the nature of preaching.

Now, the importance attached to sermons in the Calvinist tradition generally, and in the Presbyterian tradition in Scotland specifically, was more than merely an indication of religious fervor or enthusiasm for all things sacred; it was the result of long-standing positions vis-à-vis other Christian traditions. From its first years in sixteenth-century Geneva, the Reformed tradition (to use the general term designating one of two major strands of the Protestant Reformation, the other being Lutheran) produced a highly-developed doctrine of preaching. This was in many ways a consequence of the Reformers' doctrine that only the sixty-six books of canonical Scripture are the "word of God" without error, and that only they possess final authority in matters of faith. All Protestant creeds asserted this much. But the Reformed tended to go further by underscoring the degree to which that authority could be recruited and communicated through the preaching of those sixty-six books by duly appointed ministers, who consequently became known as "ministers of the Word." Among contemporary scholars Calvinism is known, in some cases known exclusively, for its doctrine of predestination; but the Calvinists on the continent and in Britain wrote as much on the "preaching of the Word," as they termed it, as on almost any other topic, predestination included. More than any other major strand of Christianity, the Reformed tradition has been characterized by its belief that revelation is made known preponderantly through the written words of the Bible as proclaimed by the minister.[22]

This emphasis is owing in some measure to the way in which John Calvin himself treated the subject of preaching. In his *Institutes of the Christian Religion* he points out various biblical passages in which pastors and teachers are described as a "blessing": "Neither could this office be more honourably advanced," Calvin comments, "than it was when He said: He that heareth you, heareth me; he that despiseth you, despiseth me, Luke x. 16 . . . If it be done not without cause, that an angel which is the interpreter of God do himself abstain from declaring the will of God, but commandeth that a man be sent for, to declare it . . . who is there now that dare despise that ministry, or pass it over as a thing superfluous, the use whereof it hath pleased God to make approved by such examples?"[23]

In other words, the very fact that God does not speak directly, but instead appoints ministers to speak for him, itself indicates vital and profound nature of the instrument by which that word is proclaimed. In another passage, Calvin argues that ministers may only assert as binding what is already written in Scripture; but this, he says, is no paltry task:

> Lo, this is the sovereign power, wherewith it behoveth the pastors of the church, to be endued, . . . that by the Word of God they may with confidence be bold to do all things; may compel all the strength, glory, wisdom and height of the world to yield and obey to his majesty: being upholden by his power, may command, all even from the highest to the lowest: may build up the house of Christ and pull down the house of Satan: may feed the sheep and drive away the wolves: may instruct and exhort the willing to learn: may reprove, rebuke, and subdue the rebellious and stubborn: may bind and loose: finally by thunder and lighten if need be: but all things in the word of God.[24]

"By the Word of God" they may do all these things: that is, by preaching. In still another passage, Calvin, reviling the Roman Catholic position that authentic revelation may be found outside the canon (i.e. in church tradition), states in essence that in preaching the canonical Scriptures ministers speak with the voice of God:

> And as in the old time he was not content with the law only, but added priests for expositors, at whose lips the people should enquire for the true meaning thereof: so at this day he not only willeth us to be heedfully bent on reading, but also appointeth masters over us, by whose labor we may be assisted: whereof cometh double profit. For on the one part a very good trial proveth our obedience, when we hear his ministers speaking as it were himself. On the other side it also provideth for our weakness, while after the manner of men, he had rather speak unto us by interpreters to allure us unto him, than with thundering drive us away from him.[25]

These appointed "masters" are really "interpreters" between God and man; they speak "as it were" God himself.

In the Reformed tradition the "preaching of the Word" occupied the most important aspect of life. In the decades after the Reformation had begun, many Reformed churches were architecturally rearranged in order to give to the pulpit a position of centrality. Further, the custom quickly evolved in which the Sacraments of baptism and Eucharist might only be administered in conjunction with a sermon, never without.[26] And the importance attached to the sermon in Genevan and other continental traditions carried over, and in some respects was even heightened, in Scotland. The *Scots Confession* of 1560 asserted that there are three "notes" (or signs) of the true church, the first of which was preaching: "The notes therefore of the trew Kirk of God we beleeve, confesse, and avow to be, first the trew preaching of the Worde of God, into the quhilk God hes revealed himselfe unto us, as the writings of the Prophets and Apostles dois declair."[27] Scottish Puritans of the seventeenth century (mostly Presbyterians, but also Episcopals and independents) placed even greater importance on the sermon than their English counterparts. While, as Calvin had before them, the Scottish Puritans resisted the idea that ministers merit a more elevated status than others, they believed fervently, as D. G. Mullan has documented, that preaching was the minister's most important duty: although the modern minister could make no claim to speak "inspired" words, yet God could and often did use their words to arouse human minds and wills.[28]

Scotland's post-Reformation legacy of mass literacy has been discussed already; but even the champions of mass literacy in the Kirk — whose enthusiasm derived mainly from the desire that all should be able to read the Bible, not necessarily anything else — insisted that *reading* the

Bible for oneself could not take the place of *hearing* the Bible preached by others. This is amply reflected in the *Westminster Confession of Faith* and its *Shorter Catechism*, documents completed in 1646 by Scottish and English theologians during the volatile reign of Charles I. The purpose of the Westminster Assembly, to forge a closer unity between the Churches of Scotland and England, was doomed from the start for political as well as theological reasons. Yet the Scottish church, for its part, held to *Westminster's* regulations with a vengeance; the *Shorter Catechism*, it has often been said, exercised a greater influence on the popular piety of Scotland than any book apart from the Bible itself. Here is Question 89 (out of 107) of the *Shorter Catechism:*

> Q. How is the Word made effectual to salvation?
> A. The Spirit of God maketh the reading, but especially the preaching, of the Word, an effectual means of convincing and converting sinners, and of building them up in holiness and comfort, through faith, unto salvation.[29]

"The Spirit of God" (in context the Holy Ghost, the third person of the Trinity) animates and employs the "reading, but especially the preaching" of the Word of God. The sentiment represented by the phrase "but especially the preaching" is reflected in almost everything Scottish Presbyterians wrote on the subject of the Bible. It was an essential part of rural popular piety, too. Robert Russell (b. 1766), Kirk minister of Yarrow (near Ecclefechan), put it this way: "The people in general had no objection as to length [of sermons] — quite the reverse ... The *reading* was not the *preaching* of the Word in their eyes ... It is [a distinction] which continues still to be made, and it is amazing how ministers of great name and fame have sunk in popular estimation from not observing it."[30] Certainly the distinction was adopted by the Seceders, those who came out of the Church of Scotland beginning with the 1733 Secession. The original leaders of the Secession, Ebenezer Erskine (1680–1754) and James Fischer (1697–1775), for example, wrote and published a commentary on the *Shorter Catechism. The Assembly's Shorter Catechism Explained* is an excruciatingly dull catechetical work that was, however, reprinted many times throughout the eighteenth and early-nineteenth centuries. Under Question 89 Erskine and Fischer write: *"May not people be more edified in reading good sermons at home, than in hearing, from the pulpit, such as are not, perhaps, so well digested?* Answ. If they are in health, and not necessarily detained from the public ordinances, they have no ground to expect any real and saving benefit to their souls, in the neglect of hearing the word preached; because it pleases *God, by the foolishness of preaching to save them that believe,* I Cor. i. 21. And *faith cometh by* hearing, Rom. x. 17."[31]

This book had profound influence among Scottish Presbyterians of all persuasions, but especially among the Seceders whose leaders authored it.[32] In a similar vein, one of the most famous of the early Seceder preachers, Adam Gib (1714–88), expressed the common Presbyterian view when he warned laymen against relying on personal Bible-reading to the exclusion of attending sermons: "It is an unspeakable mercy," he said, "that Bibles are now so common, —and that people are so commonly taught to read them; far beyond what took place in former ages. But this can nowise supersede the preaching of the Gospel. It is still a divine ordinance, as much as ever; and has the original blessing still entailed upon it."[33] Thus in an important sense the Seceders were the children of the seventeenth-century Covenanters who, in defiance of Charles I and II, met in illegal "field conventicles" to hear sermons: the Seceders left the Kirk in 1733 over the matter of "Intrusion," or the practice of imposing a minister on an unwilling congregation—the correct "preaching of the Word" was as important to them as it had been to the Covenanters.

James and Margaret Carlyle were members of the Associate or Burgher Synod, a sect that, led by Ebenezer Erskine, opposed the Antiburgher Synod after the Secession split in 1747 over the issue of the "Burgess oath" (Scottish Presbyterians worked hard during these times to earn the later designation "split P's"). Indistinguishable in most respects, both Burghers and Antiburghers were very much of the Calvinist mindset. The ecclesiastical-theological milieu in which Thomas Carlyle was raised and tutored was therefore one in which the pulpit dominated the congregant's thought and behavior to a degree rarely or never equalled in Christian history. The weight of tradition, from the Genevan Reformers to the Puritans and Covenanters, lay behind this domination: for dissenting Presbyterians in rural Scotland in the 1790s, the expounding of a biblical text by a duly appointed minister was, as the *Westminster Confession* and in their view the Bible made clear, the principal way in which God reveals himself to man.

THE CALVINIST PULPIT: ECCLEFECHAN AND AFTER

Carlyle's family was typical of Seceders in this respect. In his exhaustive biography, David Alec Wilson relates how, after a Sunday service, the Carlyle children were often asked to repeat the contents of the sermon. Thomas usually knew it better than anyone: "Tom was eagerly attentive to the preacher, and the complete fullness with which he could reproduce the sermon when required attracted admiration. It was not odd; the custom was to exhort the children to attempt this—a stimulant to the intellect hard to beat. But Tom's unusual excellence was so much remarked that in discussions on the sermon when disputes arose as to what had been said, the cry was, 'Where's Tom?' or 'Fetch Tom'; and when he came, his admiring elder brother used to say, he 'never failed to quote any part of the sermon wanted.'"[34] John Johnston, the Carlyles' minister at the Ecclefechan Meetinghouse (he had been called there in 1761), was known widely as a learned man and talented preacher; many people walked long distances to hear his sermons. Carlyle began sitting through Johnston's sermons at about age eight or nine.[35] His admiration for Johnston was, even in his hypercritical old age, unqualified: "a most exact & faithful man Mr Johnston Senior," he writes in the margin of his edition of Friedrich Althaus's 1866 biography of him; "my Father & Mother's Minister (Burgher), both of whom he esteemed. The venerablest & most venerated Clerical Person I have ever seen. White full bottom Wig; income £75 to £100 a year."[36] Carlyle's praise for George Lawson, a professor at the Associate (Burgher) Synod's seminary in Selkirk, who preached often in the Ecclefechan pulpit, was similarly copious and unqualified.[37] It is easy to see that the pulpit was the dominant image of Carlyle's youth. "Temple of my childhood," he calls the Ecclefechan Meetinghouse in one of the most moving passages in the *Reminiscences;* "Rude, rustic, bare, no Temple in the world was more so;—but there were sacred lambencies, tongues of authentic flame from Heaven, which kindled what was best in one, what was not yet gone out."[38] What made the Meetinghouse so memorable to Carlyle was not Christian charity or even the rural simplicity of its parishioners, but "sacred lambencies" and "tongues of authentic flame from Heaven."

Carlyle studied for the ministry at Divinity Hall in the University of Edinburgh, where he was required to deliver two sermons—"at least one," according to an early report, receiving "much applause" from students and faculty, which no doubt gratified him.[39] Yet in August of 1815 Carlyle was expressing weariness with the idea of preaching, at least of preaching for a living. "I am growing daily and hourly more lukewarm about this preaching business," he wrote to Thomas Murray on August 22, "The trade (for it is become a trade) is completely overstocked."[40] Still he went on preparing his "Exegesis" or academic sermon. To Robert Mitchell he explained himself thus: "You will ask me, why, since I have almost come to a determination about my fitness for the study of Divinity, why all this mighty stir—why this ado—about 'delivering' a thesis . . . ? It is not because I have altered my sentiments about the study of theology: but principally because it came into my head, to try what sort of an essay upon natural religion, I could make."[41] Already, sermons and essays were interchangeable in Carlyle's mind.

Of course, he dropped out of Divinity Hall because his Christian faith was waning. But even after he left, and long after he had ceased to assent to Christianity, he continued to entertain a strange and fascinated admiration for the sermon-centred culture of his youth; in 1866, in the *Reminiscences*, he recalls "one family, whose streaming plaids, hung up to drip, I remember to have noticed, one wet Sunday, pious Scotch weavers, . . . were in the habit of walking fifteen miles twice for their Sermon, since it was not to be had nearer. A curious phasis of things;—quite vanished now, with whatever of divine and good was in it, and whatever of merely human and not so good."[42] The use of the capitalized "Sermon" instead of "service" or "worship" is intentional. Carlyle speaks of church services in the way Seceder Presbyterians would have spoken about them; later in the same reminiscence (the third, of Edward Irving) he recalls some Scottish peasants "returning home from Sermon," and again, "At Dunscore in the evening, there was Sermon." Nor is this mere affectation: he would often speak this way, without a hint of irony, in his letters to family members.[43] Furthermore, he several times mentions going to church services with Edward Irving, always recalling what the sermon was on (or stating that he cannot remember what it was on). He mentions having heard sermons by Irving ("often"), Robert Hall (Baptist minister from Leicester), William Glen (Burgher minister of Annan), Frank Dixon (a friend of Carlyle), and Thomas Chalmers ("a great deal").

While Carlyle's philosophical outlook during the years after leaving Divinity Hall, from 1816 to 1818, drifted far from the strict Calvinism of his parents, he seems to have maintained an emotional attachment to the extravagant esteem the parishioners of Ecclefechan had had for Sermon-going. His ambivalence is apparent in the way he wrote of Chalmers. He seems sincerely to have wanted to admire this fiery and earnest preacher, indisputably the most famous preacher of his day, but Chalmers's Evangelical theology and laissez-faire political views were to him absurd. He could admire Chalmers' earnest pulpit eloquence as "muddy, thick & spirit-stirring."[44] In another letter of the same year he admires the style of Chalmers's recently published "discourses" (sermons published as essays) on Christian revelation and astronomy—

"that fiery thoroughgoing stile of writing for which the Author is so remarkable"—though he disagrees with the minister's position.[45] All the same, Carlyle could not abide Chalmers' political ideas, referring to a piece the latter had written in the *Edinburgh Review* on pauperism by grumbling that his "reasoning (so they call it) is disjointed and absurd—& his language a barbarous jargon."[46] The passage on Chalmers's oratory and ideology in the *Reminiscences*, written more than thirty years later, exhibits precisely the same ambivalence.[47]

Carlyle's fascination with sermons and sermonizing did not wane with his Christian faith; his essays from the late 1820s (as will become clear in due course) are full of the imagery of preaching. That his fascination with sermons and sermonizing endured long after Carlyle ceased to believe in the doctrines of Christianity must, it seems, have had something to do with his friendship with Irving. The years between leaving Divinity Hall and moving back to Edinburgh, 1816 to 1818, when he taught at the Kirkaldy Burgh School, were largely spent with Irving, three years Carlyle's senior; and even after Irving left for Glasgow in 1819 the two spent a great deal of time together, often attending sermons together. They must have talked a great deal about preaching, Irving's preoccupation. In his "valedictory discourse" to the congregation of St. John's, Glasgow, in 1819—when Irving and Carlyle were at their closest—Irving gives vent to his beliefs regarding the sermon. After articulating at some length his own ideas about the need for ministers to preach in different styles and with different methods according to the needs of "the age," Irving says he is pleading for *"a more natural style of preaching,* in which the various moral and religious wants of men shall be met, artlessly met, with the simple truths of revelation, delivered as ultimate facts not to be reasoned on, and expressed as Scripture expresses them—which conjunction being made, and crowned with prayer for the divine blessing, the preacher has fulfilled the true spirit of his office."[48] Irving expanded, or perhaps the word is inflated, his ideas in his eccentric collection of five sermons, *For the Oracles of God,* published in 1823, at the height of his fame. In the book's introduction he argues that the sermon could be transformed into more than an exposition delivered from a pulpit. Accordingly, the five "sermons" in this collection, four "orations" and one "argument," were originally intended, says the preacher/writer, to be read. Thus can sermons be "new vehicles for conveying the truth." Ministers, he contends in the Introduction, "ought, therefore, to lay their hand on the press as well as the pulpit . . . And as men read for entertainment and direction in their several studies and pursuits, it becomes needful that we make ourselves adept in these, and infuse into the body of science and literature the balm of salvation, that when the people consult for the present life, they may be admonished . . . of the life to come.[49] Sermons as "new vehicles for conveying the truth," as printed documents for the purpose of "in-fus[ing] into the body of science and literature the balm of salvation"— the notion was not one calculated to please the Kirk's orthodox Calvinists who would in a few years, though for entirely different rea-sons, depose Irving. Their objections would have had recourse to the *Shorter Catechism*'s Question 89: the reading, yes, but the preaching of the Word of God was the principal means of convincing and converting sinners. Yet the old Calvinist notion of the sermon—as a man's oral dis-course in which God communicates himself—has manifestly generated Irving's ideas. The sermon-centered world of his parents, then, influ-enced Carlyle not only directly, but indirectly through Irving, who was himself wondering whether the "preaching of the Word" might not be used in new ways. By all accounts Irving's theology was at this point scarcely different from that of Chalmers, though the former's egomania was already much more in evidence. Divine authority, he believed, is conveyed through the sermon; he wished merely to see if that authority might be conveyed in other media, and by means of other human apti-tudes, as well. Such an idea must have been dwelt upon by the two in their Kirkaldy days, which Carlyle portrays in the *Reminiscences* as full of "conversation and inquiry."[50] For it would emerge in Carlyle's *Life* of Schiller and especially in his essays throughout the following decade.

CARLYLE'S "SERMONS"

In 1818 Carlyle left Kirkaldy for Edinburgh, took up German, and began writing for the *Edinburgh Philosophical Journal* and the *Edinburgh Encyclopaedia*. He learned German with astonishing speed; as early as 1823 he could review Goethe's *Faust* for the short-lived *New Edinburgh Review* and translate a German treatise on geometry. In early 1823 Ir-ving approached the publisher of the *London Magazine*, John Taylor, on Carlyle's behalf, then wrote to Carlyle asking if he had any interest in writing some "portraitures of men of genius and character" for the mag-azine. By doing so, he reasoned, Carlyle would "obtain the ear of the public, which you must have, and which you cannot get, like me, by preaching." He goes on to tell Carlyle of his own book, *For the Oracles of God*, which he says is "addressed to such heads as yours."[51] A fort-night later Irving, having been told by Carlyle that he would like to

write a serialized biography of Friedrich Schiller (now lost), had nego-
tiated a deal with Taylor. After telling Carlyle the terms of the deal, he
expresses his confidence in the abilities of his friend, and implores him
to treat "that the thing which I revere above all things," the Christian
faith,

> with the reverent handling which its sacred nature deserves even from those
> that esteem it not, among which number I know that you are *not* one; for
> however you may be in darkness about the grounds of our belief, you never
> see the sincerity of it, or hear the heroism of it, without yielding to it the full
> heart of your admiration. I do most highly regard the sublime character of
> Schiller, which I understand his works exhibit under many forms. . . . What-
> ever is sacred, do touch with a serious and sacred hand, then you will be
> yourself, and you will be happy in yourself—whatever is cold-hearted, or
> unsound at heart, expose with your most powerful weapon. I would do the
> same though with weapons perhaps of a different make.[52]

Irving, at this time Carlyle's most admired and influential friend—who
at this time, it should be remembered, held more or less orthodox Calvinist views on the inspiration of the Scriptures and the preaching of
them—urges Carlyle to treat Christian revelation with reverence, and
seems to concede that great poetry, too, can exhibit "sublime character
. . . under many forms." More important, he exhorts his younger friend
to "expose with your most powerful weapon" what he, Irving, will expose with "weapons perhaps of a different make": that is, with the Bible
and the pulpit.

Counseling Carlyle to bring out Schiller's "sublime character," Irving
evidently meant to urge his friend to use Schiller's writings as an apologetic against the "satyrical character of Voltaire." Carlyle, however,
seems to have taken Irving's counsel as permission to expand his definition of Scripture, for in the *Life of Friedrich Schiller* he espouses an
almost-religious belief in "Literature" as a kind of inspired text in which
a higher truth may be found.[53] Near the end of the work Carlyle summarizes his ideas, which are no less his for being prefaced by the words
"As Schiller viewed it." "As Schiller viewed it, genuine Literature includes the essence of philosophy, religion, art; whatever speaks to the
immortal part of man. . . . The boon she bestows is truth; truth not
merely physical, political, economical, such as the sensual man in us is
perpetually demanding . . . ; but truth of moral feeling, truth of taste,
that inward truth in its thousand modifications, which only the most
ethereal portion of our nature can discern, but without which that portion of it languishes and dies. . . . The treasures of Literature are thus

celestial, imperishable, beyond all price . . . Genius, even in its faintest scintillations, is 'the inspired gift of God.' "[54]

The idea of "Literature," or "Poetry" as he would usually render it, as a source of sacred truth was, in one form or another, a common one in Romantic poetry and criticism; and while in such passages as this Carlyle may be engaging with the Romantic poets he often dismisses, yet this is more than an outworking of Romantic poetics. By attributing to Schiller's poetry the status of Scripture he is, rather, trying to fill the vacuum left in his own intellect by his loss of faith in the Christian Bible. Carlyle is attempting to replace Scripture with "Literature," which the "inspired" "Genius" writes, and which is capable of conveying "truth in its thousand modifications": the passage looks forward to *Sartor Resartus*, where the doctrine of plenary inspiration would be explicitly (if half-satirically) expanded, and where Carlyle even indicates the possibility of writing Scripture himself.[55] The author carefully avoids stating the corollary of this idea, that the critic is therefore called upon to interpret and explain this complexity of truth: "we do not aim at judging and deciding," he says at the work's commencement.[56] Over the next several years, however, beginning with "Jean Paul" (1827) and culminating in "Thoughts on History" (1830), "Characteristics" (1831), and *Sartor Resartus* (serialized 1830–31), Carlyle would express with greater clarity and fulness his belief in "Literature" and later "History" as sacred texts, and in the critic's and historian's equally sacred duty to preach those texts with, in Irving's words, his "most powerful weapon."

These early essays represent the first stage in what Christopher Vanden Bossche has depicted as Carlyle's "search for authority," his lifelong endeavor to find a source of authority that he himself could "author." Carlyle, Vanden Bossche argues, wanted to find a source of cultural authority which, like that of kirk and family in eighteenth-century rural Scotland, corresponded with the beliefs of those whom it governed—an impossible task for anyone living in metropolitan Reform-era Britain, one which sent Carlyle first to the rarified and ahistorical realms of German idealism and Romanticism, and later to the historical turmoil of the French Revolution.[57] There is much to recommend in Vanden Bossche's analysis; I wish to go further, however, by contending that the preacher-congregation relationship functioned as the template for this authority, and that Carlyle's desire to "author authority" had more to do with his regret that he had not become a literal preacher or found a way to fill that role in some other meaningful way than with any theoretical reading on his part of recent historical trends.

That overpowering need for authority led Carlyle first to the Germans. Scholars have long recognized that Carlyle's writings on German philosophy and literature are not remarkable for their interpretive accuracy, a fact which many in Carlyle's own day recognized.[58] His interest in Goethe, to him almost a god, had less to do with Goethe's works than with the impression Carlyle had of the man, an impression which itself was far from accurate.[59] To put it bluntly, Carlyle took up the cause of Goethe, and the cause of German literature generally, because the Germans provided him with plausible answers to questions he had long been unable to answer satisfactorily. For example Goethe's idea of *Entsagen* (renunciation, self-denial), when deployed in *Sartor Resartus* and elsewhere, went from being primarily an aesthetic ideal to a moral imperative; and his explanation of Kant's idealism in the essay on Novalis is little more than an impressive misinterpretation.[60] C. F. Harrold in his definitive study sums the matter up nicely: "Instead of contributing directly to the content of his thought, [the Germans] provided a stimulus, an atmosphere, and a number of new terms for what he regarded as old ideas."[61]

Harrold makes a convincing case that Carlyle extracted from Goethe, Fichte, and to a lesser degree Novalis (Friedrich von Hardenberg, the German mystic poet), the notion of God, or the "Divine Idea" (Fichte's phrase), as a being revealed in nature; or, to put it in terms of poetics, of nature as a garment behind which lies the divinity, and which it is the poet's duty to pierce. Carlyle's position contained a number of differences from that found in Goethe; Carlyle (most of the time) could not accept anything resembling pantheism, and his view tended more towards a belief in the essentially illusory nature of reality than did Goethe's; but he did adopt Goethe's belief that the world, or nature, is at bottom a revelation (*Offenbarung*) of reality, reality being variously termed by him "Nature," "the Divine," and "God." Again Harrold: "Either as pictured as the Earth-spirit's song [in *Faust*] or as stated in more intellectual terms, the theme of nature as the expression of God remained the keystone of Carlyle's world-view."[62] Thus, in Carlyle's essay on Goethe, he can speak of the truth the poet "bodies forth" as "hidden to the vulgar sight, but clear to the poet's."[63] In this sense Carlyle followed Coleridge (though he would not have admitted it) in holding that works of art should be judged according to the level of organic unity they manifest; the Divine Idea, or, alternatively, the "Open Secret," is that ultimate unifying reality which the poet seeks to portray, and which the true critic seeks to elucidate.[64]

To repeat, Harrold is right to say that these ideas provided "a stimulus, an atmosphere, and number of new terms for what Carlyle considered old ideas." He is right, furthermore, to look to eighteenth-century Scottish Calvinism for the source of those old ideas. But when it comes to defining the nature of those old ideas, specifically those of Scottish Seceder Calvinism, Harrold, otherwise scrupulously careful in the way he handles conceptual sources, resorts to grossly convoluted generalizations.[65] It is true that Calvinists believed God to be "terribly present everywhere at every moment," and true, too, as Harrold goes on to say, that Calvinism's emphasis on work and its aversion to idleness had much to do with Carlyle's outlook, both early and late; yet Harrold's description offers little insight into how, specifically, the Calvinist creed might have affected Carlyle's thinking. More helpfully, Suzy Anger has recently contended that Carlyle arrogated for his own purposes Calvinism's principles of biblical interpretation. For Carlyle, Anger writes, "the world becomes one large text on which to practice Calvin's hermeneutics," and this informs his method of biographical interpretation in *Sartor Resartus*.[66] While her assessment does justice to Carlyle's general intellectual enterprise, Anger's history-of-ideas approach causes her to attribute rather too much fine-tuned understanding of Calvin's hermeneutical methods to Carlyle, who in any case had little regard for the divinity professors through whom he might have learned Calvin's writings directly. Carlyle's use of Calvinism simply cannot be understood without reference to the centrality of the sermon in the Scottish-Presbyterian tradition.

Carlyle's first major publications, the essays published from 1827 to 1831, reveal an author endeavoring to assimilate what remained of his Calvinist Christianity—which was rather more than many of his interpreters have supposed. What remained was an irrepressible belief that God—or more broadly the "Divine," or more broadly still "Nature" or the "Open Secret"—could be understood by some gifted people, and that those people were duty-bound to proclaim the nature of what they had learned. In these early years Carlyle located this paramount reality on the pages of great capital-L "Literature," which, as "inspired" writing, served as a plausible substitute for those other inspired writings preached by "tongues of authentic flame" in the Ecclefechan Meetinghouse. By substituting Literature for Scripture and criticism for the "preaching of the Word," Carlyle was able to reconcile himself to the undeniable but for him harsh reality that he had departed from the unfeigned faith of his mother and father. And he was able at the same time to satisfy his own need—a need to which his published writings and correspondence testify time and again—to preach.

The first of these essays, "Jean Paul Friedrich Richter," appeared in 1827 in the *Edinburgh Review*. The young reviewer was searching for a new source of authority. Richter's philosophy "is not mechanical, or sceptical; it springs not from the forum or the laboratory, but from the depths of the human spirit; and yields as its fairest product a noble system of Morality, and the firmest conviction of Religion."[67] It was in the following essay, though —"The State of German Literature," the essay that first brought Carlyle wide recognition — that he expressed his ideas fully. He begins the essay denouncing (and exaggerating, as Ashton has shown) the misconceptions entertained by Britons of German literature. Then he moves to German literary criticism, which he says is more than psychological inquiry into the poet's life and thinking, and more than formal analysis of the poet's work; it is both of these, as well as an inquiry into "the essence and peculiar life of the poetry itself." "Criticism," he says, "has assumed a new form in Germany." It has assumed a "higher aim." The question to be dealt with by the critic is no longer one of mere form, "the qualities of diction, the coherence of metaphors, the fitness of sentiments, the general logical truth" of a work of art. Neither are the important questions in criticism "mainly of a psychological sort, to be answered by discovering and delineating the peculiar nature of the poet from his poetry." Rather,

it is, not indeed exclusively, but inclusively of those two other questions, properly and ultimately a question on the essence and peculiar life of the poetry itself. The first of these questions . . . relates, strictly speaking, to the *garment* of poetry; the second, indeed, to its *body* and material existence, a much higher point; but only the last to its *soul* and spiritual existence, by which alone can the body, in the movements and phases, be *informed* with significance and rational life. The problem is not now to determine by what mechanism Addison composed sentences and struck-out similitudes; but by what far finer and more mysterious mechanism Shakespeare organised his dramas, and gave life and individuality to his Ariel and his Hamlet. Wherein lies that life; how have they attained that shape and individuality? Whence comes that empyrean fire, which irradiates their whole being, and pierces, at least in starry gleams, like a diviner thing, into all hearts?[68]

As in the passage from the *Life* of Schiller, it is hard to mistake the element of personal credo here. This definition of the new criticism, supposedly German in origin though he gives no names, reveals the essayist as one struggling to discover for himself a source of paramount reality, that "*soul* and spiritual existence" no longer available to him in the Old and New Testaments. But he goes on: "Not only who was the poet, and how did he compose; but what and how was the poem, and why was it a poem and not rhymed eloquence, creation and not figured passion? . . . Criticism stands like an interpreter between the inspired and the uninspired; between the prophet and those who hear the melody of his words, and catch some glimpse of their material meaning, but understand not their deeper import."[69] Now Carlyle has begun to clarify his idea: the critic is an "interpreter between the inspired and the uninspired," between "the prophet and those who hear" him but are not sure what they hear. In this conception the author, not the critic, is the inspired prophet, even as in Calvinist thinking the prophet Isaiah or Jeremiah was inspired and without error; but just as the minister's preached interpretations of Isaiah or Jeremiah (insofar as those interpretations were correct) represented the voice of God, so here Carlyle claims for critics—for himself as a critic—the ability to speak inspired and authoritative words. Then, as if to admit what he is doing, he states that the criticism he has described is not an exclusively German phenomenon: "It is a European tendency, and springs from the general condition of intellect in Europe." These new European critics are not parochial or unduly nationalistic; rather they are part of "the ancient primitive Catholic Communion . . . It is, indeed, the most sacred article of this creed to preach and practice universal tolerance"—that is, to interpret and preach true Literature of whatever origin.[70] That he uses the language of preaching here is no coincidence: despite having disappointed his parents by failing to become a minister, Carlyle's criticism has begun to appropriate ministerial prerogatives.[71]

The next review, written for the newly begun *Foreign Review*, appeared in 1828 under the title "The Life and Writings of Werner." A review of a biography and several works by the poet-playwright, it is predominantly unfavorable toward Werner, who was, the reviewer concludes, essentially a weak if well-meaning man whose works grope for profundities that their author did not understand. The German's project of setting himself up as a prophet and evangelist irritates Carlyle. "[T]aking up the character of *Vates* in the widest sense," he sniffs, "Werner earnestly desires not only to be a poet, but a prophet." Werner had wished to join the company of "poets and preachers," "to plan and propagate" his "dogmas," which in due course were "preached abroad by the aid of Schleirmacher."[72] Werner, it seems, by assuming the vestments of the prophet and preacher, had made the critic redundant. Carlyle disapproved.

"Goethe's *Helena*" and "Goethe" appeared in the following two issues of the *Foreign Review*. The essays bear many similarities, not least Car-

lyle's propensity to speak of Goethe's writings as though they were
Scripture itself, in language that seems to mimic a Presbyterian minister's plea to reverence and study the Bible. "[T]ime is precious," he
writes in "Goethe's *Helena*," and "no book that will not improve by repeated readings deserves to be read at all. And were there an artist of a
right spirit; a man of wisdom, conscious of his high vocation, of whom
we could know beforehand that he had not written without purpose
and earnest meditation, that he knew what he had written, and had em-
bodied in it, more or less, the creations of a deep and noble soul,—
should we not draw near to him reverently, as disciples to a master; and
what task could there be more profitable than to read him as we have
described, to study him even to the minutest meanings?"[73] "In fact," he
continues, "*Faust* is to be read not once but many times, if we would
understand it: every line, every word has its purport; and only in such
minute inspection will the essential significance of the poem display itself."[74] This is exactly the way in which orthodox Presbyterians would
have spoken of the Scriptures: the doctrine of "plenary inspiration,"
holding that the Bible's every word in the original languages are inspired and without error, was thought vitally important by Scottish
Calvinists (it is stated in the opening paragraph of the 1646 *Westminster
Confession*). He applies this new doctrine to great poetry as a whole,
which embodies, as Scripture had done for the Burghers of Ecclefechan, "the Wisdom which is proper to this time; the beautiful, the
religious Wisdom, which may still, with something of its old impressive-
ness, speak to the whole soul; still, in these hard, unbelieving utilitarian
days, reveal to us glimpses of the Unseen but not unreal World."[75]
Goethe's writing, then, is simply a new manifestation of this new "religious Wisdom" of which the Bible had been for a previous era. As in
the "State of German Literature," here he is borrowing Goethe's notion
of revelation, *Offenbarung*, in order to set himself up as a preacher of a
new class, a minister capable of reading and interpreting the Divine and
proffering it to a spiritually impoverished congregation, of penetrating
the mysteries of Scripture and making them plain. "[W]e cannot but
believe," he says in "Goethe," "that there is an inward and essential
Truth in Art; a Truth far deeper than the dictates of mere Mode, and
which, could we pierce through these dictates, would be true for all nations and all men."[76]

Hence the sermonizing tone of these essays: the reviewer urges the
reader on to greater faithfulness, further study. He insists that the
poet's mind is "worthy . . . of best study from all inquiring minds," and
he applies the lessons of Goethe's writings in a kind of moral-theological

way to the reader's situation in life: "How has such a temper been attained in this so lofty and impetuous mind [i.e. the mind of Goethe himself] . . . ? How may we, each of us in his several sphere, attain it, or strengthen it, for ourselves? These are questions, this last is a question, in which no one is unconcerned."[77] Again: "Could we hope that . . . this emblematic sketch would rise before the minds of our readers in any measure as it stood before the mind of the writer; that, in considering it, they might seize only an outline of those many meanings which, at less or greater depth, lie hidden under it, we should anticipate their thanks."[78] Hence, furthermore, Carlyle's habit of comparing his task with that of the prophet Isaiah: "Reviewers, of great and small character," he says of previous attempts by British journals to promote Goethe, "have manfully endeavoured to satisfy the British world on these points: but which of us could believe their report?"—an echo of Isaiah 53:1, "Who hath believed our report? and to whom is the arm of the LORD revealed?" in which Isaiah complains that no one had taken prophecies about the Messiah seriously.[79] Carlyle is not claiming the ability to prognosticate: he is placing himself in the role of preacher, the bringer of good tidings, however those good tidings might be ignored.

The sermonlike outbursts and exhortations continue to appear in the following essays, as do the seemingly rhetorical allusions to pulpits and sermons. "Peace be with them!" says Carlyle in "Burns" (1828) to those poets who prefer to depict fanciful and otherwise nonexistent things. "But yet, as a great moralist proposed preaching to the men of this century, so would we fain preach to the poets, 'a sermon on the duty of staying at home.'"[80] So, too, would Carlyle's newfound idea that the critic can serve as a conduit by which the Divine is revealed to those willing to learn. In the 1829 essay on Novalis the idea is especially clear. Berating other reviewers as usual, Carlyle contrasts two types of reviewer—the better of which, unsurprisingly, includes himself. The "small Reviewer," a "fool" and "parasite," tries merely to triumph over the author, whereas the great reviewer, a "servant," interprets the author and conveys whatever insight may be found. "Is he the priest of Literature and Philosophy, to interpret their mysteries to the common man; as a faithful preacher, teaching him to understand what is adapted for his understanding, to reverence what is adapted for higher understandings than his? Or merely the lackey of Dulness, striving for certain wages . . . ?"[81] The servant-reviewer goes on the characterize the nature of that "understanding." For Novalis, "Nature is no longer dead, hostile matter, but the real and mysterious Garment of the Unseen; as it were, the voice with which the Deity proclaims himself to man."

"Thus," he concludes, as though from a passage of Scripture, "to live in that Light of Reason, to have, even while here and encircled with this Vision of Existence, our abode in that Eternal City, is the highest duty of man."[82]

"Signs of the Times" appeared in the *Edinburgh Review* in June of the same year. In this and the following reviews, Carlyle ceases to delineate the critic's task as he had in the essays on German literature, most of which were now behind him. In part this is because the books under review (never mentioned in the text of this "review") were not the sort of works one would wish to treat as sacred: two anonymous pamphlets, *Anticipation; or, an Hundred Years Hence* and *The Rise, Progress, and Present State of Public Opinion in Great Britain*, and Edward Irving's book on "premillenial" eschatology, *The Last Days: A Discourse on the Evil Character of These Our Times*. Still, few essays read more like a sermon than Carlyle's "Signs of the Times." In fact, he got the title of the essay from Irving himself, who in early 1829 was already publishing another tract, this one called *The Signs of the Times*, which Carlyle probably knew about through his correspondence (now lost) with Irving.[83] The book that Carlyle's essay "reviews," *The Last Days*, was a "Discourse" made up of seventeen "Sermons" and a concluding chapter entitled "IMPROVEMENT of the whole Discourse"—"improvement" customarily designating the concluding part of a sermon. Irving's book was intended to be one large sermon (586 pages) made up of seventeen smaller sermons. He was still pursuing his project of making sermons "new vehicles for conveying the truth," and Carlyle was following suit. That "Signs of the Times" is a sermon too, and not a "Review" or "Article" (nearly always pejoratives in Carlyle's nomenclature), is hinted near the beginning: accusing the Christian church of relying too much on institutions ("mechanisms"), he asks, "How did Christianity arise and spread abroad among men? Was it by institutions and establishments . . . ? Not so . . . It arose in the mystic deeps of man's soul; and was spread abroad by the 'preaching of the word.'"[84] He goes on, sermon-like, to inveigh against "Unbelief." "To what extent theological Unbelief, we mean intellectual dissent from the Church, in its view of Holy Writ, prevails at this day, were . . . an almost impossible inquiry. But the Unbelief, which is of a still more fundamental character, every man may see prevailing, with scarcely any but the faintest contradiction, all around him; even in the Pulpit itself."[85] This last reference to "the Pulpit" refers to literal pulpits, to Christian ministers. Yet he eschews the matter of religious leaders' loss of faith in the veracity of the Bible, and instead censures them for their "Unbelief" in the kind of revelation he had been enunciating in previous essays: alternately the "Divine," the "Divine Idea," "Nature," "God." He continues: "Religion . . . is no longer what it was, and should be—a thousand-voiced psalm from the heart of Man to his invisible Father, the fountain of all Goodness, Beauty, Truth, and revealed in every revelation of these." Instead religion has become "Profit; a working for wages; not Reverence, but vulgar Hope and Fear." Still, then, Carlyle was expressing his conviction that the pulpit, as traditionally conceived, had lost its power, as well as strongly implying his belief that his own works could be—or already were—the sort of natural, "un-mechanized" sermons that those of Chalmers et al. had ceased to be.

In "Thoughts on History," published in 1830, Carlyle begins to move away from imaginative literature toward history, transferring the qualities of sacredness and divinity to history itself—thus the term "Nature," for example, heretofore used to designate the paramount reality that the true poet reveals, is now applied to the manifold reality which the historian seeks to record. In this essay the poet, the writer of Scripture, is gone; now there is only the text of history.

> Let us search more and more into the Past . . . For although the whole meaning lies far beyond our ken; yet in that complex Manuscript, covered over with formless, inextricably entangled, unknown characters,—nay, which is a *Palimpsest,* and had once prophetic writing, still dimly legible there,—some letters, some words, may be deciphered; and if no complete Philosophy, here and there an intelligible precept, available in practice, be gathered, well understanding, in the mean while, that it is only a little portion we have deciphered; that much still remains to be interpreted; that History is a real prophetic Manuscript, and can be fully interpreted by no man.[86]

The object of study has shifted from poetry to "History," but the essence of the idea remains. History, the infinitely complex "Chaos of Being" as he calls it elsewhere in the essay, has become the sacred text worthy of assiduous study. Carlyle is less straightforward about the historian's duty than he had been about the literary critic's duty three years earlier in "The State of German Literature"; but it is sufficiency plain that he still wishes to don the preacher's vestments. "Of the Historian himself," he says vaguely, ". . . new and higher things are beginning to be expected." He names "Church History" as an example; it will be less concerned with institutional history than with recording the "degree of moral elevation" man can acquire by the church's instruction. "Church History, then, did it speak wisely, would have momentous secrets to teach us: nay, in its highest degree, it were a sort of continued

Holy Writ."[87] Carlyle then portrays the historian of poetry—and he was at this time writing a history of German literature—in similarly mystical language. His concluding lament that no such historian existed at the time is, of course, cutely disingenuous, for this anonymous essayist fully intended to fill that role himself. As in his previous essays on German literature, he had created a world in which he, the critic, would stand as an interpreter between God and man, between the "Divine Idea" and those needing instruction, now he expands that "Divine Idea" to envelop the entire specter of past reality, thus effectively turning over the right to interpret it to the historian—once again, to himself.

Much has been written on Carlyle's view of himself as a prophet, and certainly here he is in some sense conferring the prophetic role on himself. As early as 1827 he had been called a prophet by no less a man than Goethe, whose compliment must have seemed to him prophetic itself (though the poet was speaking of Carlyle's role as a translator, not a poet).[88] All the same, to the extent that Carlyle considered his writing prophetic at all it was only part of his belief in himself as a new kind of "minister of the word." In August of 1831 he wrote to Macvey Napier, who had two years earlier taken Jeffrey's place at the *Edinburgh*, in order to tell the new editor that he, Carlyle, would be happy to write for the journal again. The *Edinburgh Review*, he says, is the best periodical in Britain: "If you really want me to preach in your Pulpit, therefore, you have only to say so."[89] Napier responded favorably, and in short order Carlyle sent to him a long denunciation of "self-consciousness," the essay "Characteristics." In it he asks disdainfully, What is the nature of this day's religion? and takes Chalmers's 1817 book of Christian apologetics, *A Series of Discourses on the Christian Revelation*, as an example of the way in which yesterday's preachers had become irrelevant. "Is it a healthy religion, vital, unconscious of itself; that shines spontaneously in doing of the Work, or even in preaching of the Word? Unhappily, no. Instead of heroic martyr Conduct, and inspired and soul-inspiring Eloquence, whereby Religion itself were brought home to our living bosoms, to live and reign there, we have "Discourses on the Evidences," endeavoring, with smallest result, to make it probable that such a thing as Religion exists. The most enthusiastic Evangelicals do not preach a Gospel, but keep describing how it should and might be preached."[90] Despite Chalmers' reputation as a great preacher, Carlyle once again criticizes him (again without naming him) for writing apologetic treatises instead of simply proclaiming whatever it was God had said. The reference to "soul-inspiring Eloquence, whereby Religion itself were brought home to our bosoms" signifies again that the idea of the sermon as the medium through which God condescends to communicate with man, and by extension his own idea that that power could be relayed through other media, are still alive in Carlyle's mind.

These ideas continue to emerge in Carlyle's writing, particularly in *Sartor Resartus,* begun in 1829. Indeed, the preacher-text relationship seems to serve as Carlyle's rhetorical model for *Sartor,* in which the un-named "Editor" and biographer not only "exegetes" Professor Teufels-dröckh's strange text, but also preaches it.[91] He wishes the reader to be "directed rather to the Book itself than to the Editor of the Book"— even as Presbyterian ministers had worn solid black vestments in order to deflect attention from their persons. "Who or what such Editor may be," he goes on, "must remain conjectural, and even insignificant: it is a Voice publishing tidings of the Philosophy of Clothes; undoubtedly a Spirit addressing Spirits: whoso hath ears let him hear."[92]

The Presbyterian sermon influenced Carlyle's written style, too, which as early as the 1830s was referred to as "Carlylese." Throughout the 1820s, as Carlyleans have documented, his style had become less expository and more hortatory, a development that would culminate in *The French Revolution.* This stylistic transformation has been attributed, not unreasonably, to Carlyle's study of German literature, especially Jean Paul Richter.[93] Certainly in the early 1820s he began ramming words together as if in imitation of German. Yet he partially denied the influence of German when, in the margins of an 1866 biography of him, he wrote that his "poor 'style'" owed more to "Edward Irving and his admiration of the Old Puritans & Elizabethans (whom, at heart, I never could entirely adore, tho' trying hard)" than to Jean Paul. And, he added, "the most important part by far was that of Nature . . . had you ever heard my Father speak, or very often heard my Mother & her in-born melodies of heart and of voice!"[94] He made a similar remark in his reminiscence of Irving, whose high-flown oratorical style was, he confessed, influential on his own writing: Irving "affected the Miltonic or Old-English Puritan style, and strove visibly to imitate it more and more . . . there was something of preconceived intention visible in it, in fact of real 'affectation,' as there could not well help being:—to his ex-ample also, I suppose, I owe something of my own poor affections in that matter, which are now more or less visible to me, much repented of or not."[95] These two allusions to Irving as having influenced his style make sense in light of Carlyle's attempt during these years to turn his essays into sermons, or vice versa. The emphatic and hortatory style of the early essays, with their increasingly frequent use of italics and eccentric punctuation, was likely another aspect of Carlyle's sermonizing project.

In any case, by mid-1831 he saw that his "preaching" had taken effect. Writing to his brother Jack in March of that year, he admitted that he wanted to move to London where, as he had begun to believe, he could best utter forth those ideas that had been taking shape in his mind.

> [S]urely we shall have space to find a Publisher for Devilsdreck, and look round also, spying all outlooks whether there is absolutely Nothing in God's creation that will unite with me, in the way of work and well-doing. Nay, I have half a mind (but this in deepest secrecy) to start when I come there, if the ground promise well, and deliver a Dozen of Lectures, in my own Annandale accent, with my own God-created brain and heart, to such audience as will gather round me, on some section or aspect of this strange Life in this strange Era; on which my soul like Eliphaz the Temanite's is getting fuller and fuller [Job 4:2,3]. Does there seem to thee any propriety in a man that has organs of speech and even some semblance of understanding and Sincerity, sitting forever, m[u]te as millstone, while Quacks of every colour are quacking as with lungs of brass? True I have no Pulpit: but as I once said, cannot any man *make* him a pulpit, simply by inverting the nearest Tub? And what are your whigs and Lord Advocates, and Lord Chancellors, and the whole host of unspeakably gabbling Parliamenteers and Pulpiteers and Pamphleteers;—if a man suspect that "there is fire enough in his belly to burn up" the entire creation of such![96]

A year and a half later, writing to J. S. Mill after failing to get *Sartor* published between hard covers, Carlyle remarked that although reviews and magazines were often compromised by the shallowness of their content, the periodical form might yet provide a truly authoritative medium:

> I had hoped that by and by I might get out of Periodicals altogether, and write Books; but the light I got in London last winter showed me that *this* was as good as over. My Editors of Periodicals are my Booksellers, who (under certain new and singular conditions) purchase and publish my *Books* for me, a monstrous method yet still a method . . . A question often suggests itself, whether we shall never have *our own* Periodical Pulpit, and *exclude* the Philistine therefrom, above all, keep the Pew-opener (or Bibliopolist) in his place; and so preach nothing but the sound word? The Answer, meanwhile, comes not. Meanwhile: Speak! Preach! The Night Commeth. Where men are, there is an audience: "you may make a Pulpit by inverting a Tub"![97]

It would be easy, reading such passages by themselves, to assume Carlyle's use of pulpit imagery to be merely rhetorical, his way of saying that he had ideas he wished to express but had not yet found the right opportunity. But the frequent references to pulpits and preaching and sermons, however well they may serve as metaphors, reveal the author's aspiration in more than a metaphorical way. Conceiving of his essays as in some sense sermons for a new age, adopting the sermon's unquestionable moral authority and even its interpretive methods, Carlyle was able to calm the anxieties he felt over having rejected the faith and religious culture of his parents. This explains why he goes out of his way in letters from the 1820s to assure his recipients that, despite his ongoing efforts in periodical-writing, he would amount to more than a periodical-writer. "Filthiest and basest of the children of men!" he exclaims to Jane, referring to Hazlitt, Hunt, Maginn, and others, "The very best of them are ill natured weaklings: they are not red-blooded *men* at all; they are only *things* for writing 'articles.'"[98] And it also explains why he finds it necessary to denounce "Articles" and "Reviews" in his own articles and reviews.[99] He is claiming that his articles and reviews are neither, in fact, articles nor reviews.

This conclusion raises larger issues. The Calvinist Presbyterian culture in which Carlyle was raised, especially its elevation of a particular form of discourse, a form defined by rhetorical vigor and moral peremptoriness, generated in him a need to interpret, pronounce, upbraid, and praise in some analogous way. His emotionally profound attachment to parents whose faith he rejected, as well as the qualified but sincere admiration he maintained for Edward Irving and the religious culture of Dumfriesshire (as it then was), exaggerated this emotional need in Carlyle and thus made his recourse to the homiletic form all the more intense and urgent. But there is more to be seen in this than the satisfaction of an emotional need. Carlyle's extensive and quasi-overt use of the homiletic form represents an especially pronounced instance of a reluctance common among nineteenth-century Scottish men of letters to abandon the self-assurance and authority of the pulpit—an exceptional but hardly unique case of, as James Anderson had put it in 1791, "assum[ing] that dictatorial air, and dogmatic self-sufficiency of manner."

In each of the previous chapters we have seen how the Scottish periodical-writers of these decades qualified or departed from what could fairly, if a little simplistically, be called eighteenth-century ideals: Jeffrey used the concept of diffused knowledge to centralize his journal's authority, Wilson stripped polite conversation of politeness, Lockhart demoted imaginative literature by professionalizing amateurism. Carlyle was thus not unique among these others in departing from the ideals of politeness and eighteenth-century public-sphere liberalism; and that departure is nowhere clearer than in his use of the sermon. In his 1828 essay on Burns for the *Edinburgh* this becomes especially evident. He draws a parallel between the disregard and contempt the major Enlightenment figures had for Scotland—he mentions Kames, Hume, Robertson, and Smith—and the inhumanity (as he saw it) of their ideas. Scottish writing at that time was therefore, he argues, essentially derivative. He can muster only one example of authentic Scottish writing: "For a long period after Scotland became British, we had no literature: at the date when Addison and Steele were writing their *Spectators*, our good Boston was writing, with the noblest intent, but alike in defiance of grammar and philosophy, his *Fourfold State of Man*."[100]

The remark is telling, for Thomas Boston's work, *Human Nature in Its Fourfold State*, was a collection of ten sermons. Boston himself was the forerunner of the Seceder movement (he died before the Secession took place), a man whose writings are as remote from the ideals of politeness as it is possible to imagine—an eighteenth-century Bunyan, really. What Carlyle seems to suggest here is that the polite literary essays of the previous century had been merely "borrowed from the Spectators, and ill put together," as Robert Wodrow had remarked of a polite sermon in 1730. For Carlyle, the polite literary essay was fundamentally un-Scottish, and Scots who tried to write them were lamely trying to imitate their cultured betters.

In understanding the significance of Carlyle's attachment to the homiletic form it is essential to take seriously the fact that, while sermons never found a secure place in the republic of letters, they did constitute a major form of public discourse in Scotland throughout the eighteenth century, and into the nineteenth. Printed sermons attract almost no critical attention in modern times, but the sermons of John Erskine or Henry Moncrieff Wellwood were read by a far greater number of people than, say, Mackenzie's essays in *The Lounger;* the homiletic-oriented religious periodicals mentioned earlier lasted for decades, while the literary periodicals like Mackenzie's were lucky to last more than a year. The Scottish men of letters of the nineteenth century had emerged from this culture and were accordingly never entirely prepared to engage in the public sphere in the way James Anderson, among a few others, would have preferred. Peremptory authority had been witnessed, and polite reciprocity would always seem weak by comparison. When Lockhart writes in *Blackwood's* that there is "no triumph of human genius so instantaneous, so unrivalled, and so splendid, as that of the Preacher," there is no reason to suppose that he is joking or affecting irony.[101]

In 1839 Carlyle wrote to Lockhart at the *Quarterly* to ask whether he would like to print the long essay that eventually became *Chartism.* "On the whole," Carlyle remarked, "I think I partly understand what the conditions of this proposed sermon of mine would be."[102] The essay was turned down. But what is significant here is that Carlyle, obviously aware that the Tory *Quarterly* was unlikely to print that work, appeals to Lockhart as a Scot: *What I offer* (he was saying) *is something greater by far than a pretty little essay. What I offer is authority.*

Conclusion: Scottish Men of Letters
and the New Public Sphere

IN HIS 1856 ESSAY "EDINBURGH AN AGE AGO," HUGH MILLER OBSERVED that the city's golden age had ceased "within the last quarter century," which is to say some time in the 1830s. Suggesting an explanation, Miller proposed that the preeminence then increasingly accorded to the daily newspaper, and the corresponding demotion of "the bulky quarterly," had worked against a country that was too poor and unpopulated to support a daily newspaper capable of competing with the London papers. "For the highest periodic Literature London has, of consequence, become the only true mart; and the Scotchman who would live by it must of necessity make the great metropolis his home."[1] Miller was right to suppose that Scotland had achieved cultural ascendancy in large part through periodical literature, and his claim that Scottish dominance in that field had expired not because the Scots had lost their touch but because they were forced for economic reasons to emigrate to London has a great deal of truth in it, too. Henry Cockburn said much the same in his 1852 biography of Jeffrey. At the height of the *Edinburgh Review*'s preeminence, he lamented,

> The whole country had not begun to be absorbed in the ocean of London. . . . The operation of the commercial principle which tempts all superiority to try its fortune in the greatest accessible market, is perhaps irresistible; but anything is surely to be lamented which annihilates local intellect, and degrades the provincial spheres which intellect and its consequences alone can adorn. . . . The city has advantages, including its being the capital of Scotland, its old reputation, and its external beauties, which have enabled it, in a certain degree, to resist the centralising tendency, and have hitherto always supplied it with a succession of eminent men. But now, that London is at our door, how precarious is our hold of them, and how many we have lost.[2]

There is a hint of strained pathos in this, to be sure. Still it is true that whereas throughout the eighteenth century the great majority of Scotland's noteworthy intellectuals had stayed in Scotland for most or all of their lives, in the nineteenth they tended to settle in London.

But there was more to this than a "commercial principle." London dominated Britain. By 1800, the capital was ten times larger than any other British city, a proportional superiority unequalled in all the rest of Europe.[3] London was the center of authority in governmental prerogative, obviously, but also in commerce, art, literature, religion, and even (despite there being as yet no university there) education.[4] The writer with pretensions to authority had, therefore, at least to think about doing so from an authoritative location. We have seen how Carlyle, feeling that he had "fire enough in his belly to burn up," equated the state of *not yet* residing in London with "sitting forever, m[u]te as millstone."[5] That so many Scottish men of letters should have emigrated southward from the 1820s and '30s onward is a development that may be traced, in part, to the early years of the century when the *Edinburgh* reviewers and Blackwoodians began writing in ways that both assumed the reality of an open public sphere and that appropriated authority over that public sphere.

Anybody working in the field of Romantic literature will have some familiarity with the transformation that took place in the tone of reviewing, and not only of reviewing but of public discussion generally, after the *Edinburgh*'s appearance in 1802. Reviewing had been characterized by what could be called deliberate politeness, a sense that while a book under review may be a bad book, it did not represent a fundamental undermining of civilized society. True, the very act of reviewing represented at some level the reality that established beliefs and structures could be questioned.[6] But it is equally true that after 1802 periodical-writing became more aggressive, less interested in (or less enamored with) consensus, and in general more rhetorically intense and adversarial. Josiah Conder recognized the new state of affairs very early: "The authors whose works a former age would have received with gratitude, and inspected with reverence, are brow-beaten, cross-examined, and held up to ridicule by the anonymous Critic, with cold professional arrogance."[7] Of course, no account of this transformation could ignore the French Revolution—but then, no account of this transformation *has* ignored the French Revolution. That event and its ramifications in British political culture have generally, and quite properly, been summoned to explain the new tone of public debate at the turn of the century: the Revolution exposed deep political fissures in British society, and periodical-writing of every kind was bound to exhibit some measure of alienation, suspicion, and outrage. Even so, I have argued in this study

that certain aspects of the old manner of reviewing, especially the deferential and mannerly tone in which periodical-writers addressed their
audiences, were nullified by ambitious Scottish writers who, bringing
certain cultural habits and attitudes to their writing, both advocated a
version of discursive openness and asserted themselves as those who
would preside over that openness.

The four preceding chapters may be grouped, roughly, into two categories. Chapters 1 and 3 treat the manner in which Scottish periodical-
writers were prepared to invoke the ideals, or certain versions of the
ideals, of public-sphere liberalism; the manner in which, in other words,
they handled the rhetoric of the public sphere. That rhetoric came naturally to those who countenanced apparently without reservation the
myth and/or tradition of the Scottish "democratic intellect." Jeffrey
proved himself especially capable in this regard. As a fundamentally liberal Scottish Whig concerned with the potentially ameliorating affects
of widely diffused knowledge, and as an intellectually self-confident
Scot eager to participate in British literary and political life, Jeffrey arrogated authority to the journal he edited by presenting that journal as
the foremost manifestation of open intellectual exchange. Similarly, the
suspicion of the "profession" of imaginative authorship, a suspicion lasting well into the nineteenth century among a wide variety of Scottish
people, prompted the periodical-writers to challenge the privileging of
imaginative production implicit in much contemporary writing—a privileging that itself represented a challenge to the egalitarian public
sphere. These two chapters, concerning as they do the intellectual disposition of the Scottish periodical-writers, deal primarily with what
they wrote rather than how they wrote it.

Chapters 2 and 4, on the other hand, have more to do with stylistic
approaches than ideas. After a half century during which Scotland had
manifestly done its part in ensuring that Great Britain was esteemed
abroad for its cultural achievements—that is, after the bulk of what
would later be called the Scottish Enlightenment had taken place—
Scots began to evidence a greater sense of confidence in Scottishness,
and that renewed self-assurance emerged pronouncedly in the area of
conversation. In turn it became more acceptable to ignore the older
strictures of politeness in the way one conversed, and the exhibitionist
and individual-oriented mode of conversation thus made popular transferred itself to periodical-writing, which itself had long been bound up
with the customs of polite conversational interchange. The consequent
tone of writing, assertive, vigorous, and sometimes pompous and gratuitous, implicitly claimed a greater importance for reviewing and thus

elevated the status of reviewing (even as the same reviewers were busy demoting the status of imaginative literature). And if the new attitudes to conversation tended to infuse periodical-writing with greater assertiveness and self-importance, the unparalleled dominance of the sermon in large segments of Scottish culture inevitably gave aspirant young literary men in Scotland an easy familiarity with the practice of wielding authority through words. Owing to developments in the history and character of Protestantism in Scotland, published sermons, whether in books or pamphlets or periodicals, had long been among the most common works from the Scottish press: and the assumption underpinning all such works, even those by so-called Moderates, was that authority resided with the speaker, not with the listener.

These cultural forces were at work at the beginning of an era in which, thanks to recent technological advances, the periodical review and literary magazine would acquire unprecedented power and prestige. In 1798 Lord Stanhope invented the iron printing press, doubling the press's output capacity and opening the way for further inventions, and in the same year Nicholas-Louis Robert invented the paper-making machine. Moreover, for a number of economic reasons the price of books was steadily rising at the beginning of the nineteenth century, while several factors were driving the price of periodicals down.[8] The periodical-writing produced by the Scottish men of letters, characterized by the language (and often the ideas) of discursive equality and openness, as well as by an immediately apparent sense of self-assuredness and an awareness of the possession of authority—or, in other words, by the ironic and surprisingly potent combination of egalitarian humility and discursive superiority—swept early-nineteenth-century print culture to an extent many considered shocking. These were the sources of that phenomenon lamented by English men of letters who found themselves in the midst of an environment of which—to adapt Coleridge's complaint—nine-tenths was Scottish.

Notes

INTRODUCTION

1. [John Scott], "Prospectus," *London Magazine* 1 (1820): iv.

2. John Gross, *The Rise and Fall of the Man of Letters: A Study of the Idiosyncratic and the Humane in Modern Literature* (London: Macmillan, 1969), 9.

3. See Ralph Jessop, "Viragos of the Periodical Press," in *A History of Scottish Women's Writing*, ed. Douglas Gifford and Dorothy McMillan (Edinburgh: Edinburgh University Press, 1997), 216–31.

4. David Finkelstein, "Early Nineteenth-century Scottish Publishing," *Gaskell Society Journal* 8 (1994): 79.

5. Richard Sher calls this the "London-Edinburgh Publishing Axis" in his recent and definitive study, *The Enlightenment & the Book: Scottish Authors & Their Publishers in Eighteenth-Century Britain, Ireland, & America* (Chicago: University of Chicago Press, 2006), 265–440.

6. Thomas Constable, *Archibald Constable and His Literary Correspondents*, 3 vols. (Edinburgh: Edmonston and Douglas, 1873), 1:49.

7. For this information I have drawn from the appendices for the periods 1698–1788 and 1789–1836 in Alvin Sullivan, ed., *British Literary Magazines*, 4 vols. (Westport, Connecticut: Greenwood, 1983–86), appendices in all four volumes. The London journals were the *Anti-Jacobin Review*, the *British Critic*, the *Monthly Magazine*, the *Monthly Mirror*, the *Critical Review*, the *European Magazine*, and the *Universal Magazine*. In Edinburgh there were the *Edinburgh Magazine* and the *Scots Magazine*.

8. Francis Shepherd, *London: A History* (Oxford: Oxford University Press, 1998), 205; T. C. Smout, *A History of the Scottish People, 1560–1830* (London: Collins, 1969), 469.

9. Derek Roper, *Reviewing before the Edinburgh, 1788–1802* (London: Methuen, 1978), 22. Other writers mentioned in this paragraph are discussed in Roper's book, 19–24, as also in the *DNB*.

10. Benjamin Christie Nangle, *The Monthly Review, Second Series, 1790–1815: Indexes of Contributors and Articles* (Oxford: Clarendon, 1955), 21–22, 37–39, 47–48.

11. Sher, *The Enlightenment & the Book*, 118–31.

12. W. J. Couper, *The Edinburgh Periodical Press*, 2 vols. (Stirling: Eneas Mackay, 1908), 2:209. Carlyle's remark appears in *WTC* 28:25.

13. Mary Elizabeth Craig, *The Scottish Periodical Press, 1750–1789* (Edinburgh: Oliver and Boyd, 1931), 6. On the Scots' craving for the latest periodicals from the south, see the first chapter of *The Heart of Midlothian*.

14. W. S. MacDonald, "Aberdeen Periodical Publishing, 1786–1791," *Bibliotheck* 9 (1978): 1–12.

15. Marilyn Butler, *Peacock Displayed: A Satirist in His Context* (London: Routledge and Kegan Paul, 1979), 274.

16. "J. H." to an unknown correspondent, in *Letters of King George IV, 1812–1830*, 3 vols., edited by A. Aspinall (Cambridge: Cambridge University Press, 1938), 3:495 (about 1818).

17. Samuel Taylor Coleridge, *Essays on His Times*, vol. 3 of *The Collected Works of Samuel Taylor Coleridge*, ed. Kathleen Coburn, 13 vols. (Princeton: Princeton University Press, 1971–81), 275–76.

18. The English word "intellectual," used as a noun in the modern sense, only achieved currency in the early-twentieth century, and then usually in ironic and deprecatory senses. Stefan Collini has recently published a full and entertaining discussion of the origins of the word. The term "men of letters," he observes, "had been perhaps the most widely used term in the mid-Victorian period, though by the end of the century it was beginning to acquire its more restricted sense of reviewers and essayists, even (more critically), bookmen, amateurs, mere *littérateurs*": *Absent Minds: Intellectuals in Britain* (Oxford: Oxford University Press, 2006), 72–73. Though I have occasionally referred to "intellectuals" in this book, I felt the title ought to retain the historically more accurate "men of letters," especially given its association with periodical literature.

19. Jürgen Habermas, *The Structural Transformation of the Public Sphere: An Inquiry into a Category of Bourgeois Society*, trans. by Thomas Burger and Frederick Lawrence (Cambridge: Polity, 1989 [1962]), 5–14.

20. Habermas, *Structural Transformation*, 14–20.

21. Ibid., 20–26, 27–28.

22. Ibid., 29–43.

23. Ibid., 57–67 (on Fox, 65–66).

24. Peter Uwe Hohendahl, "Critical Theory, Public Sphere and Culture. Jürgen Habermas and his Critics," *New German Critique* 16 (1979): 90.

25. Habermas, *Structural Transformation*, 25–27.

26. James Van Horn Melton, *The Rise of the Public in Enlightenment Europe* (Cambridge: Cambridge University Press, 2001), 11–12.

27. T. C. W. Blanning, *The Culture of Power and the Power of Culture: Old Regime Europe 1660–1789* (Oxford: Oxford University Press, 2002), 12 (italics Blanning's).

28. Mark Parker, *Literary Magazines and British Romanticism*, Cambridge Studies in Romanticism, 45, ed. Marilyn Butler and James Chandler (Cambridge: Cambridge University Press, 2000), 19, 27.

29. Habermas, *Structural Transformation*, 29–30.

30. Blanning, *The Culture of Power and the Power of Culture*, 13–14.

31. Habermas, *Structural Transformation*, 111, 119.

32. Benjamin Nathans, "Habermas's 'Public Sphere' in the Era of the French Revolution," *French Historical Studies* 16 (1990): 631–36.

33. Jon P. Klancher, *The Making of English Reading Audiences, 1790–1832* (Madison: Wisconsin University Press, 1987), 26.

34. The terms "liberal" and "liberalism" I use in the broader sense to signify openness and general freedom of speech in political arrangements; i.e. not necessarily as opposed to conservatism.

35. Geoff Elay, "Nations, Publics, and Political Cultures: Placing Habermas in the Nineteenth Century," in *Habermas and the Public Sphere*, ed. Craig Calhoun (Cambridge, Mass.: MIT Press, 1992), 325–26.

36. Alexander Broadie, *The Scottish Enlightenment: The Historical Age of the Historical Nation* (Edinburgh: Birlinn, 2001), 15.

37. Leith Davis, *Acts of Union: Scotland and the Literary Negotiation of the British Nation, 1707–1830* (Stanford, Calif.: Stanford University Press, 1998), 12.

38. Joan Milne and Willie Smith, "Reviews and Magazines: Criticism and Polemic," in *The Nineteenth Century*, vol. 3 of *The History of Scottish Literature*, ed. Cairns Craig (Aberdeen: Aberdeen University Press, 1987–1989), 189–201.

39. Walter Bagehot, *Literary Studies*, 2 vols., Everyman's Library (London: J. M. Dent, 1911), 1:20–21.

40. George Elder Davie, *The Democratic Intellect: Scotland and Her Universities in the Nineteenth Century* (Edinburgh: Edinburgh University Press, 1961), 1–29.

41. John Clive, *Scotch Reviewers: The Edinburgh Review, 1802–1815* (Cambridge, Mass.: 1957), 25–26.

42. Margaret Oliphant, *Annals of a Publishing House: William Blackwood and His Sons, Their Magazine and Friends*, 3 vols. (Edinburgh: Blackwood, 1897), 1:102.

43. [John Gibson Lockhart], *Peter's Letters to His Kinsfolk*, 2nd ed. (i.e. 1st), 3 vols. (Edinburgh: Blackwood, 1819), 1:209–10.

44. George Gleig quotes this remark in his biographical sketch, "Life of Lockhart," *QR* 116 (1864): 465.

45. See John Robertson, *The Case for the Enlightenment: Scotland and Naples, 1680–1760* (Cambridge: Cambridge University Press, 2005), 42–43. Robertson argues, over against Roy Porter's case for a "British Enlightenment," that there was no proper Enlightenment in England, defining an "Enlightenment" as "the development of the sciences of man and of political economy, the historical investigation of the progress of society, and the critical application of ideas for human betterment to the existing social and political order." In Robertson's (in my view compelling) interpretation, there was no English counterpart to the mid-eighteenth-century Scottish intelligentsia (Hutcheson, Hume, Robertson, Smith, et al.), unless one counts the radical and unitarian minority of the 1770s, 80s, and 90s (Price, Priestly, Bentham, Wollstonecraft, and Godwin)—"but their very radicalism excluded them from a central role in English public life; they could not make up for the absence of Enlightenment thinkers in the previous four decades."

46. E. P. Thompson, "The Peculiarities of the English," in *The Poverty of Theory & Other Essays* (New York and London: Monthly Review Press, 1978), 268–69. In context Thompson is refuting the *"New Left Review* analysis" of Perry Anderson and Tom Nairn, who believed that Britain—unlike France—had never experienced a proper bourgeois revolution and had never fostered a properly oppositional intelligentsia.

47. Richard D. Altick, *The English Common Reader: A Social History of the Mass Reading Public 1800–1900* (Chicago: University of Chicago Press, 1957), 392

48. Derek Roper, *Reviewing before the Edinburgh, 1788–1802* (London: Methuen, 1978), 27–33.

49. One Edinburgh guidebook published from the period lists both the *Edinburgh Review* and the *Encyclopaedia Britanica* under "periodical literature": J. Stark, *Picture of Edinburgh* (Edinburgh: Constable; London: John Murray, 1806), 256–57.

50. Roper, *Reviewing before the Edinburgh*, 40.

51. Paul Keen, *The Crisis of Literature in the 1790s: Print Culture and the Public Sphere*, Cambridge Studies in Romanticism, 36, ed. Marilyn Butler and James Chandler (Cambridge: Cambridge University Press, 1999), 119.

52. *LLJ* 1:131.

53. Linda Colley, *Britons: Forging the Nation 1707–1837* (New Haven: Yale University Press, 1992), 120–37, passim.

54. Sir Walter Scott to William Knighton, in *Letters of King George IV*, 2:540 (September 22, 1822). This letter is omitted from the Grierson collection.

55. Terry Eagleton, *The Function of Criticism: from the Spectator to Post-Structuralism* (London: Verso, 1984), 17.

56. Clive James, "Echoes from another century," *The Guardian*, June 23, 2001, Saturday Pages, 2.

57. Edmund Wilson, "The Historical Interpretation of Literature," in *The Triple Thinkers: Twelve Essays on Literary Subjects* (New York: Oxford University Press, 1963), 268.

58. Andrew Noble, "John Wilson (Christopher North) and the Tory Hegemony," in *The Nineteenth Century*, vol. 3 of *The History of Scottish Literature*, ed. Cairns Craig (Aberdeen: Aberdeen University Press, 1987–89), 125–51.

59. Commonplace book of John Dunlop, National Library of Scotland MS 9262, 138.

60. David Craig, *Scottish Literature and the Scottish People, 1680–1830* (London: Chatto and Windus, 1961), 203.

61. Sydney Smith, *The Letters of Sydney Smith*, ed. Nowell Smith, 2 vols. (Oxford: Oxford University Press, 1953), 1:21–2. Smith had just arrived in Edinburgh in 1798 when he wrote this.

62. [Lockhart], *Peter's Letters*, 3:69, 74.

63. Thomas Carlyle, *Reminiscences*, ed. Kenneth J. Fielding and Ian Campbell, Oxford World's Classics (Oxford: Oxford University Press, 1997), 208.

64. Robert Gillies, *Memoirs of a Literary Veteran*, 3 vols. (London: Richard Bentley, 1851), 1:166–67; Mary Gordon, *"Christopher North": A Memoir of John Wilson*, 2 vols (Edinburgh: Edmonston and Douglas, 1862), 1:5.

65. Walter Houghton, "A Brief History of the *Wellesley Index:* Its Origin, Evaluation, and Variety of Uses," *Victorian Periodicals Review*, 18 (1972), 49.

66. Klancher, *The Making of English Reading Audiences*, 52.

67. Parker, *Literary Magazines and British Romanticism*, 3.

CHAPTER 1. "A MERE INTELLECTUAL BAZAAR"

1. R. A. Houston, *Scottish Literacy and the Scottish Identity: Illiteracy and Society in Scotland and Northern England, 1600–1800*, Cambridge Studies in Population, Economy and Society, ed. by Peter Laslett and others (London: Cambridge University Press, 1985), 1–7.

2. T. C. Smout, *A History of the Scottish People, 1560–1830* (London: Collins, 1969), 449.

3. Tobias Smollett, *The Expedition of Humphry Clinker*, ed. Angus Ross, Penguin Classics (Harmondsworth: Penguin, 1967 [1771]), 307 (September 15); *The Adventures of Roderick Random*, ed. Paul-Gabriel Boucé, Oxford World's Classics (Oxford: Oxford University Press, 1979 [1748]), 224 (chapter 40).

4. Mary Brunton, *Emmeline, with Some Other Pieces* (Edinburgh: Manners and Miller, 1819), 167.

5. John Gibson Lockhart, *Reginald Dalton* (Edinburgh: Blackwood, 1823), 97.

6. Quoted in Alan Lang Strout, *Life and Letters of James Hogg, the Ettrick Shepherd* (Lubbock, Texas: Texas Tech Press, 1946), 47.

7. As e.g. in John Wilson, "Some Observations on the Poetry of the Agricultural and That of the Pastoral Districts of Scotland," *BEM* 4 (1819): 521–29.

8. John Gibson Lockhart, *Memoirs of the Life of Sir Walter Scott*, 5 vols. (London: Macmillan 1900), 4:183 (chapter 25, 1824). In context, Scott does concede there to have been an element of truth in Johnson's remark with regard to classical learning.

9. R. D. Anderson, *Education and the Scottish People, 1750–1918* (Oxford: Clarendon, 1995), 33–39.

10. J. V. Smith, "Manners, Morals, and Mentalities: Reflections of the Popular Enlightenment of Early Nineteenth-Century Scotland," in *Scottish Culture and Scottish Education*, ed. Walter M. Humes and Hamish M. Paterson (Edinburgh: John Donald, 1983): 25–54.

11. Jonathan Rose, "A Conservative Canon: Cultural Lag in British Working Class Reading Habits," *Libraries and Culture* 33 (1998), 98; John C. Crawford, "Reading and Book use in 18th-century Scotland," *The Bibliotheck* 19 (1994), 37.

12. Asa Briggs, *The Age of Improvement, 1783–1867* (London: Longmans, 1959), 223–25.

13. J. V. Smith, "Manners, Morals, and Mentalities," 28.

14. Robert Henry, *The History of Great Britain, from the First Invasion of It by the Romans under Julius Cæsar*, 6 vols. (London: T. Cadell, 1771–1793), 6:564–65. On Henry, see *DNB*.

15. John Millar, *An Historical View of the English Government*, 4 vols. (London: J. Mawman, 1803), 3:87–89; cf. 3:92–93.

16. James Mill, "Education of the Poor," *ER* 21 (1813): 208.

17. See his tract *Schools for All* in *James Mill on Education*, ed. W. H. Burston (Cambridge: Cambridge University Press, 1969), 120–93.

18. Alexander Christison, *The General Diffusion of Knowledge One Great Cause of the Prosperity of North Britain* (Edinburgh: Peter Hill, 1802), esp. 6–15.

19. Quoted in R. H. M. Buddle Atkinson and G. A. Jackson, *Brougham and His Early Friends*, 3 vols. (London: Darling and Pead, 1908), 3:19. Italics in the original.

20. Jon P. Klancher, *The Making of English Reading Audiences, 1790–1832* (Madison: Wisconsin University Press, 1987), 18–26.

21. Klancher, *The Making of English Reading Audiences*, 26–38.

22. Greg Laugero, "Infrastructures of Enlightenment: Road-making, the Public Sphere, and the Emergence of Literature," *Eighteenth-Century Studies* 29 (1995), 51–64. Laugero also discusses Thomas Hardy, founder of the London Corresponding Society, who was Scottish.

23. Paul Keen, *The Crisis of Literature in the 1790s: Print Culture and the Public Sphere*, Cambridge Studies in Romanticism, 36, ed. Marilyn Butler and James Chandler (Cambridge: Cambridge University Press, 1999), 32–53.

24. Alexander Murdoch, "Scotland and the Idea of Britain in the Eighteenth Century," in *Eighteenth Century Scotland: New Perspectives*, ed. T. M. Devine and J. R. Young (East Lothian: Tuckwell, 1999), 106–120. Also Paola Bono, *Radicals and Reformers in Late Eighteenth-Century Scotland: An Annotated Checklist of Books, Pamphlets, and Documents Printed in Scotland 1775–1800*, Scottish Studies, 6 (Frankfurt am Main: Peter Lang, 1989), 14–19 and passim.

25. To the extent such a sphere existed, of course—a debatable question I shall not address directly, though it is indisputable that many people *thought* such a sphere existed.

26. See John Clive, "The Earl of Buchan's Kick: A Footnote to the history of the *Edinburgh Review*," *Harvard Library Bulletin* 5 (1951): 362–70.

27. The remark appears in *Elements of the Philosophy of the Human Mind* (1792): *Collected Works of Dugald Stewart*, ed. William Hamilton, 11 vols. (Edinburgh: Constable, 1854), 2:229–30.

28. Dugald Stewart, "Dissertation: Exhibiting the Progress of Metaphysical, Ethical, and Political Philosophy Since the Revival of Letters in Europe," in ibid., 1:504–5.

29. Francis Horner, *The Horner Papers: Selections from the Letters and Miscellaneous Writings of Francis Horner, M.P., 1795–1817*, ed. Kenneth Bourne and William Banks Taylor (Edinburgh: Edinburgh University Press, 1994), 89–90.

30. Ina Ferris, *The Achievement of Literary Authority: Gender, History, and the Waverley Novels* (Ithaca: Cornell University Press, 1991), 24.

31. In his forthcoming critical biography, William Christie discusses Jeffrey's intrusive editorial practices by reproducing passages from a number of unpublished letters between Jeffrey and his contributors (see chapter 1).

32. Edward Copleston, *A Reply to the Calumnies of the Edinburgh Review against Oxford* (Oxford: J. Cooke and J. Parker, 1810), 4.

33. Walter Scott, *Letters of Sir Walter Scott*, ed. H. J. C. Grierson, 12 vols. (London: Constable, 1932), 2:121, 126 (November 2, 1808).

34. Scott, *Letters of Sir Walter Scott*, 2:107 (October 25, 1808).

35. "Cornelius Scipio," *A Sketch of the Politics of the Edinburgh Reviewers, as Exhibited in Their Three First Numbers for the Year 1807* (London: R. S. Kirkby and J. Hatchard, 1807), 2.

36. Scipio, Cornelius, *A Sketch of the Politics of the Edinburgh Reviewers*, 66–67.

37. R. Wharton, *Remarks on the Jacobinical Tendency of the Edinburgh Review, in a Letter to Lord Lonsdale* (London: J. Hatchard, 1809), 5–6.

38. Benjamin Christie Nangle, *The Monthly Review, Second Series, 1790–1815: Indexes of Contributors and Articles* (Oxford: Clarendon, 1955), x.

39. Roper, *Reviewing before the Edinburgh*, 45, 80, 173.

40. In a letter to Jeffrey: *Horner Papers*, 349 (September 12, 1804). (The "hypostatic union" is the ancient Christian doctrine of the two natures of Christ, human and divine.)

41. *Complete Works of William Hazlitt*, ed. P. P. Howe, 22 vols. (London: J. M. Dent, 1930–1934), 11:127–28.

42. Emma Vincent Macleod, *A War of Ideas: British Attitudes to the Wars against Revolutionary France, 1792–1802* (Aldershot: Ashgate, 1998).

43. Cockburn, *LLJ* 2:151–52 (March 12, 1815).

44. Jeffrey, Contributions to the Edinburgh Review *CER* 1:ix. The allusion is to Hebrews 5:12: "For when for the time ye ought to be teachers, ye have need that one teach you again which be the first principles of the oracles of God; and are become such as have need of milk, and not of strong meat."

45. [Francis Jeffrey], "The Dangers of the Country," *ER* 10 (1807): 10–18.

46. Michael Roberts, *The Whig Party: 1807–1812* (London: Macmillan, 1939), 178.

47. [Francis Jeffrey], "Cobbett's Political Register," *ER* 10 (1807): 407–9.

48. Cookburn, *LLJ* 2:110–11 (September 18, 1806).

49. John Clive, *Scotch Reviewers: The Edinburgh Review, 1802–1815* (Cambridge, Mass: 1957), 104–10.

50. Philip Flynn, *Francis Jeffrey* (Newark: University of Delaware Press, 1978), 120.

51. "Cobbett's Political Register," 387.

52. Elizabeth Schneider, John D. Kern, and Irwin Griggs, "Brougham's Early Contributions to the *Edinburgh Review:* A New List," *Modern Philology* 42 (1944): 170–71.

53. Francis Jeffrey and Henry Broughan "Don Pedro Cevallos on the French Usurpation of Spain," *ER* 13 (1808): 215–34 (esp. 221–23).

54. Ibid., 224.

55. Quoted in *Memoirs and Correspondence of Francis Horner, M.P.*, ed. Leonard Horner, 2 vols. (London: John Murray, 1843), 1:437–39 (December 6, 1808).

56. Thomas Love Peacaock, *Crotchet Castle*, together with *Nightmare Abbey*, ed. Raymond Wright, Penguin Classics (Harmondsworth: Penguin, 1969 [1831]), 158.

57. Marilyn Butler, *Peacock Displayed: A Satirist in His Context* (London: Routledge and Kegan Paul, 1979), 278.

58. See Walter E. Houghton, *Wellesley Index to Victorian Periodicals, 1824–1900*, 4 vols. (London: Routledge and Kegan Paul, 1966–87), 2:173–76.

59. David Nokes, *Jonathan Swift, A Hypocrite Reversed: A Critical Biography* (Oxford: Oxford University Press, 1985), 123.

60. In fact, the *Wellesley Index of Victorian Periodicals* is itself an excellent example of the way in which these periodicals' readers—twentieth-century scholars, in this case—have sometimes mistakenly conflated preeminent Victorian periodicals, on the one hand, and the Victorian culture of which those periodicals were a part, on the other. See P. G. Scott, "Unmasking the Mandarins: Wellesley II," *Victorian Periodicals Newsletter* 6 (December 1973): 41–49 (esp. 46–48).

61. Jürgen Habermas, *The Structural Transformation of the Public Sphere: An Inquiry into a Category of Bourgeois Society*, trans. by Thomas Burger and Frederick Lawrence (Cambridge: Polity, 1989 [1962]), 130–31.

62. Ibid., 129–40 (esp. 136–37).

63. Keen, *The Crisis of Literature in the 1790s*, 111–15.

64. James Van Horn Melton, *The Rise of the Public in Enlightenment Europe* (Cambridge: Cambridge University Press, 2001), 117.

65. James Mill, in a long article on the *Edinburgh Review* in 1824, interpreted the journal's Whig disposition as mere lack of principle: "Periodical Literature: 1. Edinburgh Review," *Westminster Review* 1 (1824): 206–49.

66. On the Scientific Whigs' theories of law as an institution that develops by adapting to changing social contexts, see Peter Stein, "Law and Society in Eighteenth-Century Scotland," in *Scotland in the Age of Improvement: Essays in Scottish History in the Eighteenth Century*, ed. N. T. Phillipson and Rosalind Mitchison (Edinburgh: Edinburgh University Press, 1970), 148–68.

67. Cockburn, *LLJ* 1:170–71.

68. Biancamaria Fontana, *Rethinking the Politics of Commercial Society: The Edinburgh Review 1802–1832* (Cambridge: Cambridge University Press, 1985), 7; cf. 112–46; and Clive, *Scotch Reviewers*, 86–123.

69. Smith, *Letters of Sydney Smith*, ed. Nowell Smith, 2 vols. (Oxford: Oxford University Press, 1953), 1:186 (April 17, 1810).

70. Quoted in David Groves, "Francis Jeffrey and the 'Peterloo' Massacre of 1819," *Notes and Queries* 235 (1990): 418.

71. Francis Jeffrey, *Commonplace Book of Notes and Books*, Thomas Cooper Library, University of South Carolina, 4825.J2 A16 1798, 103–4. The quotation may be found in a transcription: David Wayne Pitre, *Francis Jeffrey's Journal* (unpublished PhD dissertation, University of South Carolina, 1980), 118–19.

72. *LLJ* 2:19–20 (December 22, 1795).

73. *LLJ* 2:112 (September 18, 1806); cf. 1:195–96.

74. "Parliamentary Reform," *ER* 17 (1811), 253–90 (288).

75. Clive, *Scotch Reviewers*, 122.

76. One example: In 1810 he advocated an alliance between Whigs and radicals. He confessed to John Allen a few months later: "I know I stated the danger of the thing coming to a crisis too strongly, and I knew it at the time; but what I meant . . . [was] that if the present miserable system is ever to be corrected by the sense and spirit of the nation—that nation would then appear under these two divisions": *LLJ* 2:128 (May 4, 1810).

77. Cockburn, *LLJ* 1:129–30.

78. Henry Braugham, *Life and Times of Henry Lord Brougham, written by himself*, 3 vols. (Edinburgh: Blackwood, 1871), 1:253.

79. Francis Jeffrey, "Mounier, De L'Influence des Philosophes," *ER* 1 (1802): 1–18 (8).

80. Ibid., 14.

81. Neil Berry, "The Reviewer Triumphant," *London Magazine*, new series, 33 (February/March 1994): 34–49 (41).

82. "Mounier," 8.

83. "Southey's Thalaba," *ER* 1 (1802), 63–83 (63).

84. Ibid., 64.

85. Jerome Christensen, *Romanticism at the End of History* (Baltimore: Johns Hopkins University Press, 2000), 109.

86. "Southey's Thalaba," 71. Jeffrey expresses profound admiration for the reading public in "De Lille, Malheur et Pitié: Poëme," *ER* 3 (1803): 26–27.

87. *CER,* ix–x.

88. Frances Jeffrey, "Thelwall's Poems," *ER* 2 (1802): 197–202 (197). "Effusions of Relative and Social Feeling" is one of the subdivisions in Thelwall's *Poems Chiefly Written in Retirement.*

89. Francis Jeffrey, "Millar's View of the English Government," *ER* 3 (1803): 154–81 (175).

90. Stefan Collini, Donald Winch, and John Burrow, *That Noble Science of Politics: A Study in Nineteenth-century Intellectual History* (Cambridge: Cambridge University Press, 1983), 53–55.

91. Clive, *Scotch Reviewers*, 175.

92. "Bentham, Princepes de Legislation, par Dumont," *ER* 4 (1804): 19–20; *CER,* III, 318.

93. Francis Jeffrey, "Memoirs de Bailly," *ER* 6 (1805): 138; *CER,* 2:39.

94. Ibid., 139–40; *CER,* 2:41.

95. Francis Jeffrey, "Drummond's Academical Questions," *ER* 7 (1805): 163–85 (185).

96. Francis Jeffrey, "The Works of Dr. Franklin," *ER* 8 (1806): 329–30; *CER,* 1:139–40.

97. The book itself is dedicated to "Francis, Earl of Moira," and in it there are poems dedicated to "Lord Viscount Strangford," "Marchioness Dowager of D— —n— —g——ll," "Lord Viscount Forbes, from Washington," "His Serene Highness the Duke of Montpensier," "Honourable William Spencer, from Buffalo," "Lady Charlotte R— —wd——on," and "Lady H— — — —."

98. Francis Jeffrey, "Moore's Poems," *ER* 8 (1806): 460.

99. Francis Jeffrey, "Pamphlets on the Catholic Question," *ER* 11 (1807): 116; "Montgomery's Poems," *ER* 9 (1807): 348.

100. "Poems by W. Wordsworth," *ER* 11 (1807): 214.

101. Ibid., 215–16.

102. Peter Uwe Hohendahl, *The Institution of Criticism* (Ithaca: Cornell University Press, 1982), 49–51. "The contradiction within the liberal public sphere becomes evident—it does not do justice to its own idea. Although in principle the capacity to form an accurate opinion is considered present in everyone, in practice it is limited to the educated": 51.

103. William H. Christie, "Francis Jeffrey's Associationist Aesthetics," *British Journal of Aesthetics* 33 (1993): 267–68.

104. Philip Flynn, "Francis Jeffrey and the Scottish Critical Tradition," in *British Romanticism and the Edinburgh Review*, ed. Massimiliano Demata and Duncan Wu (New York: Palgrave Macmillan, 2002), 28–30.

105. Francis Jeffrey, "Reliques of Burns," *ER* 13 (1809): 250.

106. Francis Jeffrey to Thomas Carlyle, October 17, 1827, NLS MS 787, ff. 9–10. I am grateful to Professor Will Christie for sharing with me his transcriptions of Jeffrey's letters to Carlyle.

107. Francis Jeffrey, "Mrs. Hamilton's Cottagers," *ER* 12 (1808): 410.

108. [John Gibson Lockhart], *Peter's Letters to His Kinsfolk*, 2nd ed. (i.e. 1st), 3 vols. (Edinburgh: Blackwood, 1819), 1:118–20; cf. Russell Noyes, *Wordsworth and Jeffrey in Controversy* (Bloomington: Indiana University Publications, 1941), 38–39.

109. James A. Greig, *Francis Jeffrey of the Edinburgh Review* (London: Oliver and Boyd, 1948), 68–69. Greig quotes George Saintsbury: "He arranged his critical judgments on something like a regular and co-ordinated system. Even his prejudices and injustices were systematic."

110. Allan Massie, "Maddest of Tribunals," *Times Literary Supplement*, August 9, 2002, 12–13.

111. Leslie Stephen, "The First Edinburgh Reviewers," in *Hours in a Library*, 3rd series (London: Smith, Elder, 1879), 176.

112. John Clive, "The *Edinburgh Review*: the life and death of a periodical," in *Essays on the History of Publishing, in celebration of the 250th anniversary of the House of Longman*, ed. Asa Briggs (London: Longman, 1974), 121.

113. Leslie Mitchell, *Holland House* (London: Duckworth, 1980), 191.

114. Terry Eagleton, *The Function of Criticism: from the Spectator to Post-Structuralism* (London: Verso, 1984), 37.

115. Francis Jeffrey, "Southey's Thalaba," 65–66.

116. Marilyn Butler is (so far as I know) alone in pointing this out. "The probable reason for concocting this digressive review was to stir up a controversy that would win publicity for the new journal": Marilyn Butler, "Culture's Medium: the Role of the Review," in *The Cambridge Companion to British Romanticism*, ed. Stuart Curran (Cambridge: Cambridge University Press, 1993), 133. Still, coming as this statement does in an essay on periodicals as retrospectively coherent enterprises, it necessarily implies that the review's straightforward snobbery was central to the *Edinburgh*'s general cultural disposition, which is not quite the case.

117. William Wordsworth, *Prose Works of William Wordsworth*, ed. W. J. B. Owen and J. W. Smyser, 3 vols. (Oxford: Clarendon, 1974), 1:129.

118. William H. Christie, "A Recent History of Poetic Difficulty," *ELH* 67 (2000): 545. Christie's emphasis on the importance of the public's judgment in Jeffrey's criticism, indeed in all his writing, has been greatly needed; his recourse to public judgment has been incorrectly portrayed as an insurance policy against the failure of his aesthetic principles; as in John U. Peters, "Jeffrey's Keats Criticism," *Studies in Scottish Literature*, 10 (1972–73), 175–85.

119. Peter F. Morgan, *Literary Critics and Reviewers in Early 19th-Century Britain* (London: Croom Helm, 1983), 12.

120. William Wordsworth, *Poetical Works of William Wordsworth*, ed. E. de Selincourt and Helen Darbishire, 5 vols. (Oxford: Clarendon, 1940–49), 5:1–312.

121. Francis Jeffrey, "Wordsworth's Excursion," *ER* 24 (1814): 4; *CER* 3:237–38.

122. Ibid., 6; *CER* 3:241.

123. Ibid., 30; *CER* 3:267.

124. Dan Jacobson, "Border Crossings," *Times Literary Supplement*, November 2, 2007, 14–15.

125. James K. Chandler, *Wordsworth's Second Nature: A Study of the Poetry and Politics* (Chicago: University of Chicago Press, 1984), 90–92. Cf. *The Excursion*, 9:245–49.

126. Ibid., xix. On Jeffrey's and other Scottish Whigs' views of Burke, see Fontana, *Rethinking the Politics of Commercial Society*, 25–28. I am aware that many Wordsworth scholars have not espoused Chandler's reading; e.g. Alan Grob, "Wordsworth and the Politics of Consciousness," in *Critical Essays on William Wordsworth*, ed. George H. Gilpin (Boston: Hall, 1990), 339–56. The point in this context, however, is not that Chandler is right, but that Jeffrey discerned in Wordsworth's poems the same elements Chandler has found in them, fairly or otherwise.

127. Francis Jeffrey, "Wordsworth's Excursion," 27; *CER* 3:263; cf. *The Excursion*, 9:237–47, 336–54.

128. John Wilson, "Preface to a Review of the Chronicles of the Canongate," *BEM* 22 (1827): 546.

129. *Evidence, Oral and Documentary: Taken and Received by the Commissioners for Visiting the Universities of Scotland*, 4 vols. (London: Clowes and Sons, 1837), 1:393.

130. Richard D. Altick, *The English Common Reader: A Social History of the Mass Reading Public 1800–1900* (Chicago: University of Chicago Press, 1957), 318.

131. Ian Parsons, "Copyright and Society," in *Essays in the History of Publishing in celebration of the 250th anniversary of the House of Longman*, ed. Asa Briggs (London: Longman, 1974), 39–40.

132. Warren McDougall, "Copyright Litigation in the Court of Session, 1783–1749, and the Rise of the Scottish Book Trade," *Edinburgh Bibliographical Society Transactions* 5:5 (1988): 10–11; John Feather, *A History of British Publishing* (London: Croom Helm, 1988), 82; Richard B. Sher, *The Enlightenment & the Book: Scottish Authors & Their Publishers in Eighteenth-Century Britain, Ireland, & America* (Chicago: University of Chicago Press, 2006), 315.

133. Scott A. McLean, "Cleansing the Hawker's Basket: Popular Literature and the Cheap Periodical Press in Scotland," *Studies in Scottish Literature* 32 (2001): 88–91.

134. Quoted in Marjorie King, "*Illudo Chartis:* An Initial Study in Carlyle's Mode of Composition," *Modern Languages Review* 49 (1954): 166.

135. Francis Horner, *Horner Papers*, 412.

CHAPTER 2. "EDINBURGH IS A TALKING TOWN"

1. Samuel Johnson, *Journey to the Western Isles of Scotland*, together with James Boswell's *Journey of a Tour to the Hebrides*, Penguin Classics, ed. Primo Levi (Harmondsworth: Penguin, 1988), 151.

2. Quoted in Richard B. Sher, *Church and University in the Scottish Enlightenment: The Moderate Literati of Edinburgh* (Edinburgh: Edinburgh University Press, 1985), 108. The complaint was almost commonplace; here e.g. is Thomas Blacklock writing apologetically to the publisher Robert Dodsley: "Experience has made it plain to me, how great, & how numerous the difficulties are, which a Scotch Man has to encounter, before he can write with that facility & Chastness [sic] which occur naturally to an Englishman . . . I am sensible that the strictest Attention & Care are too little to guard us against harsh Periods, & exotick Idioms which are rendered familiar to us from our Infancy by the Difference of our manners, Conversation & Accent': *The Correspondence of Robert Dodsley, 1733–1764*, ed. James E. Tierney (Cambridge: Cambridge University Press, 1988), 283 (June 27, 1757).

3. Alexander Law, *Education in Edinburgh in the Eighteenth Century* (London: University of London Press, 1965), 157–61.

4. On voluntary associations in eighteenth-century England: John Brewer, "Credit, Clubs, and Independence," in John Brewer, Neil McKendrick, and J. H. Plumb, *The Birth of a Consumer Society: The Commercialization of Eighteenth-century England* (London: Europa, 1982), 203–30.

5. David McElroy, *Scotland's Age of Improvement: a Survey of Eighteenth-Century Literary Clubs and Societies* (Pullman: Washington State University Press, 1969), 14, 55, 88–89, 111.

6. Richard B. Sher, *The Enlightenment & the Book: Scottish Authors & Their Publishers in Eighteenth-Century Britain, Ireland, & America* (Chicago: University of Chicago Press, 2006), 106–8.

7. "On Conversation," *The North-British Intelligencer or Constitutional Miscellany* 1 (1776): 163–64.

8. Anonymous, "The Charms of Conversation," *Scots Magazine* 59 (1797): 59–60; cf. "Tea Table Conversation," *Scots Magazine* 57 (1795): 518.

9. Hugh Blair, *Lectures on Rhetoric and Belles Lettres*, 2 vols (Edinburgh: William Creech, 1783). Blair's lectures were reprinted by Scottish firms many times throughout the first half of the nineteenth century.

10. E.g. Hugh Mitchell, *Scotticisms, Vulgar Anglicisms, and Grammatical Improprieties Corrected* (Glasgow: Falconer and Willison, 1799). Note that "Vulgar" only attaches to Anglicisms; all Scoticisms were so. (Sometimes "Scoticism" was spelt with one "t," sometimes with two.)

11. James Beattie, *Scoticisms* [so spelt], *Arranged in Alphabetical Order, Designed to Correct Improprieties of Speech and Writing* (Edinburgh: William Creech, 1787).

12. Boswell, *Journal*, 480.

13. George Elder Davie, *The Democratic Intellect: Scotland and Her Universities in the Nineteenth Century* (Edinburgh: Edinburgh University Press, 1961), 14–15.

14. Paul Langford, *A Polite and Commercial People: England, 1727–1783* (Oxford: Clarendon, 1989), 59–121.

15. Nicholas Phillipson, "The Scottish Enlightenment," in *The Enlightenment in Na-*

tional Context, ed. Roy Porter and Mikuláš Teich (Cambridge: Cambridge University Press, 1981), 19–40.

16. Lawrence Klein, *Shaftesbury and the Culture of Politeness: Moral Discourse and Cultural Politics in Early Eighteenth-Century England* (Cambridge: Cambridge University Press, 1994), 4–5; cf. 96–101; or, more fully, the same author's "The Rise of Politeness in England, 1660–1715" (unpublished doctoral thesis, Johns Hopkins University, 1984), 65–85.

17. Francis Horner, *Memoirs and Correspondence of Francis Horner, M.P.,* ed. Leonard Horner, 2 vols. (London: John Murray, 1843), 1:90.

18. Henry Cockburn, *Memorials of His Time* (Edinburgh: Adam and Charles Black, 1856), 268. The *Memorials* were written throughout the 1820s and '30s.

19. Ann Grant, *Memoir and Correspondence of Mrs. Grant of Laggan,* ed. J. P. Grant, 2 vols. (London: Longman, Brown, Green, and Longmans, 1844), 2:24 (19 November 1812).

20. Henry Mackenzie, *An Account of the Life and Writings of John Home* (Edinburgh: Constable, 1822), 23.

21. Charles Kirkpatrick Sharpe, *Letters to and from Charles Kirkpatrick Sharpe,* ed. Alexander Allardyce, 2 vols. (Edinburgh: Blackwood, 1888), 2:52 (November 1812).

22. Susan Ferrier, *Marriage,* ed. Herbert Foltinek, Oxford World's Classics (Oxford: Oxford University Press, 1997 [1818]), 414–25 (Volume 3, chapter 18).

23. Thomas Hamilton, *The Youth and Manhood of Cyril Thornton,* ed. Maurice Lindsay (Aberdeen: Association for Scottish Literary Studies, 1990 [1820]), 46.

24. John Galt, *The Ayrshire Legatees* [1821], vol. 2 of *The Works of John Galt,* ed. D. S. Meldrum and William Roughead, 10 vols. (Edinburgh: John Grant, 1936), 120, 219 (Letter 25).

25. *CL* 4:416 (November 21, 1828).

26. Joseph Farington, *The Diary of Joseph Farington,* ed. Kenneth Garlick, Angus Macintyre and Kathryn Cave, 15 vols. (New Haven: Yale University Press, 1970–1984), 15:5395 (August 5, 1819).

27. Quoted in David Masson, *Edinburgh Sketches and Memories* (London: Adam and Charles Black, 1892), 280.

28. [John Gibson Lockhart], *Peter's Letters to His Kinsfolk,* 2nd ed. (i.e. 1st), 3 vols. (Edinburgh: Blackwood, 1819), 2:309–14.

29. Ibid., 1:69.

30. Ibid., 2:301.

31. Eliza Fletcher, *Autobiography of Mrs. Fletcher,* 3rd ed. (Edinburgh: Edmonston and Douglas, 1876), 102.

32. William Hazlitt, *Spirit of the Age,* vol. 11 of *Collected Works of William Hazlitt,* ed. P. P. Howe, 22 vols. (London: J. M. Dent, 1930–34), 133.

33. On the various accounts of the series' origin: Alan Strout, "Concerning the Noctes Ambrosianæ," *Modern Language Notes* 51 (1936): 493–504.

34. Scott wrote this on August 29, 1829: *The Journal of Sir Walter Scott,* ed. W. E. K. Anderson (Oxford: Clarendon Press, 1972), 191. Cf. May 7, 1828: "In general the English understand conversation well. There is that ready deference for the claims of every one who wishes to speak . . . and it is seldom now a days that '*A la stoccata*' carries it away thus."

35. Cockburn, *LLJ* 1:152.

36. [John Gibson Lockhart and Thomas Hamilton], "Two Reviews of a Military Work," Hamilton, *BEM* 5 (1819): 552–53.

37. J. H. Alexander, *"Blackwood's:* Magazine as Romantic Form," *Wordsworth Circle* 15 (1984): 57–68. Compare Mark Parker's discussion of the ways in which the dialogic criticism of the "Noctes" series both defined and historicized Romantic literature in *Literary Magazines and British Romanticism,* Cambridge Studies in Romanticism, 45, ed. Marilyn Butler and James Chandler (Cambridge: Cambridge University Press, 2000), 106–34.

38. Douglas Mack has discussed Wilson's uses of Hogg in "John Wilson, James Hogg, 'Christopher North,' and 'The Ettrick Shepherd,'" *Studies in Hogg and His World* 12 (2001): 5–24.

39. *WPW* 1:36.

40. Wilson's criticisms of Wordsworth were consistent only in their inconsistency: Alan Lang Strout, "John Wilson, 'Champion' of Wordsworth," *Modern Philology* 31 (1934): 383–94.

41. Quoted in Margaret Oliphant, *Annals of a Publishing House: William Blackwood and His Sons, Their Magazine and Friends,* 3 vols (Edinburgh: William Blackwood and Sons, 1897), I, 296.

42. Harriet Martineu recalls that Wilson and Thomas Campbell were once seen early in the morning leaving a tavern, where they had been, as she retells it, for "twenty-four hours, discussing poetry and wine to the top of their bent": *Biographical Sketches* (London: Macmillan, 1862), 340–41.

43. [John Wilson], "Noctes Ambrosianæ," *BEM* 25 (1829): 525–48 (542–43); Wilson, *WPW* 2:239–40.

44. Terry Eagleton, *The Function of Criticism: from the Spectator to Post-Structuralism* (London: Verso, 1984), 17.

45. Irene Elizabeth Mannion, "Criticism 'Con Amore': A Study of Blackwood's Magazine" (unpublished doctoral dissertation, University of California Los Angeles, 1984), 99. The manuscripts are now among the Blackwood Papers at the NLS.

46. [John Wilson], "Speech Delivered by an Eminent Barrister," *BEM* 4 (1818): 215.

47. [John Wilson], "Account of Some Curious Clubs in London, About the Beginning of the Eighteenth Century," *BEM* 3 (1818): 552.

48. [John Wilson], "Pilgrimage to the Kirk of Shotts," *BEM* 5 (1819): 671. Italics Wilson's.

49. [John Wilson], "The Literary Character . . . by Mr. D'Israeli," *BEM* 4 (1818): 14.

50. [John Wilson], "The General Question," *BEM* 14 (1823): 337.

51. As e.g. in [John Wilson], "The Works of Charles Lamb," *BEM* 4 (1818): 600.

52. [John Wilson and others], "Preface," *BEM* 19 (1826): xxiv. This was a collaboration between William Maginn, David Robinson, John Galt, and Wilson; 20 to 29 are obviously Wilson's: see Brian M. Murray, "The Authorship of Some Unidentified or Disputed Articles in *Blackwood's Magazine," Studies in Scottish Literature* 4 (1966–67): 153."[T]houghts that breathe, words that burn" is an allusion is to Gray's *Progress of Poetry:* "Bright-eyed Fancy, hov'ring o'er, / Scatters from her pictured urn / Thouoghts that breathe and words that burn" (3:3:2).

53. Jon Klancher, *The Making of English Reading Audiences, 1790–1832* (Madison: University of Wisconsin Press, 1987), 54–55.

54. Fiona Stafford, "The *Edinburgh Review* and the Representation of Scotland," in *British Romanticism and the Edinburgh Review,* ed. Massimiliano Demata and Duncan Wu (New York: Palgrave Macmillan, 2002), 44.

55. [John Stuart Mill], "Periodical Literature: 2. Edinburgh Review," *Westminster Review* 1 (1824): 521.

56. Colin Kidd, *Subverting Scotland's Past: Scottish whig historians and the creation of an Anglo-British identity, 1689–c.1830* (Cambridge: Cambridge University Press, 1993), 255.

57. W. G., "The Lord Advocate's Address to Auld Reekie's Sons," Edinburgh, 1832. The words quoted are taken from a song, "Francis Jeffrey," following this short "address." "W. G." seems to have been a Tory satirist—the song is in mock praise.

58. Sydney Smith, *The Letters of Sydney Smith*, ed. Nowell Smith, 2 vols. (Oxford: Oxford University Press, 1953), 1:331–32 (August 7, 1819). Mill's article and Smith's comment are both discussed in Stafford's essay.

59. Francis Jeffrey to Thomas Carlyle, September 23, 1828, NLS MS 787, ff. 28–29.

60. Macvey Napier, *Selections from the Correspondence of the Late Macvey Napier*, ed. Macvey Napier (London: Macmillan, 1879), 65.

61. [John Wilson], "Meg Dods's Cookery," *BEM* 19 (1826): 656; Wilson, *WPW* 4:61.

62. [John Wilson], "Cruickshank on Time," *BEM* 21 (1827): 786; Wilson, *WPW* 4:145.

63. [John Wilson], "Preface to a Review of the Chronicles of the Canongate," *BEM* 22 (1827): 554.

64. Ibid., 546.

65. Thomas Carlyle, *Reminiscences*, ed. Kenneth J. Fielding and Ian Campbell, Oxford World's Classics (Oxford: Oxford University Press, 1997), 420.

66. [Wilson], "Meg Dods's Cookery," 659; *WPW*, V, 72–73.

67. [Wilson], "Cruickshank on Time," 779.

68. [Wilson], "Preface to a Review," 546.

69. [John Wilson], "Green's Guide to the Lakes of England," *BEM* 12 (1822): 87.

70. Carey McIntosh, *The Evolution of English Prose, 1700–1800: Style, Politeness, and Print Culture* (Cambridge: Cambridge University Press, 1998), esp. 36–37.

71. Ian Gordon, *The Movement of English Prose*, English Language Series (London: Longmans, 1966), 153–61.

72. Adam Potkay, *The Fate of Eloquence in the Age of Hume* (Ithaca: Cornell University Press, 1994), 67–70, 69, 95.

73. The interplay between the conversation and the periodical has been observed before. As Clifford Siskin has noted, the editors of many literary magazines around the middle of the eighteenth century marketed their magazines as "conversations" with readers, hence effectively soliciting from those same readers cost-free contributions, usually contributions of fiction: *The Work of Writing: Literature and Social Change in Britain, 1700–1830* (Baltimore: Johns Hopkins University Press, 1988), 163–70.

74. Jürgen Habermas, *The Structural Transformation of the Public Sphere: An Inquiry into a Category of Bourgeois Society*, trans. Thomas Burger and Frederick Lawrence (London: Polity, 1989), 40–43. In his recent and important study of the European Enlightenment, John Robertson notes that by the 1740s Scotland, with its abundance of voluntary societies, had developed a public sphere in ways that other hotbeds of Enlightenment thought (e.g. France and the Italian provinces) had not: *The Case for the Enlightenment: Scotland and Naples 1680–1760* (Cambridge: Cambridge University Press, 2005), 372–73.

75. Stephen Copley, "Commerce, Conversation, and Politeness in the Early Eighteenth-Century Periodical," *British Journal for Eighteenth-Century Studies* 18 (1995): 63–77.

76. Polite society was to be found in coffeehouses and salons, where "men and women met each other as friends and equals and were able to enjoy the sense of ease that good conversation could bring. Addison and Steele saw coffee-house conversation as a form of social interaction that taught men tolerance, moderation and the pleasures of consensus": Phillipson, "The Scottish Enlightenment," 26–27.

77. David Hume, "On Essay-Writing," in *Selected Essays*, ed. Stephen Copley, World's Classics (London: Oxford Univesity Press: 1998), 1–5.

78. McElroy, *Scotland's Age of Improvement*, 15.

79. Quoted in W. J. Couper, *The Edinburgh Periodical Press*, 2 vols. (Stirling: Eneas Mackay, 1908), 1:143.

80. Quoted in Couper, *The Edinburgh Periodical Press*, 2:151.

81. Derek Roper, *Reviewing before the Edinburgh, 1788–1802* (London: Methuen, 1978), 45.

82. Walter Scott, *Letters of Sir Walter Scott*, ed. H. J. C. Grierson, 12 vols (London: Constable, 1932), 1:216 (March 10, 1804).

83. Lawrence Dundas Campbell, *Reply to the Strictures of the Edinburgh Review on the Foreign Policy of Marquis Wellesley's Administration in India* (London: T. Cadell and W. Davies, 1807), 7.

84. Alexander Boswell, *Epistle to the Edinburgh Reviewers* (Edinburgh: Mundell, 1803), 4, 7.

85. Cockburn, *LLJ* 1:31–32.

86. [Walter Scott and William Laidlaw], "The Sagacity of a Shepherd's Dog," *BEM* 2 (1818): 417–20.

87. John Gibson Lockhart, *Memoirs of the Life of Sir Walter Scott*, 5 vols. (London: Macmillan, 1900), 3:187.

88. Quoted in Gerald Bullett, *Sydney Smith: A Biography and a Selection* (London: Michael Joseph, 1951), 44–45.

89. On which see Kenneth Simpson, *The Protean Scot: The Crisis of Identity in Eighteenth-Century Scottish Literature* (Aberdeen: Aberdeen University Press, 1988), passim but esp. 6.

90. On the increasing availability of periodicals over the course of the eighteenth century: T. C. W. Blanning, *The Culture of Power and the Power of Culture: Old Regime Europe 1660–1789* (Oxford: Oxford University Press, 2002), 156–57. On periodical reading at the century's end: Richard D. Altick, *The English Common Reader: a Social History of the Mass Reading Public 1800–1900* (Chicago: University of Chicago Press, 1957), 47, 392.

91. "Restoration of the Parthenon for the National Monument," *Scots Magazine* 85 (1820): 99–105 (99).

92. [James Hogg, John Gibson Lockhart, and John Wilson], "Translation from an Ancient Chaldee Manuscript," *BEM* 2 (1817): 89.

93. Ian Duncan, *Scott's Shadow: The Novel in Romantic Edinburgh* (Princeton: Princeton University Press, 2007), 46–69.

94. Janet Adam Smith, "Some Eighteenth-century Ideas of Scotland," in *Scotland in the Age of Improvement: Essays in Scottish History in the Eighteenth Century*, ed. N. T. Phillipson and Rosalind Mitchison (Edinburgh: Edinburgh University Press, 1970), 107–24; cf. T. C. Smout, "Problems of Nationalism, Identity and Improvement in Later Eighteenth-century Scotland," in *Improvement and Enlightenment*, ed. T. M. Devine (Edinburgh: John Donald, 1989), 1–21.

95. [Thomas Carlyle], "Burns," *ER* 48 (1828): 289; *WTC* 24: 289–90.

96. Cockburn, *LLJ* 2:83 (September 8, 1803).

97. Ernest Gellner, *Nations and Nationalism*, New Perspectives on the Past, ed. R. I. Moore (Ithaca: Cornell University Press, 1983), 39–52, and esp. 50–51.

98. Joanne Shattock, "The 'Review-like Essay' and the 'Essay-like Review,'" in *Politics and Reviewers: The Edinburgh and the Quarterly in the Early Victorian Age* (Leicester: Leicester University Press, 1989), 104–24.

99. Ina Ferris, *The Achievement of Literary Authority: Gender, History, and the Waverley Novels* (Ithaca: Cornell University Press, 1991), 29–30.

100. Paul Keen, *The Crisis of Literature in the 1790s: Print Culture and the Public Sphere*, Cambridge Studies in Romanticism, 36, ed. Marilyn Butler and James Chandler (Cambridge: Cambridge University Press, 1999), 115–25.

101. J. H. Alexander provides an excellent study of reviewing in the period 1800 to 1802 in *Two Studies in Romantic Reviewing: Edinburgh Reviewers and the English Tradition*, ed. James Hogg, 2 vols., Romantic Reassessment, 49 (Salzburg: Institut für Englische Sprache und Literatur, Universität Salzburg, 1976), 1:55–102; the quotation from the *Critical* appears on 57.

102. "John Charles O'Reid" [i.e. Josiah Conder], *Reviewers Reviewed; Including an Inquiry into the Moral and Intellectual Habits of Criticism* (Oxford: J. Bartlett, 1811), 5–6. In 1814 Conder became the proprietor of the nonconformist *Eclectic Review*, founded in 1805 on the older, humbler model.

103. [Conder], *Reviewers Reviewed*, 63.

104. Parker, *Literary Magazines and British Romanticism*, 27. Italics mine.

105. Henry Crabb Robinson, *Henry Crabb Robinson on Books and Their Writers*, ed. Edith Morley, 3 vols. (London: J. M. Dent, 1938), 1:28 (March 29, 1811).

CHAPTER 3. "A DEAL MORE SAFE . . ."

1. David Allan, *Virtue, Learning, and Scottish Enlightenment* (Edinburgh: Edinburgh University Press, 1993), 29–66.

2. This is why art forms such as painting and architecture, which at least in theory lent themselves to specific purposes, were both practiced and encouraged by Scottish Calvinists since the Reformation; see M. P. Ramsay, *Calvin and Art Considered in Relation to Scotland* (Edinburgh: Moray Press, 1938), 41–83.

3. Herbert Lüthy, "Variations on a Theme by Max Weber," in *International Calvinism, 1541–1715*, ed. Menna Prestwich (Oxford: Clarendon Press, 1985), 369–90; John T. MacNeill, *The History and Character of Calvinism* (Oxford: Oxford University Press, 1954), 222, 419, 431.

4. [Thomas M'Crie], 'Review of Tales of My Landlord,' *Edinburgh Christian Instructor*, 7 (1817), 41–73 (41).

5. Walter Scott, *The Tale of Old Mortality*, ed. Douglas S. Mack (Harmondsworth: Penguin, 1999 [1816]), 188 (chapter 23); John Galt, *Annals of the Parish* (1821), vol. 2 of *The Works of John Galt*, 10 vols., ed. D. S. Meldrum and William Roughead (Edinburgh: John Grant, 1936), 25 (chapter 42).

6. Lawrence E. Klein, *Shaftesbury and the Culture of Politeness: Moral Discourse and Cultural Politics in Early Eighteenth-Century England* (Cambridge: Cambridge University Press, 1994), 5–6.

7. See Klein, *Shaftesbury*, 9–10, 154–94. Allegiances were somewhat more compli-

cated that this, to be sure: the above-named figures were attempting to fashion a new Whig-dominated polity; they were all Whigs, as were most (though not all) Evangelicals in the Kirk throughout the eighteenth century. Still, for Evangelicals there was always something of deism and skepticism in talk of politeness.

8. See Richard B. Sher, *Church and University in the Scottish Enlightenment: The Moderate Literati of Edinburgh* (Edinburgh: Edinburgh University Press, 1985), 57–58.

9. John Erskine, *Discourses Preached on Several Occasions*, 2 vols (Edinburgh: Ogle and Aikman, 1804), II, 318.

10. Quoted in a favorable review of Charters's 1810 volume, *Sermons*, in *The Works of Thomas Chalmers*, 25 vols. (Edinburgh: Constable, 1851–54), 12:304–5.

11. So recalled Hogg's brother William in "Some Particulars Relative to the Ettrick Shepherd," *New Monthly Review* 46 (1836): 445.

12. Since the terms "polite" and "elegant" began to fall out of use around the beginning of the nineteenth century, where this chapter is headed, I will begin here to use the term "imaginative"; by "imaginative literature" I mean, roughly, poetry and fiction that is not exclusively religious or devotional.

13. Which was the attitude of many in Glasgow business circles who objected to the University's emphasis on non-"useful" subjects such as classical literature; see Richard B. Sher, "Commerce, Religion, and the Enlightenment in Eighteenth-century Glasgow," in *Glasgow*, ed. T. M. Devine and Gordon Jackson (Manchester: Manchester University Press, 1995), I: *Beginnings to 1830*, 342–351.

14. Henry Mackenzie, *The Anecdotes and Egotisms of Henry Mackenzie*, ed. Harold William Thomson (Oxford: Oxford University Press, 1927), 184–85.

15. James Mackintosh, *Memoirs of the Life of the Right Honourable Sir James Mackintosh*, ed. Robert James Mackintosh, 2 vols. (London: Edward Moxon, 1835), 1:15. "It is not improbable," records Mackintosh's son and editor of these memoirs, "that during the latter part of his residence [at university] he wished to shake off the poet."

16. Quoted in D. M. Moir's memoir of Balfour in a collection of the latter's poems, *Weeds and Wildflowers* (Edinburgh: Daniel Lizars, 1830), xiii–xiv.

17. John Galt, *Literary Life and Miscellanies*, 3 vols. (Edinburgh, 1834), 1:57.

18. Much, of course, has been written about the ways in which Scott used his anonymity as the Author of Waverley for his own literary and cultural purposes: see, most recently, Jerome McGann, "My Kinsman Walter Scott," in *The Scholar's Art: Literary Studies in a Managed World* (Chicago: University of Chicago Press, 2006), 71–87. McGann understands Scott's use of his own authorial personality as part of a "postmodern" tradition in which the author's presence determines important characteristics of narrative dynamics. I tend toward a less highfalutin explanation. Scott, I think, was simply embarrassed about the idea of himself as a writer of fiction, and endeavored—sometimes cleverly, often halfheartedly—to complicate or obscure the association in common parlance between Walter Scott and novels.

19. Sir Walter Scott, *Letters of Sir Walter Scott*, ed. H. J. C. Grierson, 12 vols. (London: Constable, 1932), 3:479 (June 28, 1814). John Sutherland has speculated that Scott's ballad-collecting activities in 1799 and 1800 (and the "minstrelsy" theory behind them—namely that the Border ballads had come originally from court-employed minstrels) appealed to him partly because the ballads represented literary works by men firmly ensconced within hierarchy of professional life: John Sutherland, *The Life of Walter Scott: A Critical Biography* (Oxford: Blackwell, 1995), 76.

20. William Beattie, *Life and Letters of Thomas Campbell*, 3 vols. (London: Hall, Virtue, 1850), 1:110.

21. Robert P. Gillies, *Memoirs of a Literary Veteran*, 3 vols (London: Richard Bentley, 1851), I: 203.

22. Quoted in *The Poetical Works of David Macbeth Moir*, ed. Thomas Aird, 2 vols (Edinburgh: Blackwood, 1852), 1:xxxvii.

23. *LLJ* 1:62.

24. [Francis Jeffrey], "Southey's Madoc: A Poem," *ER* 7 (1805): 1–29 (1); "Raymond's Life of Dermody," *ER* 8 (1806): 159.

25. Richard B. Sher, "Literature and the Church of Scotland," in *1660–1800*, ed. Andrew Hook, vol. 2 of *The History of Scottish Literature*, ed. Cairns Craig (Aberdeen: Aberdeen University Press, 1987–89), 259–71.

26. Ian D. L. Clark, "From Protest to Reaction: The Moderate Regime in the Church of Scotland, 1752–1805," in *Scotland in the Age of Improvement: Essays in Scottish History in the Eighteenth Century*, ed. N. T. Phillipson and Rosalind Mitchison (Edinburgh: Edinburgh University Press, 1970), 200–223.

27. See John R. McIntosh, *Church and Theology in Enlightenment Scotland: The Popular Party, 1740–1800* (East Linton: Tuckwell Press, 1998), 84–91.

28. Quoted in George Otto Trevelyan, *The Life and Letters of Lord Macaulay*, 2 vols. (London: Longmans, Green, 1876), 1:60.

29. *The Caledonian Mercury*, April 23, 1783.

30. E.g. Elizabeth Hamilton, *The Cottagers of Glenburnie*, 2nd ed. (Edinburgh: Ballantyne, 1808), 297 (chapter 5); or Susan Ferrier, *Marriage*, ed. Herbert Foltinek, World's Classics (Oxford: Oxford world's Classics, 1997 [1818]), 205 (volume 2, chapter 9).

31. Such apprehensions are not confined to the eighteenth and nineteenth centuries. The contemporary American Jewish novelist Cynthia Ozick has expressed serious doubts about the activity of writing fiction; she suggests in one of her essays that the idea of being a Jewish writer may be "what rhetoricians call an 'oxymoron'—a pointed contradiction, in which one arm of the phrase clashes so profoundly with the other as to annihilate it": see Hillel Halkin, "What is Cynthia Ozick About?" *Commentary* 119:1 (January 2005): 53.

32. Paul Keen, *The Crisis of Literature in the 1790s: Print Culture and Public Sphere*, Cambridge Studies in Romanticism, 36, ed. Marilyn Butler and James Chandler (Cambridge: Cambridge University Press, 1999), 78.

33. William Wordsworth, *Prose Works of William Wordsworth*, ed. W. J. B. Owen and J. W. Smyser, 3 vols. (Oxford: Clarendon, 1974), 1:138–39.

34. M. H. Abrams, *The Mirror and the Lamp: Romantic Theory and the Critical Tradition* (London: Oxford University Press, 1953), 97–99.

35. Michael O'Neill, *Romanticism and the Self-conscious Poem* (Oxford: Clarendon, 1997), xxiii.

36. Frank Kermode discusses isolation in Romantic writing in *Romantic Image* (London: Routledge and Kegan Paul, 1957), 1–29.

37. Ian Duncan, with Leith Davis and Janet Sorenson, "Introduction," in *Scotland and the Borders of Romanticism*, ed. Davis, Duncan, and Sorenson (Cambridge: Cambridge University Press, 2004), 6, 10. In addition to the chapters in this volume, note Leith Davis, "From Fingal's Harp to Flora's Song: Scotland, Music, and Romanticism," *Wordsworth Circle* 31 (2000): 93–97; and the entries for James Beattie, Robert Burns, James Hogg, James MacPherson, and Walter Scott in *A Handbook to English Romanticism*, ed. Jean Raimond and J. R. Watson (New York: St. Martin's, 1992).

38. Kenneth Simpson, *The Protean Scot: The Crisis of Identity in Eighteenth Century Scottish Literature* (Aberdeen: Aberdeen University Press, 1988), 9.

39. Alvin Kernan, *Printing Technology, Letters, and Samuel Johnson* (Princeton: Princeton University Press, 1987), esp. 8–23; also Terry Belanger, "Publishers and Writers in Eighteenth-Century England," in *Books and Their Readers in Eighteenth-century England*, ed. Isabel Rivers (London: St. Martin's, 1982), 5–25.

40. Mark Rose, *Authors and Owners: The Invention of Copyright* (Oxford: Oxford University Press, 1993), 92–97.

41. Clifford Siskin, *The Work of Writing: Literature and Social Change in Britain, 1700–1830* (Baltimore: Johns Hopkins University Press, 1988), 155–63.

42. See Iain McCalman's excellent overview, "Publishing," in *The Oxford Companion to the Romantic Age*, ed. Iain McCalman (Oxford: Oxford University Press, 1999), 197–206.

43. Quoted in Thomas Constable, *Archibald Constable and His Literary Correspondents*, 3 vols. (Edinburgh: Edmonston and Douglas, 1873), 3:151 (December 29, 1814).

44. [John Gibson Lockhart], *Peter's Letters to His Kinsfolk*, 2nd ed. (i.e. 1st), 3 vols. (Edinburgh: Blackwood, 1819), 1:209–12 and 2:174–201.

45. Andrew Lang, *The Life and Letters of John Gibson Lockhart*, 2 vols. (London: J. C. Nimmo, 1897), 1:1–15; Marion Lochhead, *John Gibson Lockhart* (London: John Murray, 1954), 4–8.

46. See Peter Murphy on the contrasting approaches to profit-making adopted by Wordsworth and Scott in *Poetry as an Occupation and an Art in Britain, 1760–1830*, Cambridge Studies in Romanticism, 4, ed. Marilyn Butler and James Chandler (Cambridge: Cambridge University Press, 1993), 136–240.

47. J. W. Saunders, *The Profession of English Letters* (London: Routledge and Kegan Paul, 1964), 158–159. More recently Jerome McGann has called this the "Romantic Ideology," that conception of poetic life, advocated first by Romantic poets themselves and later by generations of critics and scholars, in which "only a poet and his works can transcend a corrupting appropriation by 'the world' of politics and money": *The Romantic Ideology: A Critical Investigation* (Chicago: University of Chicago Press, 1983), 13.

48. [Walter Scott], "On the Present State of Periodical Criticism," *Edinburgh Annual Register* 2, Part 2 (1811): 566.

49. Jeffrey Cox, *Poetry and Politics in the Cockney School: Keats, Shelley, Hunt and their Circle*, Cambridge Studies in Romanticism, 31, ed. Marilyn Butler and James Chandler (Cambridge: Cambridge University Press, 1998), 22; Nicholas Roe, "Introduction," in *Keats and History*, ed. Nicholas Roe (Cambridge: Cambridge University Press, 1995), 3.

50. Scott expressed his complaints in his essay "On the Present State of Periodical Criticism," 574–79.

51. Sutherland, *Life of Walter Scott*, 233.

52. [John Gibson Lockhart], "On the Periodical Criticism of England," *BEM* 2 (1818): 671.

53. [Lockhart], *Peter's Letters*, 1:118–20; [Lockhart] *Reginald Dalton*, 3 vols. (Edinburgh: Blackwood, 1823), II, 36.

54. John Gibson Lockhart, *John Bull's Letter to Lord Byron*, ed. Alan Lang Strout (Norman: Oklahoma University Press, 1947 [1821]), 68.

55. [John Gibson Lockhart], "On the Cockney School of Poetry. No. 1," *BEM* 2 (1817): 39.

56. Ibid., 40. The two volumes of *The Life of John Buncle*, by the devoutly Unitarian Thomas Amory, appeared in 1756 and 1766; "The Flower and the Leaf," a fifteenth-century imitation of Chaucer, was translated by Dryden; "Launcelot" is Malory's.

57. Peter T. Murphy, "Impersonation and Authorship in Romantic Britain," *ELH* 59 (1992): 628. Murphy subsumes Lockhart's maneuver in this review under the Blackwoodians' general strategy of conflating people and their writing, the real and the representational.

58. [John Gibson Lockhart], "On the Cockney School of Poetry. No. 4," *BEM* 3 (1818): 520. The quotation comes from "Sleep and Poetry": "O Poesy! for thee I hold my pen / That am not yet a glorious denizen / Of thy wide heaven — Should I rather kneel / Upon some mountain-top until I feel."

59. M. C. Hildyard, *Lockhart's Literary Criticism* (Oxford: Basil Blackwell, 1931), 8.

60. [John Gibson Lockhart], "On the Cockney School of Poetry. No. 5," *BEM* 5 (1819): 97.

61. Ibid., 98.

62. [Lockhart], *Peter's Letters*, 2:300.

63. Ibid., 1:102–3.

64. [John Gibson Lockhart], "Sir Egerton Brydges's Recollections," *BEM* 17 (1825): 506.

65. Martha Woodmansee, "The Genius and the Copyright: Economic and Legal Conditions of the Emergence of the 'Author,'" *Eighteenth-century Studies* 17 (1984): 425–48.

66. [Lockhart], "Sir Egerton Brydges's Recollections," 507.

67. [John Gibson Lockhart], "Lives of the Novelists," *QR* 34 (1826): 367.

68. [John Gibson Lockhart], "Croker's Edition of Boswell," *QR* 46 (1831): 23. Cf. Lockhart's *Life of Robert Burns*, Everyman's Library, 156 (London: J. M. Dent, 1907 [1828]), 194.

69. [John Gibson Lockhart], "Moore's Life of Lord Byron," *QR* 44 (1831): 189–90.

70. ibid., 191–92.

71. [John Gibson Lockhart], "Life of Crabbe, by his Son," *QR* 50 (1834): 488–89.

72. [John Gibson Lockhart], "Coleridge's Table-Talk," *QR* 53 (1835): 82. Lockhart has brought together two passages in chapter 11 of the *Biographia*, several paragraphs apart in the original. The capitals are Coleridge's.

73. [Lockhart], "Coleridge's Table-Talk," 89.

74. John Gibson Lockhart, *Memoirs of the Life of Sir Walter Scott*, 5 vols. (London: Macmillan, 1900 [1837–38]), 1:274 (chapter 9, 1798–99).

75. Lockhart, *Life of Sir Walter Scott*, 2:23 (chapter 27, 1808).

76. Ibid., 2:335 (chapter 27, 1814).

77. Ibid., 4:294 (chapter 63, 1825).

78. Deprecation of his own writings is a theme running through Scott's correspondence. John Sutherland reckons it had something to do with the fact that Scott was unable to become a full-fledged soldier: "Was he," asks Sutherland, surmising Scott's thinking, "anything more than a lawyer with a limp, a lively imagination, and a happy knack with words? Other men were dying, or winning glory, in his place": Sutherland, *Life of Walter Scott*, 145.

79. Lockhart, *Life of Sir Walter Scott*, 3:94 (chapter 38, 1817). In truth, of course, Scott had little chance of getting a judgeship.

80. Ibid., 4:294 (chapter 63, 1825).

81. Ibid., 1:396–400 (chapter 14, 1805).

82. Ibid., 1:454 (chapter 15, 1806).

83. Ibid., 2:224 (chapter 25, 1812).

84. Ibid., 4:46–47 (chapter 61, 1822).

85. Ibid., 4:95–96 (chapter 63, 1823).

86. Ibid., 1:417–18 (chapter 14, 1805).

87. Ibid., 4:342 (chapter 64, 1825).

88. Ibid., 5:445–49 (Conclusion).

89. Ibid., 5, 440 (chapter 84, Conclusion).

90. [Thomas Carlyle], "Memoirs of the Life of Scott," *London and Westminster Review* 28 (1838): 336.

91. Francis Hart, *Lockhart as Romantic Biographer* (Edinburgh: Edinburgh University Press, 1971), 164–69.

92. Alba H. Warren, *English Poetic Theory 1825–1865* (Princeton: Princeton University Press, 1950), 21.

93. [John Gibson Lockhart], "Autobiography of Sir Egerton Brydges," *QR* 51 (1834): 342–65. The book under review is the second installment of Brydges's memoir, Lockhart having reviewed the first in *Blackwood's* in 1825.

94. Virginia Blain, "Anonymity and the Discourse of Amateurism: Caroline Bowles Southey negotiates *Blackwood's*, 1820–1847," in *Victorian Journalism: Exotic and Domestic*, ed. Barbara Garlick and Margaret Harris (Queensland: Queensland University Press, 1988), 1–18; and Joanne Shattock, "Work for Women: Margaret Oliphant's Journalism," in *Nineteenth-Century Media and the Construction of Identities*, ed. Laurel Brake, Bill Bell, and David Finkelstein (New York: Palgrave, 2000), 165–77.

95. Cockburn, *LLJ* 1:126–27.

96. [Lockhart], *Peter's Letters*, 2:194–95.

97. Lockhart to Croker, July 21, 1838, NLS 1819, f. 1.

98. *Poetical Works of David Macbeth Moir*, xxix. At the time Moir was a junior partner in a Musselburgh medical practice; once he acquired seniority, it seems, being known as a poet became less problematic for his career.

99. Henry Peter Brougham, *Life and Times of Henry Lord Brougham, written by himself*, 3 vols. (Edinburgh: Blackwood, 1871), 1:255.

100. Cobkburn, *LLJ* 2:4 (October 25, 1791).

101. Cockburn, *LLJ* 2:34 (August 6, 1798). Italics mine.

102. Cockburn, *LLJ* 1:145 (May 11, 1803).

103. Francis Horner, *Memoirs and Correspondence of Francis Horner, M.P.*, ed. Leonard Horner, 2 vols. (London: John Murray, 1843), 1:212 (December 12, 1802).

104. John Galt, *Autobiography* (London: Cochrane and M'Crone, 1833), 200–1.

105. Hugh Miller, *My Schools and Schoolmasters; or, The Story of My Education* (Edinburgh: W. Johnstone and Hunter, 1854), 438.

106. [Francis Jeffrey], "Crabbe's Poems," [Francis Jeffrey], *ER* 12 (1808): 134 [Francis Jeffrey], "Keats's Poems," *ER* 34 (1820): 206; cf. "Thelwall's Poems," *ER* 2 (1802): 200.

107. [Henry Peter Brougham], "Lord Byron's Poems," *ER* 11 (1808): 288.

108. [John Wilson], "Some Observations on the 'Biographia Literaria' of S. T. Coleridge, Esq.—1817," *BEM* 2 (1818): 5.

109. [John Wilson], "Tennyson's Poems," *BEM* 31 (1832): 725; *WPW* 6:117.

110. Philip Harling, "The Perils of 'French Philosophy': Enlightenment and revolution in Tory journalism, 1800–1832," *Studies in Voltaire and the Eighteenth Century* 6 (2004): 202–4.

111. Thomas Carlyle, "The Poetry *he* liked (he did not call it Poetry) was Truth and

the Wisdom of Reality": *Reminiscences,* ed. Kenneth J. Fielding and Ian Campbell, Oxford World's Classics (Oxford: Oxford University Press, 1997), 12.

112. [Thomas Carlyle], "Novalis," *FR* 4 (1829): 97–141 (6); *WTC* 27, 7. More examples of this kind of language appear in the next chapter.

CHAPTER 4. *"OUR OWN* PERIODICAL PULPIT"

1. Terry Eagleton, *The Function of Criticism: from the Spectator to Post-Structuralism* (London: Verso, 1984), 49.

2. John Feather, "British Publishing in the Eighteenth Century: a Preliminary Subject Analysis," *The Library,* sixth series, 8 (1986): 32–46.

3. To take one quantifiable indication that this was so, the lists of new publications in the *Scots Magazine* from the 1780s and '90s were divided into two sections, "London" and "Edinburgh," and although there were far more books listed under the former, a much higher proportion of the latter were religious in content, especially sermons and collections of sermons.

4. Robert Wodrow, *Analecta: or Materials for a history of remarkable providences; mostly relating to Scotch ministers and Christians,* 4 vols. (Edinburgh: The Maitland Club, 1843), 4:129.

5. Anonymous, "Review of Bishop Horsley's Sermons," *Edinburgh Christian Instructor* 7 (1813): 178; "On the Present State of the Scottish Pulpit," *Scots Magazine,* new series, 4 (1819): 132.

6. [James Anderson], "Further Reflections on the Utility of Periodical Performance," *The Bee* 1 (1791): 171.

7. Jon Klancher, *The Making of English Reading Audiences, 1790–1832* (Madison: Wisconsin University Press, 1987), 24.

8. All of the above periodicals are discussed in W. J. Couper, *The Edinburgh Periodical Press,* 2 vols. (Stirling: Eneas Mackay, 1908), 2:178–260.

9. "This sermon, preached at Newlands, was directed against the 'new doctrine of French philosophy, the monstrous doctrine of equality.' Few of his parishioners could have understood a word of it": M. G. Watkins in the DNB.

10. "Preface," *Evangelical Magazine* 1 (1803): iv.

11. Francis Jeffrey, "Southey's Thalaba," *ER* 1 (1802): 63.

12. "Hogg would undoubtedly have expected his reader of 1834 to recognize the literary context of *Lay Sermons* as including both the Christian sermon and the essay-periodical tradition": Introduction to the *Lay Sermons,* ed. Gillian Hughes, in *The Works of James Hogg,* ed. Douglas Mack, Stirling/South Carolina Edition (Edinburgh: Edinburgh University Press, 1992), xix.

13. Ralph Jessop in "Recontextualizing Carlyle within Scottish Philosophical Discourse," *The Carlyle Society Occasional Papers* 13 (2000–2001): 34–47.

14. Ruth apRoberts, *The Ancient Dialect: Thomas Carlyle and Comparative Religion* (Berkeley: University of California Press, 1988), 27–45.

15. *CL* 4:165 (December 9, 1826).

16. *CL* 8:19 (January 28, 1835); *CL* 11:75 (April 13, 1839).

17. Ian Campbell, "Carlyle's Religion: The Scottish Background," in *Carlyle and His Contemporaries: Essays in Honor of Charles Richard Sanders* (Durham, North Carolina:

Duke University Press, 1976), 3–20. Campbell also discusses Carlyle's concept of faith, or as he usually rendered it "Belief."

18. Carlyle seems to have recognized that Lockhart semi-amateurishness: he referred to him, in his customary praise-then-damn mode, as "a dandiacal not without force, but barren and unfruitful": *CL* 6:126.

19. *WTC* 13:330–31.

20. A point not sufficiently acknowledged in M. H. Abrams, *Natural Supernaturalism: Tradition and Revolution in Romantic Literature* (New York: Norton, 1973), 375–77.

21. One exception is Roderick Watson's essay "Carlyle: the World as Text and the Text as Voice," in *The Nineteenth Century,* vol. 3 of *The History of Scottish Literature,* ed. Cairns Craig (Aberdeen: Aberdeen University Press, 1987–89), 153–67. Watson has contended that in *Sartor Resartus* Carlyle borrows from his Calvinist heritage the notion of exegeting biblical texts: *Sartor's* "Editor" exegetes not the Bible but the world itself, and that the work's emphatic style mimics the preaching of that exegesis. Watson's aim is to establish Carlyle as a forerunner of twentieth-century modernism (which he does successfully), while mine is to explain Carlyle's pre-*Sartor* interests in German literature, and to draw conclusions about Scottish culture at large. On Carlyle's use of Calvinist methods of exegesis, see also Suzy Anger's article, referenced below.

22. See *e.g.* John H. Leith, *Introduction to the Reformed Tradition* (Edinburgh: Saint Andrew Press, 1978), 78–81, 226–27.

23. John Calvin, *Institution of the Christian Religion,* trans. by Thomas Norton (Glasgow: Alexander Irvine, 1762), 504–5 (book 4, chapter 3, paragraph 3). For the sake of argument, I have quoted this rather stilted translation published in Scotland in the eighteenth century; it would probably have been available to John Johnston, the Carlyles' minister.

24. Ibid., 552 (book 4, chapter 8, paragraph 9).

25. Ibid., 485 (book 4, chapter 1, paragraph 5).

26. James L. Ainslie, *The Doctrines of Ministerial Order in the Reformed Churches of the 16th and 17th Centuries* (Edinburgh: T. & T. Clark, 1940), 40–57.

27. Quoted in Philip Schaff, *The Evangelical Protestant Creeds,* vol. 3 of *The Creeds of Christendom,* 3 vols. (New York: Harper, 1878), 461–62.

28. David George Mullan, *Scottish Puritanism, 1590–1638* (Oxford: Oxford University Press, 2000), 57; on preaching see 56–62.

29. Quoted in Schaff, *Creeds of Christendom,* 3:695–96.

30. James Russell, *Reminiscences of Yarrow* (Edinburgh: Blackwood, 1886), 21–22. "The rites of the Scottish Church," wrote the Swiss traveler H. C. Escher after attending church in Glasgow in 1814, "are different from those of the Anglican service but very similar to our rites in Switzerland. The only difference is that the sermon—two hours in length—is divided into two parts . . . And our host was by no means a member of one of the religious sects that flourish here": W. O. Henderson, ed. and trans., *Industrial Britain Under the Regency: The Diaries of Escher, Bodmer, May and de Gallois, 1814–18,* (New York: Augustus M. Kelly, 1968), 38–39.

31. Ebenezer Erskine and James Fischer, *The Assembly's Shorter Catechism Explained by Way of Question and Answer* (Glasgow: John Brown, 1760), 238–39.

32. On the influence of this work see John Macleod, *Scottish Theology in Relation to Church History Since the Reformation* (Edinburgh: Publications Committee of the Free Church of Scotland, 1943), 179.

33. Adam Gib, *A Sermon Preached at the Ordination of Mr Thomas Beveridge* (Edinburgh: Neill and Company, 1783), 32.

34. David Alec Wilson, *Carlyle Till Marriage (1795–1826)* (London: Kegan Paul, Trench, Trubner, 1923), 29. Wilson footnotes this anecdote, saying that several of Carlyle's surviving relatives told him the story, none of whom "knew [he] had heard it before." It was also "village tradition" in Ecclefechan.

35. Ian Campbell, "Carlyle and the Secession," *Records of the Scottish Church History Society* 18 (1972–74): 51–53.

36. Thomas Carlyle, *Two Reminiscences of Thomas Carlyle*, ed. John Clubbe (Durham: Duke University Press, 1974), 30.

37. See Andrew Thomson, *Life of Principal Harper* (Edinburgh: Andrew Elliot, 1881), 16–17. The letter was written to Lawson's biographer, James Macfarlane, who had sent the finished product to Carlyle.

38. Thomas Carlyle, *Reminiscences*, ed. Ian Campbell and Kenneth J. Fielding, Oxford World's Classics (Oxford: Oxford University Press, 1997), 210.

39. See Ian Campbell, "Thomas Carlyle: Borderer," *Carlyle Newsletter* 7 (1986): 4–7.

40. Thomas Carlyle, *CL* 1:60 (August 22, 1815).

41. Ibid., (December 11, 1815).

42. Carlyle, *Reminiscences*, 209.

43. Ibid., 274, 327. See e.g. from Carlyle to Jack, *CL* 5:21 (August 11, 1829): "The afternoon, after morning sermon, we spent with Mrs Richardson." Carlyle's parents spoke this way: "I am just come from sermon," Margaret Carlyle writes in 1823, as usual urging her son to persist in sermon-attendance, "and am thinking which [church] Jack and you have been attending [or] whether at all": Margaret Carlyle to Thomas Carlyle, February 15, 1823, NLS 1763, f. 84.

44. *CL* 1:113–14 (November 19, 1817).

45. Ibid. 1:103–4 (June 5, 1817).

46. Ibid. 1:130 (May 25, 1818).

47. Carlyle, *Reminiscences*, 251. "A very eminent vivacity lay in him, which could rise to complete impetuosity (glowing conviction, passionate eloquence, fiery play of heart and head),—all in a kind of *rustic* type, one might say, though wonderfully true and tender . . . his tones, in preaching, would rise to the piercingly pathetic." Yet he was a man of "little culture . . . ill-*read*, so ignorant in all that lay beyond the horizon in place or in time"; characterized by "soaking indolence, lazy brooding, and donothingism" and yet "capable of using such impetuous activity and blazing audacity as his latter years shewed. I suppose there will never again be such a Preacher in any Christian Church."

48. Quoted in Washington Wilks, *Edward Irving: An Ecclesiastical and Literary Biography* (London: Simpkin, Marshall, 1860), 18–19 (italics in original).

49. Edward Irving, *For the Oracles of God, Four Orations; For Judgment to Come, an Argument* (London: T. Hamilton, 1824), v–vi.

50. Carlyle, *Reminiscences*, 219–20.

51. Irving to Carlyle, February 23, 1823, NLS 665, f. 15.

52. Ibid., March 6 1823, NLS 665, f. 16.

53. This certainly had not been Irving's idea. Several years later, in the winter of 1832, Irving explained his and his church's excesses to Carlyle and Jane by referring continually and exclusively, as Carlyle would recall in the *Reminiscences*, to "the 13th of Corinthians" (he means the fourteenth chapter, the one about speaking in tongues—the thirteenth is the famous one about love). He recalls retorting that "an ancient Book" is not the only place where "the Most High" has revealed himself; "Authentic 'writings' of the Most High, were they found in old Books only? They were in the stars and on

the rocks, and in the brain and heart of every mortal, —*not* dubious there, to any person, as this '13th of Corinthians' very greatly was": Carlyle, *Reminiscences,* 339.

54. Carlyle, *WTC* 25:200–201. "[T]he inspired gift of God" is difficult to identify. My guess is that he has in mind 2 Timothy 3:16, "All scripture is given by inspiration of God, and is profitable for doctrine, for reproof," etc.

55. Thomas Carlyle, *Sartor Resartus,* ed. Kerry McSweeney and Peter Sabor, Oxford World's Classics (Oxford: Oxford University Press, 1987), 140–49, esp. 147.

56. Carlyle, *WTC* 25:3.

57. Christopher R. Vanden Bossche, *Carlyle and the Search for Authority* (Columbus: Ohio State University Press, 1991), chapters 1 and 2.

58. Such as Henry Crabb Robinson, Richard Holt Hutton, and G. H. Lewes; see Rosemary Ashton, *The German Idea: Four English Writers and the Reception of German Thought, 1800–1860* (Cambridge: Cambridge University Press, 1980), 90–91.

59. See Gregory Maertz, "Carlyle's Critique of Goethe: Literature and the Cult of Personality," *Studies in Scottish Literature* 29 (1986): 205–26.

60. On Carlyle's uses and misuses of Goethe, see Rosemary Ashton, "Carlyle's Apprenticeship: His Early German Criticism and His Relationship with Goethe," *Modern Language Review* 71 (1976): 1–18. On Carlyle's failure to understand Kant see Ashton, *The German Idea,* 84–86.

61. Charles Frederick Harrold, *Carlyle and German Thought, 1819–1834,* Yale Studies in English, 82 (New Haven: Yale University Press, 1934), 18.

62. Harrold, *Carlyle and German Thought,* 80; see 76–87.

63. [Thomas Carlyle], "Goethe," *FR* 2 (1828): 101; Carlyle, *WTC* 26:225.

64. See G. B. Tennyson, *"Sartor" Called "Resartus": The Genesis, Structure, and Style of Thomas Carlyle's First Major Work* (Princeton: Princeton University Press, 1965), 90–98.

65. The belief system adhered to by the Carlyles "naturally exalted labor and suffering as the chief realities of life. There was little place for Love and the other tenderer elements of Christianity. If the Maker drives a hard bargain, men will be likely to do the same with each other: they will not be inclined to give or accept mercy." The believer "strives to achieve a fierce joy in measuring up to austere standards; and the guiding spirit of one's conduct is a patient, sad stoicism which is to substitute for the 'peace which passeth understanding'"; to the Scottish Calvinist believer, "God was believed to be terribly present everywhere at every moment, testing, rewarding, judging, punishing," etc.: Harrold, *Carlyle and German Thought,* 26–27. Harrold seems to have assumed that Scottish Calvinists were all more or less like Carlyle (only not so literate).

66. Suzy Anger, "Carlyle: Between Biblical Exegesis and Romantic Hermeneutics," *Texas Studies in Literature and Language* 40 (1998): 78–96.

67. [Thomas Carlyle], "Jean Paul F. Richter," *ER* 46 (1827): 192; Carlyle, *WTC* 26:22.

68. [Thomas Carlyle], "The State of German Literature," *ER* 46 (1827): 323–24; Carlyle, *WTC* 26:51.

69. [Carlyle], "State," 324; *WTC* 26:52.

70. [Carlyle], "State," 326; *WTC* 26:53.

71. Carlyle's mother did read some of his early reviews; see Carlyle, *CL* 4:298.

72. [Thomas Carlyle], "Life and Writings of Werner," *FR* 1 (1828): 117–20; Carlyle, *WTC* 26:115–18.

73. [Thomas Carlyle], "Goethe's *Helena*," *FR* 1 (1828): 432; Carlyle, *WTC,* 26, 150–51.

74. [Carlyle], "Goethe's *Helena*," 434; Carlyle, *WTC* 26:153.

75. [Carlyle], "Goethe," 88; Carlyle, *WTC* 26:208.

76. [Carlyle], "Goethe," 105; Carlyle, *WTC* 26:230.

77. [Carlyle], "Goethe," 101; Carlyle, *WTC* 26:225–26.

78. [Carlyle], "Goethe," 115; Carlyle, *WTC* 26:242.

79. [Carlyle], "Goethe," 81; Carlyle, *WTC* 26:199.

80. [Thomas Carlyle], "Burns," *ER* 48 (1828): 277; *WTC* 26:271.

81. [Thomas Carlyle], "Novalis," *FR* 4 (1829): 97–141 (101); *WTC*, XXVII, 7.

82. [Carlyle], "Novalis," 20; Carlyle, *WTC* 27:29.

83. Carlyle refers to Irving's hand in the essay's title in a letter to his brother; see *CL* 5:81 (March 19, 1830).

84. [Thomas Carlyle], "Signs of the Times," *ER* 49 (1829): 450; Carlyle, *WTC* 27:70.

85. [Carlyle], "Signs of the Times," 454; Carlyle, *WTC* 27:76.

86. [Thomas Carlyle], "Thoughts on History," *Fraser's Magazine* 2 (1830): 416; Carlyle, *WTC* 27:90.

87. [Carlyle], "Thoughts on History," 417; Carlyle, *WTC* 27:92–93.

88. See *Correspondence between Goethe and Carlyle*, ed. Charles Eliot Norton (London: Macmillan, 1887), 18–19, 26.

89. *CL* 5:311 (August 1, 1831).

90. [Thomas Carlyle], "Characteristics," *ER* 54 (1831): 368; Carlyle, *WTC* 28:22–23.

91. Articles already mentioned by Suzy Anger and Roderick Watson reproduce many passages in *Sartor* that suggest that Teufelsdröckh's book is being treated by its "Editor," however ironically, in the manner of Scripture.

92. Carlyle, *Sartor Resartus*, 10.

93. "[T]he influence of the German language, with its declamations and sonorities, begins to be detected in his hitherto simple, educated Scots style. His letters (except to his family . . .) begin to sound high-flown and rather pompous, marking an important development in what the world would call 'Carlylese'": Simon Heffer, *Moral Desperado: A Life of Thomas Carlyle* (London: Weidenfield and Nicolson, 1995), 52–53. Cf. Tennyson, "*Sartor*" Called "*Resartus*," 36–44.

94. Quoted in Carlyle, *Two Reminiscences*, 59.

95. Carlyle, *Reminiscences*, 228.

96. *CL* 5:243–44 (March 4, 1831).

97. Ibid., 6:241 (October 16, 1832).

98. Ibid., 3:233–34 (December 20, 1824); cf. Ibid., 3:244–45 (January 9, 1825).

99. [Carlyle], "Characteristics," 354; Carlyle, *WTC* 28:25; Carlyle, "Signs," 443; Carlyle, *WTC* 27:61.

100. [Carlyle], "Burns," 267–312 (288); Carlyle, *WTC* 26:288–89.

101. [John Gibson Lockhart], "On the Pulpit Eloquence of Scotland. No. I.—Chalmers," *BEM* 2 (1817): 131.

102. *CL* 11:104 (February 16, 1839).

Conclusion

1. Hugh Miller, *Essays: Historical and Biographical, Political and Social, Literary and Scientific* (Edinburgh: William P. Nimmo, 1869), 126–27.

2. Cockburn, *LLJ* 1:160.

3. Ian Christie, *Wars and Revolution, 1760–1815* (London: Edward Arnold, 1982), 7, 158–59.

4. Francis Shepherd, *London: A History* (Oxford: Oxford University Press, 1998), 239–49.

5. See chapter 4, note 96.

6. "What is spoken or written, within this rational space, pays due deference to the niceties of class and rank; but the speech act itself, the énonciation as opposed to the énonceé, figures in its very form an equality, autonomy and reciprocity at odds with its class bound content": Terry Eagleton, *The Function of Criticism: from the Spectator to Post-Structuralism* (London: Verso, 1984), 14–15.

7. "John Charles O'Reid" [i.e. Josiah Conder], *Reviewers Reviewed; Including an Inquiry into the Moral and Intellectual Habits of Criticism* (Oxford: J. Bartlett, 1811), 26.

8. John O. Hayden, "Introduction," in *The Romantic Age, 1789–1836*, vol. 2 of *British Literary Magazines*, ed. by Alvin Sullivan, 4 vols. (Westport, Conn.: Greenwood, 1983–86), xv–xvi.

Bibliography

Primary Sources

"Address to the Public." *The Christian Magazine; or, Evangelical Repository* 1 (1797): i–v.

Advice to the Whigs; with Hints to the Democrats; and Cautions to the Edinburgh Reviewers (London: J. Hatchard, 1810).

[Anderson, James]. "Further Remarks on the Utility of Periodical Performance." *The Bee* 1 (1791): 167–71.

Aspinall, A., ed. *The Letters of King George IV, 1812–1830.* 3 vols. Cambridge: Cambridge University Press, 1938.

Bagehot, Walter. *Literary Studies.* 2 vols. Everyman's Library. London: J. M. Dent, 1911.

Balfour, Alexander. *Weeds and Wildflowers.* Edinburgh: Daniel Lizars, 1830.

Beattie, James. *Scoticisms, Arranged in Alphabetical Order, Designed to Correct Improprieties of Speech and Writing.* Edinburgh: William Creech, 1787.

Beattie, William. *Life and Letters of Thomas Campbell.* 3 vols. London: Hall, Virtue, 1850.

Blair, Hugh. *Lectures on Rhetoric and Belle Lettres.* 2 vols. Edinburgh: William Creech, 1783.

[Boswell, Alexander]. *Epistle to the Edinburgh Reviewers.* Edinburgh: Mundell, 1803.

Boswell, James. *Boswell in Extremes, 1776–1778.* Edited by Charles Weis and Frederick Pottle. London: Heinemann, 1971.

Brougham, Henry Peter. *Life and Times of Henry Lord Brougham, written by himself.* 3 vols. Edinburgh: Blackwood, 1871.

[————], "Lord Byron's Poems." *Edinburgh Review* 11 (1808): 285–89.

Brunton, Mary. *Emmeline, with Some Other Pieces.* Edinburgh: Manners and Miller, 1819.

Calvin, John. *Institution of the Christian Religion.* Translated by Thomas Norton. Glasgow: Alexander Irvine, 1762.

Campbell, Lawrence Dundas. *A Reply to the Strictures of the Edinburgh Review on the Foreign Policy of Marquis Wellesley's Administration in India.* London: T. Cadell and W. Davies, 1807.

Carlyle, Thomas. "Burns." *Edinburgh Review* 48 (1828): 267–312.

[————]. "Characteristics." *Edinburgh Review* 54 (1831): 351–83.

————. *The Collected Letters of Thomas Carlyle and Jane Welsh Carlyle,* edited by Charles Richard Sanders, Clyde de L. Ryals, et al. 32 vols. Durham, North Carolina: Duke University Press, 1970–).

[————]. "Goethe." *Foreign Review* 2 (1828): 80–127.

197

[————]. "Goethe's *Helena.*" *Foreign Review,* 1 (1828): 429–68.

[————]. "Jean Paul F. Richter." *Edinburgh Review* 46 (1827): 177–95.

[————]. "Life and Writings of Werner." *Foreign Review* 1 (1828): 95–141.

[————]. "The Life of Heyne." *Foreign Review* 2 (1828): 437–64.

[————]. "Memoirs of the Life of Scott." *London and Westminster Review* 28 (1838): 293–345.

[————]. "Novalis." *Foreign Review* 4 (1829): 97–141.

————. *Reminiscences.* Edited by Ian Campbell and Kenneth J. Fielding. Oxford World's Classics. Oxford: Oxford University Press, 1997.

————. *Sartor Resartus.* Edited by Kerry McSweeney and Peter Sabor. Oxford World's Classics (Oxford: Oxford University Press, 1987).

[————]. "Signs of the Times." *Edinburgh Review* 49 (1829): 439–59.

[————]. "The State of German Literature." *Edinburgh Review* 46 (1827): 304–51.

[————]. "Thoughts on History." *Fraser's Magazine* 2 (1830): 413–18.

————. *Two Reminiscences of Thomas Carlyle.* Edited by John Clubbe. Durham: Duke University Press, 1974.

————. *The Works of Thomas Carlyle.* Edited by H. D. Traill. Centenary Edition. 30 vols. London: Chapman and Hall, 1896–99.

Chalmers, Thomas. *The Works of Thomas Chalmers.* 25 vols. Edinburgh: Constable, 1851–54.

"The Charms of Conversation." *Scots Magazine* 59 (1797): 59–60.

Christison, Alexander. *The General Diffusion of Knowledge One Great Cause of the Prosperity of North Britain.* Edinburgh: Peter Hill, 1802.

Cockburn, Henry. *Life of Lord Jeffrey.* 2 vols. Edinburgh: Adam and Charles Black, 1852.

————. *Memorials of His Time.* Edinburgh: Adam and Charles Black, 1856.

Coleridge, Samuel Taylor. *The Collected Works of Samuel Taylor Coleridge.* 13 vols. Edited by Kathleen Coburn. Princeton: Princeton University Press, 1971–81.

[Conder, Josiah]. *Reviewers Reviewed; Including an Inquiry into the Moral and Intellectual Habits of Criticism.* Oxford: J. Bartlett, 1811.

Constable, Thomas. *Archibald Constable and His Literary Correspondents.* 3 vols. Edinburgh: Edmonston and Douglas, 1873.

Copleston, Edward. A Reply to the Calumnies of the Edinburgh Review against Oxford (Oxford: J. Cooke and J. Parker, 1808).Dodsley, Robert, *The Correspondence of Robert Dodsley, 1733–1764.* Edited by James E. Tierney. Cambridge: Cambridge University Press, 1988.

Edward, Copleston. *A Reply to the Calumnies of the Edinburgh Review against Oxford.* Oxford: J. Cooke and J. Parker, 1810.

Erskine, Ebenezer, and John Fisher. *The Assembly's Shorter Catechism Explained by Way of Question and Answer.* Glasgow: John Brown, 1760.

Erskine, John. *Discourses Preached on Several Occasions.* 2 vols. Edinburgh: Ogle and Aikman, 1804.

Farington, Joseph. *The Diary of Joseph Farington.* Edited by Kenneth Garlick, Angus Macintyre, and Kathryn Cave. 15 vols. New Haven: Yale University Press, 1970–84.

Ferrier, Susan. *Marriage*. Edited by Herbert Foltinek. Oxford World's Classics. Oxford: Oxford University Press, 1997.

Fletcher, Eliza. *Autobiography of Mrs. Fletcher*. 3rd ed. Edinburgh: Edmonston and Douglas, 1876.

Galt, John, *Autobiography*. London: Cochrane and M'Crone, 1833.

————. *Literary Life and Miscellanies*. 3 vols. Edinburgh: Blackwood, 1834.

————. *The Works of John Galt*. Edited by D. S. Meldrum and William Roughead, 10 vols. Edinburgh: John Grant, 1936.

Gib, Adam. *A Sermon Preached at the Ordination of Mr Thomas Beveridge*. Edinburgh: Neill and Company, 1783.

Gillies, Robert P. *Memoirs of a Literary Veteran*. 3 vols. London: Richard Bentley, 1851.

Grant, Ann. *Memoir and Correspondence of Mrs. Ann Grant of Laggan*. Ed. J. P. Grant. 2 vols. London: Longman, Brown, Green, and Longmans, 1844.Hamilton, Elizabeth, *The Cottagers of Glenburnie*. 2nd ed. Edinburgh: Ballantyne, 1808.

[Hamilton, Thomas; and J. G. Lockhart]. "Two Reviews of a Military Work." *Blackwood's Edinburgh Magazine* 5 (1819): 552–53.

Hamilton, Thomas. *The Youth and Manhood of Cyril Thornton*. Edited by Maurice Lindsay. Aberdeen: Association for Scottish Literary Studies, 1990.

Hazlitt, William. *Complete Works of William Hazlitt*. Edited by P. P. Howe. 22 vols. London: J. M. Dent.

Henry, Robert. *The History of Great Britain, from the First Invasion of It by the Romans under Julius Cæsar*. 6 vols. London: T. Cadell, 1771–93.

Hogg, James. *Lay Sermons*. Ed. Gillian Hughes. In *Works of James Hogg*, Stirling/South Carolina Edition, ed. Douglas Mack. Edinburgh: Edinburgh University Press, 1995– .

[Hogg, William], "Some Particulars Relative to the Ettrick Shepherd." *New Monthly Magazine* 46 (1836): 443–46.

[————]. John Gibson Lockhart, and John Wilson]. "Translation from an Ancient Chaldee Manuscript." *Blackwood's Edinburgh Magazine* 2 (1817): 89–96.

Horner, Francis. *The Horner Papers: Selections from the Letters and Miscellaneous Writings of Francis Horner, M.P., 1795–1817*. Edited by Kenneth Bourne and William Banks Taylor. Edinburgh: Edinburgh University Press, 1994.

————. *Memoirs and Correspondence of Francis Horner, M.P.* Edited by Leonard Horner. 2 vols. London: John Murray, 1843.

Irving, Edward, *For the Oracles of God, Four Orations; For the Judgment to Come, an Argument*. London: T. Hamilton, 1824.

————. *The Last Days: A Discourse on the Evil Character of These Our Times*. (London: Sheeley and Burnside, 1828.

————. *The Signs of the Times*. (London: Andrew Panton, 1829.

[Jeffrey, Francis]. "Bentham, Princepes de Legislation, par Dumont." *Edinburgh Review* 4 (1804): 1–26.

————. Commonplace Book of Notes and Books. Thomas Cooper Library, University of South Carolina 4825.J2. 1798.————. *Contributions to the Edinburgh Review*. 4 vols. London: Longman, Brown, Green, and Longmans, 1844.

[————]. "Crabbe's Poems." *Edinburgh Review* 12 (1808): 131–51.

[————]. "The Dangers of the Country." *Edinburgh Review* 10 (1807): 1–29.

[————]. "De Lille, Malheur et Pitié: Poëme." *Edinburgh Review* 3 (1803): 26–42.

[————]. "Keats's Poems." *Edinburgh Review* 34 (1820): 203–13.

[————]. "Mounier, De L"Influence des Philosophes." *Edinburgh Review* 1 (1802): 1–18.

[————]. "Memoirs de Bailly." *Edinburgh Review* 6 (1805): 137–61.

[————]. "Millar's View of the English Government." *Edinburgh Review* 3 (1803): 154–81.

[————]. "Montgomery's Poems." *Edinburgh Review* 9 (1807): 347–54.

[————]. "Mrs. Hamilton's Cottagers." *Edinburgh Review* 12 (1808): 401–10.

[————]. "Pamphlets on the Catholic Question." *Edinburgh Review* 11 (1807): 116–44.

[————]. "Poems by W. Wordsworth." *Edinburgh Review* 11 (1807): 214–31.

[————]. "Raymond's Life of Dermody." *Edinburgh Review* 8 (1806): 159–67.

[————]. "Reliques of Burns." *Edinburgh Review* 13 (1809): 249–76.

[————], 'southey's Madoc: A Poem." *Edinburgh Review* 7 (1805): 1–29.

[————], 'southey's Thalaba." *Edinburgh Review* 1 (1802): 63–83.

[————]. "Thelwall's Poems." *Edinburgh Review* 2 (1802): 197–202.

[————]. "Wordsworth's Excursion." *Edinburgh Review* 24 (1814): 1–30.

[————]. "The Works of Benjamin Franklin." *Edinburgh Review* 8 (1806): 327–44.

[————. and Henry Brougham]. "Don Pedro Cevallos on the French Usurpation of Spain." *Edinburgh Review* 12 (1808): 215–34.

[————. and Henry Brougham]. "Parliamentary Reform." *Edinburgh Review* 17 (1811): 253–90.

Johnson, Samuel. *Journey to the Western Isles of Scotland.* James Boswell. *Journal of a Tour to the Hebrides.* Penguin Classics. Ed. Primo Levi. Harmondsworth: Penguin, 1988.[Lockhart, John Gibson]. "Autobiography of Sir Egerton Brydges." *Quarterly Review* 51 (1834): 342–65.

[————]. "Coleridge's Table-Talk." *Quarterly Review* 53 (1835): 79–103.

[————]. "Croker's Edition of Boswell." *Quarterly Review* 46 (1831): 1–46.

[————]. "Extracts from Mr. Wastle's Diary No. II." *Blackwood's Edinburgh Magazine* 7 (1820): 317–22.

[————], *John Bull's Letter to Lord Byron.* Edited by Alan Lang Strout. 1821. Reprint, Norman: Oklahoma University Press, 1947.

[————]. "Life of Crabbe, by his Son." *Quarterly Review*, 50 (1834): 468–508.

————. *Life of Robert Burns.* Everyman's Library, 156. London: J. M. Dent, 1907.

[————]. "Lives of the Novelists." *Quarterly Review* 34 (1826): 349–78.

[————], *Memoirs of the Life of Sir Walter Scott,* 5 vols. London: Macmillan, 1900.

[————]. "Moore's Life of Lord Byron." *Quarterly Review* 44 (1831): 168–226.

[————]. "On the Cockney School of Poetry. No. 1." *Blackwood's Edinburgh Magazine* 2 (1817): 38–41.

[————]. "On the Cockney School of Poetry. No. 4." *Blackwood's Edinburgh Magazine* 2 (1818): 519–24.

[———]. "On the Cockney School of Poetry. No. 5." *Blackwood's Edinburgh Magazine* 5 (1819): 97–100.

[———]. "On the Pulpit Eloquence of Scotland. No. 1—Chalmers." *Blackwood's Edinburgh Magazine* 2 (1817): 131–40.

———. "On the Periodical Criticism of England." *Blackwood's Edinburgh Magazine*. 2 (1818): 670–79.[———]; *Peter's Letters to His Kinsfolk*. 2nd ed. [i.e. 1st]. 3 vols. Edinburgh: Blackwood, 1819.

[———]; *Reginald Dalton*. 3 vols. Edinburgh: Blackwood, 1823.

[———]. "Remarks on the Periodical Criticism of England." *Blackwood's Edinburgh Magazine* 2 (1818): 670–79.

[———], "Sir Egerton Brydges's Recollections." *Blackwood's Edinburgh Magazine* 17 (1825): 504–17.

Mackenzie, Henry. *The Anecdotes and Egotisms of Henry Mackenzie*. Edited by Harold William Thomson. Oxford: Oxford University Press, 1927.

Mackintosh, James. *Memoirs of the Life of the Right Honourable Sir James Mackintosh*. Edited by Robert James Mackintosh. 2 vols. London: Edward Moxon, 1835.

Martineau, Harriet. *Biographical Sketches*. London: Macmillan, 1862.

Masson, David. *Edinburgh Sketches and Memories*. London: Adam and Charles Black, 1892.

[M'Crie, Thomas]. "Review of Tales of My Landlord." *Edinburgh Christian Instructor* 7 (1817): 41–73.

[Mill, James]. "Education and the Poor." *Edinburgh Review* 21 (1813): 207–19.

[———]. "Periodical Criticism: 1. Edinburgh Review." *Westminster Review* 1 (1824): 206–49.

[Mill, John Stuart]. "Periodical Literature: 2. Edinburgh Review." *Westminster Review* 1 (1824): 505–41.

Millar, John. *An Historical View of the English Government*. 4 vols. 1787. Reprint, London: J. Mawman, 1803.

Miller, Hugh. *Essays: Historical and Biographical, Political and Social, Literary and Scientific*. Edinburgh: William P. Nimmo, 1869.

———. *My Schools and Schoolmasters; or, The Story of My Education* (Edinburgh: Johnstone and Hunter, 1854.

Mitchell, Hugh. *Scotticisms, Vulgar Anglicisms, and Grammatical Improprieties Corrected*. Glasgow: Falconer and Willison, 1799.

Moir, David Macbeth. *The Poetical Works of David Macbeth Moir*. Edited by Thomas Aird. 2 vols. Edinburgh: Blackwood, 1852.

Moore, Thomas. *Epistles, Odes, and Other Poems*. London: James Carpenter, 1806.

Napier, Macvey. *Selections from the Correspondence of the Late Macvey Napier*. Edited by Macvey Napier. London: Macmillan, 1879.

Norton, Charles Eliot. *Correspondence between Goethe and Carlyle*. London: Macmillan, 1887.

"On Conversation." *The North British Intelligencer or Constitutional Miscellany* 1 (1776): 163–64.

"On the Present State of the Scottish Pulpit." *Scots Magazine* 4 (1819): 131–35.

"Pantheon." *The Caledonian Mercury,* April 23, 1783.

"Pantheon." *The Caledonian Mercury,* May 24, 1783.

Peacock, Thomas Love. *Crotchet Castle.* Edited by Raymond Wright, Penguin Classics. 1831. Reprint, Harmondsworth: Penguin, 1969.

"Preface." *Evangelical Magazine* 1 (1803): iv.

"Restoration of the Parthenon for the National Monument." *Scots Magazine* 85 (1820): 99–105.

"Review of Bishop Horsley's Sermons." *Edinburgh Christian Instructor* 7 (1813): 176–95.

Robinson, Henry Crabb. *Henry Crabb Robinson on Books and Their Writers.* Edited by Edith Morley. 3 vols. London: J. M. Dent, 1938.

———. Royal Commission of Inquiry into the State of the Universities of Scotland. Evidence, Oral and Documentary: Taken and Received by the Commissioners for Visiting the Universities of Scotland. 4 vols. London: Clowes and Sons, 1837.

Russell, James. *Reminiscences of Yarrow.* Edinburgh: Blackwood, 1886.

"Scipio, Cornelius." *A Sketch of the Politics of the Edinburgh Reviewers, as Exhibited in Their Three First Numbers for the Year 1807.* London: R. S. Kirkby and J. Hatchard, 1807.

[Scott, John]. "Prospectus." *London Magazine* 1 (1820): iv.

Scott, Walter. *The Heart of Midlothian.* Edited by Claire Lamont. Oxford World's Classics 1818. Reprint, Oxford: Oxford University Press, 1982.

———. Journal of Walter Scott. Ed. WEK Anderson. Oxford: Clarendon Press, 1972.[———]. *Letters of Sir Walter Scott.* Edited by H. J. C. Grierson. 12 vols. London: Constable, 1932.

[———]. "On the Present State of Periodical Criticism." *Edinburgh Annual Register* 2, Part 2 (1811): 556–81.

———. *The Tale of Old Mortality.* Edited by Douglas S. Mack. Penguin Classics. 1816. Reprint, Harmondsworth: Penguin, 1993.

[———. and William Laidlaw]. "Sagacity of a Shepherd's Dog." *Blackwood's Edinburgh Magazine* 2 (1818): 417–20.

Scottish Universities Commission. *Evidence, Oral and Documentary, Taken by the Commissioners Appointed . . . for Visiting the Universities of Scotland.* 4 vols. London: Clowes and Sons, 1837.

Sharpe, Charles Kirkpatrick. *Letters from and to Charles Kirkpatrick Sharpe.* Edited by Alexander Allardyce. 2 vols. Edinburgh: Blackwood, 1888.

Smith, Sydney. *The Letters of Sydney Smith.* Edited by Nowell Smith. 2 vols. Oxford: Oxford University Press, 1953.

Smollett, Tobias. *The Adventures of Roderick Random.* Edited by Paul-Gabriel Boucé. 1748. Oxford World's Classics. Oxford: Oxford University Press, 1979.

———. *The Expedition of Humphry Clinker.* Edited by Angus Ross. 1771. Reprint, Penguin Classics. Harmondsworth: Penguin, 1967.

Stark, J. *Picture of Edinburgh.* Edinburgh: Constable; London: John Murray, 1806.

Stephen, Leslie. *Hours in a Library.* 3rd series. London: Smith, Elder, 1879.

Stewart, Dugald. *Collected Works of Dugald Stewart.* Edited by William Hamilton. 11 vols. Edinburgh: Constable, 1854.

"Tea Table Conversation." *Scots Magazine* 57 (1795): 578.

["W. G."]. "The Lord Advocate's Address to Auld Reekie's Sons." Edinburgh, 1832.

Wharton, R. *Remarks on the Jacobinical Tendency of the Edinburgh Review in a Letter to Lord Lonsdale.* London: J. Hatchard, 1809.

[Wilson, John]. "Account of Some Curious Clubs in London, About the Beginning of the Eighteenth Century." *Blackwood's Edinburgh Magazine* 3 (1818): 552–56.

[———]. "Cruickshank on Time." *Blackwood's Edinburgh Magazine* 21 (1827): 777–92.

[———]. "The General Question." *Blackwood's Edinburgh Magazine* 14 (1823): 332–42.

[———]. "A Glance over Selby's Ornithology." *Blackwood's Edinburgh Magazine* 20 (1826): 657–80.

[———]. "Green's Guide to the Lakes of England." *Blackwood's Edinburgh Magazine* 12 (1822): 84–90.

[———]. "The Literary Character . . . by Mr. D'Israeli." *Blackwood's Edinburgh Magazine* 4 (1818): 14–19.

[———]. "Meg Dods's Cookery." *Blackwood's Edinburgh Magazine* 19 (1826): 651–60.

[———]. "Noctes Ambrosianæ." *Blackwood's Edinburgh Magazine* 25 (1829): 525–48.

[———]. "Pilgrimage to the Kirk of Shotts." *Blackwood's Edinburgh Magazine* 5 (1819): 671–80.

[———]. "Preface to a Review of the Chronicles of the Canongate." *Blackwood's Edinburgh Magazine* 22 (1827): 533–56.

[———], "Some Observations on the Poetry of the Agricultural and That of the Pastoral Districts of Scotland." *Blackwood's Edinburgh Magazine* 4 (1819): 521–29.

[———]. "Speech Delivered by an Eminent Barrister." *Blackwood's Edinburgh Magazine* 4 (1818): 213–17.

[———]. "Tennyson's Poems." *Blackwood's Edinburgh Magazine* 31 (1832): 721–41.

[———]. "The Works of Charles Lamb." *Blackwood's Edinburgh Magazine* 4 (1818): 599–611.

———. *Works of Professor Wilson.* Edited by James Ferrier. 12 vols. Edinburgh: Blackwood and Sons, 1865.

[———. and others]. "Preface." *Blackwood's Edinburgh Magazine* 19 (1826): i–xxx.

Wodrow, Robert. *Analecta: or Materials for a history of remarkable providences; mostly relating to Scotch ministers and Christians.* 4 vols. Edinburgh: The Maitland Club, 1843.

Wordsworth, William. *Poetical Works of William Wordsworth.* Edited by E. de Selincourt and Helen Darbishire. 5 vols. Oxford: Clarendon, 1940–49.

———. *Prose Works of William Wordsworth.* Edited by W. J. B. Owen and J. W. Smyser. 3 vols. Oxford: Clarendon, 1974.

SECONDARY SOURCES

Abrams, M. H., *The Mirror and the Lamp: Romantic Theory and the Critical Tradition.* London: Oxford University Press, 1953.

———. *Natural Supernaturalism: Tradition and Revolution in Romantic Literature* (New York: Norton, 1973.

Ainslie, James L. *The Doctrines of Ministerial Order in the Reformed Churches of the 16th and 17th Centuries.* Edinburgh T. & T. Clark, 1940.

Allan, David. *Virtue, Learning, and Scottish Enlightenment.* Edinburgh: Edinburgh University Press, 1993.

Alexander, J. H.. *"Blackwood's:* Magazine as Romantic Form." *The Wordsworth Circle* 15 (1984): 57–67.

———. *Two Studies in Romantic Reviewing: Edinburgh Reviewers and the English Tradition.* Edited by James Hogg. Romantic Reassessment, 49. Salzburg: Institut für Englische Sprache und Literatur, Universität Salzburg, 1976.

Altick, Richard D. *The English Common Reader: A Social History of the Mass Reading Public 1800–1900.* Chicago: University of Chicago Press, 1957.

Anderson, R. D. *Education and the Scottish People, 1750–1918.* Oxford: Clarendon, 1995.

Anger, Suzy. "Carlyle: Between Biblical Exegesis and Romantic Hermeneutics." *Texas Studies in Literature and Language* 40 (1998): 78–96.

apRoberts, Ruth, *The Ancient Dialect: Thomas Carlyle and Comparative Religion.* Berkeley: University of California Press, 1988.

Ashton, Rosemary. "Carlyle's Apprenticeship: His Early German Criticism and His Relationship with Goethe, 1822–32." *Modern Language Review* 71 (1976): 1–18.

———. *The German Idea: Four English Writers and the Reception of German Thought, 1800–1860.* Cambridge: Cambridge University Press, 1980.

———. *Thomas and Jane Carlyle: Portrait of a Marriage.* London: Chatto and Windus, 2002.

Atkinson, R. H. M. Buddle, and G. A. Jackson. *Brougham and His Early Friends.* 3 vols. London: Darling and Pead, 1908.

Belanger, Terry. "Publishers and Writers in Eighteenth-Century England." In *Books and Their Readers in Eighteenth-century England.* Edited by Isabel Rivers. London: St. Martin's, 1982.

Berry, Neil. "The Reviewer Triumphant." *London Magazine,* new series, 33 (February/March 1994): 34–49.

Blaine, Virginia. "Anonymity and the Discourse of Amateurism: Caroline Bowles Southey negotiates *Blackwood's,* 1820–1847." In *Victorian Journalism: Exotic and Domestic.* Edited by Barbara Garlick and Margaret Harris. Queensland: Queensland University Press, 1988.

Blanning, T. C. W., *The Power of Culture and the Culture of Power: Old Regime Europe, 1660–1789.* Oxford: Oxford University Press, 2002.

Bono, Paola, *Radicals and Reformers in Late Eighteenth-Century Scotland: An Annotated Checklist of Books, Pamphlets, and Documents Printed in Scotland 1775–1800.* Scottish Studies, 6. Frankfurt am Main: Peter Lang, 1989.

Brewer, John; Neil McKendrick; and J. H. Plumb. *The Birth of a Consumer Society: The Commercialization of Eighteenth-century England.* London: Europa, 1982.

Briggs, Asa. *The Age of Improvement, 1783–1867.* London: Longmans, 1959.

Broadie, Alexander. *The Scottish Enlightenment: The Historical Age of the Historical Nation.* Edinburgh: Birlinn, 2001.

Bullett, Gerald. *Sydney Smith: A Biography and a Selection.* London: Michael Joseph, 1951.

Butler, Marilyn. "Culture's Medium: the Role of the Review." In *The Cambridge Com-*

panion to British Romanticism. Edited by Stuart Curran. Cambridge: Cambridge University Press, 1993.

———. *Peacock Displayed: A Satirist in His Context*. London: Routledge and Kegan Paul, 1979.

Campbell, Ian. "Carlyle and the Secession." *Records of the Scottish Church History Society* 18 (1972–74): 48–64.

———. "Carlyle: Style and Sense." *Carlyle Studies Annual* 14 (1994): 12–23.

———. "Carlyle's Borrowings from the Theological Library of Edinburgh University." *The Bibliotheck* 5 (1967–76): 165–68.

———. "Carlyle's Religion: The Scottish Background." In *Carlyle and his Contemporaries: Essays in Honor of Charles Richard Sanders*. Edited by John Clubbe. Durham, North Carolina: Duke University Press, 1976.

———. "Thomas Carlyle: Borderer." *Carlyle Newsletter*, 7 (1986): 4–7.

Chandler, James K. *Wordsworth's Second Nature: A Study of the Poetry and Politics*. Chicago: University of Chicago Press, 1984.

Christensen, Jerome, *Romanticism at the End of History*. Baltimore: Johns Hopkins University Press, 2000.

Christie, Ian. *Wars and Revolution, 1760–1815*. London: Edward Arnold, 1982.

Christie, William H. "Francis Jeffrey's Associationist Aesthetics." *British Journal of Aesthetics* 33 (1993): 257–70.

———. "A Recent History of Poetic Difficulty." *ELH* 67 (2000): 539–64.

Clark, Ian D. L. "From Protest to Reaction: The Moderate Regime in the Church of Scotland, 1752–1805." In *Scotland in the Age of Improvement: Essays in Scottish History in the Eighteenth Century*. Edited by N. T. Phillipson and Rosalind Mitchison. Edinburgh: Edinburgh University Press, 1970.

Clive, John. "The Earl of Buchan's Kick: A Footnote to the history of the *Edinburgh Review*." *Harvard Library Bulletin* 5 (1951): 362–70.

———. "The *Edinburgh Review*: the life and death of a periodical." In *Essays in the History of Publishing in celebration of the 250th anniversary of the House of Longman, 1724- 1974*. Edited by Asa Briggs. London: Longman, 1974): 113–39.

———. *Scotch Reviewers: The Edinburgh Review 1802–1815*. Cambridge, Mass., 1957.

Colley, Linda. *Britons: Forging the Nation 1707–1837*. New Haven: Yale University Press, 1992.

Collini, Stefan. *Absent Minds: Intellectuals in Britain*. Oxford: Oxford University Press, 2006.

———. Donald Winch, and John Burrow. *That Noble Science of Politics: A Study in Nineteenth-century Intellectual History*. Cambridge: Cambridge University Press, 1983.

Copley, Stephen. "Commerce, Conversation, and Politeness in the Early Eighteenth-Century Periodical." *British Journal for Eighteenth-Century Studies* 18 (1995): 63–77.

Couper, W. J. *The Edinburgh Periodical Press*. 2 vols. Stirling: Eneas Mackay, 1908.

Cox, Jeffrey. *Poetry and Politics in the Cockney School: Keats, Shelley, Hunt and their Circle*. Cambridge Studies in Romanticism, 31. Edited by Marilyn Butler and James Chandler Cambridge: Cambridge University Press, 1998.

Craig, David. *Scottish Literature and the Scottish People, 1680–1830*. London: Chatto and Windus, 1961.

Craig, Mary Elizabeth. *The Scottish Periodical Press, 1750–1789* Edinburgh: Oliver and Boyd, 1931.

Crawford, John. "Reading and Book use in 18th-century Scotland." The Bibliotheck 19 (1994), 23–43.Crawford, Robert. *Devolving English Literature.* Oxford: Clarendon, 1992.

Daiches, David, *Literary Essays.* Chicago: University of Chicago Press, 1956.

Davie, George Elder. *The Democratic Intellect: Scotland and Her Universities in the Nineteenth Century.* Edinburgh: Edinburgh University Press, 1961.

Davis, Leith. *Acts of Union: Scotland and the Literary Negotiation of the British Nation, 1707–1830.* Stanford, Calif.: Stanford University Press, 1998.

————. "From Fingal's Harp to Flora's Song: Scotland, Music, and Romanticism." *Wordsworth Circle* 31 (2000): 93–97.

————, Ian Duncan, and Janet Sorensen, ed. *Scotland and the Borders of Romanticism.* Cambridge: Cambridge University Press, 2004.

Duncan, Ian. *Scott's Shadow: The Novel in Romantic Edinburgh.* Princeton: Princeton University Press, 2007.

Eagleton, Terry. *The Function of Criticism: from the Spectator to Post-Structuralism.* London: Verso, 1984.

Elay, Geoff. "Nations, Publics, and Political Cultures: Placing Habermas in the Nineteenth Century." In *Habermas and the Public Sphere.* Edited by Craig Calhoun. Cambridge, Mass.: MIT Press, 1992): 289–339.

Feather, John. "British Publishing in the Eighteenth Century: a Preliminary Subject Analysis." *The Library*, sixth series, 8 (1986): 32–46.

————. *A History of British Publishing.* London: Croom Helm, 1988.

Ferris, Ina. *The Achievement of Literary Authority: Gender, History, and the Waverley Novels.* Ithaca: Cornell University Press, 1991.

Finkelstein, David. "Early Nineteenth-century Scottish Publishing." *Gaskell Society Journal* 8 (1994): 77–86

Flynn, Philip. *Francis Jeffrey.* Newark: University of Delaware Press, 1978.

————. "Francis Jeffrey and the Scottish Critical Tradition." In *British Romanticism and the Edinburgh Review.* Edited by Massimiliano Demata and Duncan Wu. New York: Palgrave Macmillan, 2002.

Fontana, Biancamaria. *Rethinking the Politics of Commercial Society: The Edinburgh Review 1802–1832.* Cambridge: Cambridge University Press, 1985.

Gellner, Ernest. *Nations and Nationalism*, New Perspectives on the Past. Edited by R. I. Moore. Ithaca: Cornell University Press, 1983.

[Gleig, George]. "Life of Lockhart." *Quarterly Review*, 116 (1864): 439–82.

Gordon, Ian A. *The Movement of English Prose.* English Language Series. London: Longmans, 1966.

Gordon, Mary. *"Christopher North": A Memoir of John Wilson.* 2 vols. Edinburgh: Edmonston and Douglas, 1862.

Greig, James A. *Francis Jeffrey of the Edinburgh Review.* London: Oliver and Boyd, 1948.

Grob, Alan. "Wordsworth and the Politics of Consciousness." In *Critical Essays on William Wordsworth.* Edited by George H. Gilpin. Boston: Hall, 1990.

Gross, John. *The Rise and Fall of the Man of Letters: A Study of the Idiosyncratic and the Humane in Modern Literature.* London: Macmillan, 1969.

Groves, David. "Francis Jeffrey and the 'Peterloo' Massacre of 1819." *Notes and Queries* 235 (1990): 418.

Habermas, Jürgen. *The Structural Transformation of the Public Sphere: An Inquiry into a Category of Bourgeois Society.* 1962. Translated by Thomas Burger and Frederick Lawrence. Reprint, Cambridge: Polity, 1989.

Halkin, Hillel. "What Is Cynthia Ozick About?" *Commentary* 119:1 (January 2005): 49–55

Harling, Philip. "The Perils of 'French philosophy': Enlightenment and revolution in Tory journalism, 1800–1832." *Studies in Voltaire and the Eighteenth Century* 2004:06. 199–220.

Harrold, Charles Frederick. *Carlyle and German Thought: 1819–1834.* Yale Studies in English, 82. New Haven: Yale University Press, 1934.

Hart, Francis. *Lockhart as Romantic Biographer.* Edinburgh: Edinburgh University Press, 1971.

Hayden, John O. "Introduction." In *British Literary Magazines.* Edited by Alvin Sullivan. 4 vols. Westport, Conn.: Greenwood, 1983–86.

Heffer, Simon. *Moral Desperado: A Life of Thomas Carlyle.* London: Weidenfeld and Nicolson, 1995.

Henderson, W. O., ed. and trans. *Industrial Britain Under the Regency: The Diaries of Escher, Bodmer, May and de Gallois. 1814–18.* New York: Augustus M. Kelly, 1968.

Hildyard, H. Clive. *Lockhart's Literary Criticism.* Oxford: Basil Blackwell, 1931.

Hohendahl, Peter Uwe. "Critical Theory, Public Sphere and Culture. Jürgen Habermas and his Critics." *New German Critique* 16 (1979): 89–118.

———. *The Institution of Criticism.* Ithaca: Cornell University Press, 1982.

Houghton, Walter. "A Brief History of the *Wellesley Index:* Its Origin, Evaluation, and Variety of Uses." *Victorian Periodicals Review* 18 (1972): 48–51.

Houston, R. A. *Scottish Literacy and the Scottish Identity: Illiteracy and Society in Scotland and Northern England, 1600–1800,* Cambridge Studies in Population, Economy and Society. Edited by Peter Laslett. London: Cambridge University Press, 1985.

Hume, David, "On Essay-Writing," in *Selected Essays,* ed. Stephen Copley, Word's Classics (London: Oxford University Press, 1998), 1–5.

Jacobson, Dan. "Border Crossings." Times Literary Supplement. November 2, 2007: 14–15.

James, Clive. "Echoes from Another Century." *The Guardian,* June 23, 2001, Saturday Pages.

Jessop, Ralph. "Recontextualizing Carlyle within Scottish Philosophical Discourse." *The Carlyle Society Occasional Papers* 13 (session 2000–2001): 34–47

———. "Viragos of the Periodical Press." In *A History of Scottish Women's Writing,* edited by Douglas Gifford and Dorothy McMillan, 216–31. Edinburgh: Edinburgh University Press, 1997.

Keen, Paul. *The Crisis of Literature in the 1790s: Print Culture and the Public Sphere.* Cambridge Studies in Romanticism, 36. Edited by Marilyn Butler and James Chandler. Cambridge: Cambridge University Press, 1999.

Kermode, Frank. *Romantic Image*. London: Routledge and Kegan Paul, 1957.

Kernan, Alvin. *Printing Technology, Letters, and Samuel Johnson*. Princeton: Princeton University Press, 1987.

Kidd, Colin. *Subverting Scotland's Past: Scottish whig historians and the creation of an Anglo-British identity, 1689–c.1830*. Cambridge: Cambridge University Press, 1993.

King, Marjorie. *"Illudo Chartis:* An Initial Study in Carlyle's Mode of Composition." *Modern Languages Review* 49 (1954): 164–75.

Klancher, Jon P. *The Making of English Reading Audiences, 1790–1832*. Madison: Wisconsin University Press, 1987.

Klein, Lawrence. "The Rise of Politeness in England, 1660–1715." Unpublished doctoral dissertation. Johns Hopkins University, 1984.

———. *Shaftesbury and the Culture of Politeness: Moral Discourse and Cultural Politics in Early Eighteenth-Century England*. Cambridge: Cambridge University Press, 1994.

Knight, Charles A. "The Created World of the Edinburgh Periodicals." *Scottish Literary Journal* 6 (1979): 20–36.

Lang, Andrew. *Life and Letters of John Gibson Lockhart*. 2 vols. London: J. C. Nimmo, 1897.

Langford, Paul. *A Polite and Commercial People: England, 1727–1783*. Oxford: Clarendon, 1989.

Laugero, Greg. "Infrastructures of Enlightenment: Road-making, the Public Sphere, and the Emergence of Literature." *Eighteenth-Century Studies* 29 (1995): 45–67.

Law, Alexander. *Education in Edinburgh in the Eighteenth Century*. London: University of London Press, 1965.

Leith, John H. *Introduction to the Reformed Tradition*. Edinburgh: Saint Andrew Press, 1978.

Lochhead, Marion. *John Gibson Lockhart*. London: John Murray, 1954.

Lüthy, Herbert. "Variations on a Theme by Max Weber." In *International Calvinism, 1541–1715*. Edited by Menna Prestwich. Oxford: Clarendon, 1985.

Macbeth, Gilbert. "John Gibson Lockhart: a Critical Study." *University of Illinois Bulletin*, 32 (1935).

MacDonald, W. R. "Aberdeen Periodical Publishing, 1786–1791." *The Bibliotheck* 9 (1978): 1–12.

Mack, Douglas. "John Wilson, James Hogg. 'Christopher North,' and 'The Ettrick Shepherd.'" *Studies in Hogg and His World* 12 (2001): 5–24.

Mackenzie, Henry. An Account of the Life and Writings of John Home. Edinburgh: Constable, 1822.

Macleod, John. *Scottish Theology in Relation to Church History Since the Reformation*. Edinburgh: Publications Committee of the Free Church of Scotland, 1943.

MacNeill, John T. *The History and Character of Calvinism*. Oxford: Oxford University Press, 1954.

Maertz, Gregory. "Carlyle's Critique of Goethe: Literature and the Cult of Personality." *Studies in Scottish Literature* 29 (1986): 205–26.

Mannion, Irene Elizabeth. "Criticism 'Con Amore': A Study of *Blackwood's Magazine*." Unpublished doctoral dissertation. University of California Los Angeles, 1984.

Massie, Alan. "Maddest of Tribunals." Review of *British Romanticism and the Edinburgh Review*. Edited by Duncan Wu. *Times Literary Supplement*, (August 9, 2002): 12–13.

McCalman, Iain. "Publishing." In *The Oxford Companion to the Romantic Age*. Edited by Iain McCalman. Oxford: Oxford University Press, 1999.

McDougall, Warren. "Copyright Litigation in the Court of Session, 1738–1749, and the Rise of the Scottish Book Trade." *Edinburgh Bibliographical Society Transactions* 5, part 5 (1988): 2–31.

McElroy, Davis D. *Scotland's Age of Improvement: A Survey of Eighteenth-Century Literary Clubs and Societies*. Pullman: Washington State University Press, 1969.

McGann, Jerome. *The Romantic Ideology: A Critical Investigation* (Chicago: University of Chicago Press, 1983.

———. *The Scholar's Art: Literary Studies in a Managed World*. Chicago: University of Chicago Press, 2006.

McIntosh, Carey. *The Evolution of English Prose, 1700–1800: Style, Politeness, and Print Culture*. Cambridge: Cambridge University Press, 1998.

McIntosh, John R. *Church and Theology in Enlightenment Scotland: The Popular Party, 1740-1800*. East Lothian: Tuckwell Press, 1998.

McLean, Scott A. "Cleansing the Hawker's Basket: Popular Literature and the Cheap Periodical Press in Scotland." *Studies in Scottish Literature* 32 (2001): 88–100.

Macleod, Emma Vincent. *A War of Ideas: British Attitudes to the Wars Against Revolutionary France, 1792–1802*. Aldershot: Ashgate, 1998.

Melton, James Van Horn. *The Rise of the Public in Enlightenment Europe*. Cambridge: Cambridge University Press, 2001.

Milne, Joan, and Willie Smith. "Reviews and Magazines: Criticism and Polemic." In *The History of Scottish Literature*. Edited by Cairns Craig. Vol. 3, *The Nineteenth Century*. Edited by Douglas Gifford. Aberdeen: Aberdeen University Press, 1989.

Mitchell, Leslie. *Holland House*. London: Duckworth, 1980.

M'Kerrow, John. *History of the Secession Church*. Glasgow: A. Fullarton, 1841.

Morgan, Peter F. *Literary Critics and Reviewers in Early 19th-Century Britain*. London: Croom Helm, 1983.

———. "Lockhart's Literary Personality." *Scottish Literary Journal* 2 (1975): 27–35.

Morrison, Robert. "John Wilson and the Editorship of *Blackwood's Magazine*." *Notes and Queries* 46:1 (March 1999): 48–50.

Mullan, David George. *Scottish Puritanism, 1590–1638*. Oxford: Oxford University Press, 2000.

Murdoch, Alexander. "Scotland and the Idea of Britain in the Eighteenth Century." In *Eighteenth Century Scotland: New Perspectives*. Edited by T. M. Devine and J. R. Young. East Lothian: Tuckwell, 1999.

Murphy, Peter T. "Impersonation and Authorship in Romantic Britain." *ELH* 59 (1992): 625–49.

———. *Poetry as an Occupation and an Art in Britain, 1760–1830*. Cambridge Studies in Romanticism, 3. Edited by Marilyn Butler and James Chandler. Cambridge: Cambridge University Press, 1993.

Nangle, Benjamin Christie. *The Monthly Review, Second Series, 1790–1815: Indexes of Contributors and Articles*. Oxford: Clarendon, 1955.

Nathans, Benjamin. "Habermas's 'Public Sphere' in the Era of the French Revolution." *French Historical Studies* 16 (1990): 620–44.

Noble, Andrew. "John Wilson (Christopher North) and the Tory Hegemony." In *The History of Scottish Literature.* Edited by Cairns Craig. Vol. 3, *The Nineteenth Century.* Edited by Douglas Gifford. Aberdeen: Aberdeen University Press, 1989.

Nokes, David. *Jonathan Swift, A Hypocrite Reversed: A Critical Biography.* Oxford: Oxford University Press, 1985.

Noyes, Russell. *Wordsworth and Jeffrey in Controversy.* Bloomington: Indiana University Publications, 1941.

Oliphant, Margaret. *Annals of a Publishing House: William Blackwood and His Sons, Their Magazine and Friends.* 3 vols. Edinburgh: Blackwood, 1897.

O'Neill, Michael. *Romanticism and the Self-conscious Poem.* Oxford: Clarendon, 1997.

Parker, Mark. *Literary Magazines and British Romanticism.* Cambridge Studies in Romanticism, 45. Edited by Marilyn Butler and James Chandler. Cambridge: Cambridge University Press, 2000.

Parsons, Ian. "Copyright and Society." In *Essays in the History of Publishing in celebration of the 250th anniversary of the House of Longman, 1724–1974.* Edited by Asa Briggs. London: Longman, 1974.

Peters, John U. "Jeffrey's Keats Criticism." *Studies in Scottish Literature* 10 (1972–73): 175–85.

Phillipson, Nicholas. "The Scottish Enlightenment." In *The Enlightenment in National Context.* Edited by Roy Porter and Mikulá Teich. Cambridge: Cambridge University Press, 1981.

Pitrie, David Wayne. "Francis Jeffrey's Journal." Unpublished doctoral dissertation. University of South Carolina, 1980.

Potkay, Adam. *The Fate of Eloquence in the Age of Hume.* Ithaca: Cornell University Press, 1994.

Raimond, Jean, and J. R. Watson, ed. *A Handbook to English Romanticism.* New York: St. Martin's, 1992.

Ramsay, M. P. *Calvin and Art Considered in Relation to Scotland.* Edinburgh: Moray Press, 1938.

Richardson, Thomas. "Character and Craft in Lockhart's *Adam Blair.*" In *Nineteenth-Century Scottish Fiction.* Edited by Ian Campbell. Manchester: Carcanet New Press, 1979.

Roberts, Michael. *The Whig Party: 1807–1812.* London: Macmillan, 1939.

Robertson, John. *The Case for the Enlightenment: Scotland and Naples, 1680–1760.* Cambridge: Cambridge University Press, 2005.

Roe, Nicholas. "Introduction." In *Keats and History.* Edited by Nicholas Roe. Cambridge: Cambridge University Press, 1995.

Roellinger, Francis X. "The Early Development of Carlyle's Style." *PMLA,* 72 (1957): 936–51.

Roper, Derek. *Reviewing before the Edinburgh, 1788–1802.* London: Methuen, 1978.

Rose, Jonathan. "A Conservative Canon: Cultural Lag in British Working Class Reading Habits." *Libraries and Culture,* 33 (1998): 98–104.

Rose, Mark. *Authors and Owners: The Invention of Copyright.* Oxford: Oxford University Press, 1993.

Rundle, Margaret. "Perhaps the Greatest Paradox of All: Carlyle's Greater Success as Prophet in the 1820s and 1830s." *Carlyle Studies Annual,* special issue (1995): 111–23.

Saintsbury, George. "Lockhart." In *The Collected Essays and Papers of George Saintsbury.* 4 vols. London: J. M. Dent, 1923.

Saunders, J. W. *The Profession of English Letters.* London: Routledge and Kegan Paul, 1964.

Schaff, Philip. *Creeds of Christendom.* 3 vols. New York: Harper, 1878.

Scott, P. G. "Unmasking the Mandarins: Wellesley II." *Victorian Periodicals Newsletter* 6 (December 1973): 41–49.

Shattock, Joanne. "The 'Review-like Essay' and the 'Essay-like Review.'" In *Politics and Reviewers: The Edinburgh and the Quarterly in the Early Victorian Age.* Leicester: Leicester University Press, 1989.

———. "Work for Women: Margaret Oliphant's Journalism." In *Nineteenth-Century Media and the Construction of Identities.* Edited by Laurel Brake, Bill Bell, and David Finkelstein. New York: Palgrave, 2000.

Shepherd, Francis. *London: A History.* Oxford: Oxford University Press, 1998.

Sher, Richard B. *Church and University in the Scottish Enlightenment: The Moderate Literati of Edinburgh.* Edinburgh: Edinburgh University Press, 1985.

———. "Commerce, Religion, and the Enlightenment in Eighteenth-century Glasgow." In *Glasgow.* Edited by T. M. Devine and Gordon Jackson. Manchester: Manchester University Press, 1995.

———. *The Enlightenment & the Book: Scottish Authors & Their Publishers in Eighteenth-Century Britain, Ireland, & America.* Chicago: University of Chicago Press, 2006.

———. "Literature and the Church of Scotland." In *The History of Scottish Literature.* Edited by Cairns Craig. Vol. 2, *1660–1800.* Edited by Andrew Hook. Aberdeen: Aberdeen University Press, 1987–89.

Simpson, Kenneth. *The Protean Scot: The Crisis of Identity in Eighteenth Century Scottish Literature.* Aberdeen: Aberdeen University Press, 1988.

Siskin, Clifford. *The Work of Writing: Literature and Social Change in Britain, 1700–1830.* Baltimore: Johns Hopkins University Press, 1998.

Skelton, John. *The Table-Talk of Shirley.* Edinburgh: Blackwood and Sons, 1895.

Smith, J. V. "Manners, Morals, and Mentalities: Reflections on the Popular Enlightenment of Early Nineteenth-Century Scotland." In *Scottish Culture and Scottish Education.* Ed. Walter M. Humes and Hamish M. Patterson (Edinburgh: John Donald, 1983). 25–54.Smith, Janet Adam. "Some Eighteenth-century Ideas of Scotland." In *Scotland in the Age of Improvement: Essays in Scottish History in the Eighteenth Century.* Edited by N. T. Phillipson and Rosalind Mitchison. Edinburgh: Edinburgh University Press, 1970.

Smout, T. C. *A History of the Scottish People, 1560–1830.* London: Collins, 1969.

———. "Problems of Nationalism, Identity and Improvement in Later Eighteenth-century Scotland." In *Improvement and Enlightenment.* Edited by T. M. Devine. Edinburgh: John Donald, 1989.

Stafford, Fiona. "The *Edinburgh Review* and the Representation of Scotland." In *British*

Romanticism and the Edinburgh Review. Edited by Massimiliano Demata and Duncan Wu. New York: Palgrave Macmillan, 2002.

Stein, Peter. "Law in Eighteenth-Century Scotland." In *Scotland in the Age of Improvement: Essays in Scottish History in the Eighteenth Century*. Edited by N. T. Phillipson and Rosalind Mitchison. Edinburgh: Edinburgh University Press, 1970.

Stephen, Leslie. "The First Edinburgh Reviewers." In *Hours in a Library*. 3rd series. London: Smith, Elder, 1879.

Strout, Alan. "Concerning the *Noctes Ambrosianae*." *Modern Language Notes* 51 (1936): 493–504.

———. *Life and Letters of James Hogg, the Ettrick Shepherd*. Lubbock: Texas Tech Press, 1946.

———. "John Wilson, 'Champion' of Wordsworth." *Modern Philology* 31 (1934): 383–94.

Sullivan, Alvin, ed. *British Literary Magazines*, 4 vols. Westport, CT.: Greenwood, 1983–1986.

Sutherland, John. *The Life of Walter Scott: A Critical Biography*. Oxford: Blackwell, 1995.

Swann, Elsie. *John Wilson—Christopher North*. Edinburgh and London: Oliver and Boyd, 1934.

Tennyson, G. B. *"Sartor" Called "Resartus": The Genesis, Structure, and Style of Thomas Carlyle's First Major Work*. Princeton: Princeton University Press, 1965.

Thompson, E. P. *The Poverty of Theory & Other Essays*. New York and London: Monthly Review Press, 1978.

Thomson, Andrew. *Life of Principal Harper*. Edinburgh: Andrew Elliot, 1881.

Trevelyan, George Otto. *The Life and Letters of Lord Macaulay*. 2 vols. London: Longmans, Green, 1876.

Vanden Bossche, Christopher R. *Carlyle and the Search for Authority*. Columbus: Ohio State University Press, 1991.

Warren, Alba H. *English Poetic Theory 1825–1865*. Princeton: Princeton University Press, 1950.

Watson, Roderick. "Carlyle: the World as Text and the Text as Voice." In *The History of Scottish Literature*. Edited by Cairns Craig. Volume 3, *The Nineteenth Century*. Aberdeen: Aberdeen University Press, 1987–1989.

Wilks, Washington. *Edward Irving: An Ecclesiastical and Literary Biography*. London: Simpkin, Marshall, 1860.

Wilson, David Alec. *Carlyle Till Marriage (1795–1826)*. London: Kegan Paul, Trench, Trubner, 1923.

Wilson, Edmund. *The Triple Thinkers: Twelve Essays on Literary Subjects*. New York: Oxford University Press, 1963.

Woodmansee, Martha. "The Genius and the Copyright: Economic and Legal Conditions of the Emergence of the 'Author.'" *Eighteenth-century Studies* 17 (1984): 425–48.

AUTHOR IDENTIFICATION

Houghton, Walter E. *Wellesley Index to Victorian Periodicals, 1824–1900*. 4 vols. London: Routledge and Kegan Paul, 1966–1987.

Murray, Brian M. "The Authorship of some Unidentified or Disputed Articles in *Black-wood's Magazine*." *Studies in Scottish Literature* 4 (1966): 144–54.

Schneider, Elizabeth; John D. Kern; and Irwin Griggs. "Brougham's Early Contributions to the *Edinburgh Review*: A New List." *Modern Philology* 42 (1944): 152–73.

Strout, Alan Lang. *Bibliography of Articles in Blackwood's Magazine: 1817–1825*. Library Bulletin, 5. Lubbock: Texas Technical College, 1959.

MANUSCRIPTS

Commonplace Book Notes on Books, by Francis Jeffrey, University of South Carolina, 4825.J2 A16.

Commonplace Book of John Dunlop, National Library of Scotland, Edinburgh, MS 9262.

Letters of Francis Jeffrey, National Library of Scotland, Edinburgh, MS 787.

Letters to Thomas Carlyle, National Library of Scotland, Edinburgh, MS 665.

Letters to Thomas Carlyle from his family, National Library of Scotland, Edinburgh, MS 1763.

Lockhart-Croker correspondence, National Library of Scotland, Edinburgh, MS 1819.

Index